Internal Auditing:
Directions
and Opportunities

Internal Auditing: Directions and Opportunities

by Robert K. Mautz, Ph.D.
Peter Tiessen, Ph.D.
Robert H. Colson, Ph.D.

The Institute of Internal Auditors Research Foundation
Altamonte Springs, Florida

The Institute of Internal Auditors

Copyright © 1984 by The Institute of Internal Auditors, Inc. All rights reserved. Printed in the United States of America. No part of this book may be reproduced, stored in a retrieval system, or transmitted in any form by any means — electronic, mechanical, photocopying, recording, or otherwise — without the written permission of the publisher.

ISBN 0-89413-122-2
84227 OCT84
Library of Congress Catalog Card Number: 84-82310

Foreword

Internal auditors, members of a growing profession, have been bombarded by changes in recent years. These changes include expanding business use of computers, diversification of business organizations, new government regulations and other demands on business accountability, greater involvement by audit committees, and a renewed concern for productivity, responsibility, and security. In short, the changes impact overall business management today, particularly those impacting corporate controls and profitability.

The IIA Research Committee and trustees of The IIA Research Foundation decided that a comprehensive study was needed to determine more specifically how these changes influence internal auditors. Three years ago, a major proposal from The University of Michigan was approved to research and present to the internal audit profession the information and findings of such a study. This study was undertaken as part of our overall research program directed at the leading edge of auditing state of the art. The depth of this research project dictated certain practical limits. The limits selected were "recent developments impacting internal auditing at major United States and Canadian corporations." Our principal objectives were to increase knowledge about internal auditing, to identify future educational needs for internal auditors, and to develop recommendations on directions for The Institute of Internal Auditors and other professional development efforts.

Research questionnaires for this project were quite detailed. They were sent to audit committee members, senior management, external auditors, internal audit directors, and staff auditors. We received over 2,000 responses, and the researchers found the data useful and comprehensive. Many of the comments and answers relating to specific issues are presented from the prospective of different levels of management or audit responsibilities.

A project of this magnitude could not have been completed without the involvement, support, and assistance of many people. On behalf of The IIA Research Foundation and it membership, I express my sincere appreciation to all who had a part in this project. Particularly helpful to the research effort was the consultation and the guidance provided by internal audit leaders from several corporations, members of the Steering and Advisory Committee, other interested reviewers, and participants at the project seminars to test and evaluate research findings. William C. Anderson, our immediate past president, provided the leadership for the successful coordination of internal auditing consultation to meet the requests of the researchers. We are especially thankful to the four major sponsors of this project: General Electric Company, IDS/American Express, Inc., Price Waterhouse, and Ernst & Whinney.

C. W. Gissel, CIA, CPA	Hugh L. Marsh, CMA
President	Chairman of the Board
IIA Research Foundation	The Institute of Internal Auditors
1984-85	1984-85

Acknowledgments

Although we accept full responsibility for any errors or deficiencies in this report, many others contributed directly to its completion. We are especially appreciative of the time and the effort expended by the hundreds of internal auditors and others who responded to our questionnaires, participated in our research seminars, and submitted to interviews. The burden of cooperation was significant. Without such generous assistance, the research assignment could never have been completed.

Members of The Institute of Internal Auditors' steering committee were always available to arrange interviews, to consult on specific questions, to critique tentative conclusions, and to share their considerable experience. We are also grateful for the cooperation and assistance provided by John Dattola, director of research; Rob Muirhead, CIA, manager of research; Richard Holman, Ed.D., research editor, of The Institute of Internal Auditors; Linda Costa, consulting editor; and Eleanor Avni, word processing specialist.

Mrs. Gloria Crosswait typed and retyped the lengthy manuscript, its tables and appendices, with patience and skill. Charles F. Klemstine, as a research assistant, approached full participation in the project and added Appendix C as its sole author.

As researchers, we found the assignment a long and difficult one. We acknowledge that more information lies within our reported data than we have yet identified and analyzed. Our hope is that others will find these data as interesting and challenging as we did and that they will add their efforts to ours in making the most of this new and rich data base.

Finally, we express our appreciation to the Research Foundation for the financial support and the opportunity to complete a strenuous, challenging, and productive study.

Robert K. Mautz, Ph.D.
Peter Tiessen, Ph.D
Robert H. Colson, Ph.D

Altamonte Springs, Florida
October 1984

Special Recognition

The trustees of the IIA Research Foundation express their sincere gratitude to the four major sponsors of this research study.

Ernst & Whinney Foundation
General Electric Foundation
IDS/American Express, Inc.
Price Waterhouse

About the Authors

Robert K. Mautz, Ph.D., is professor of accounting in the Graduate School of Business Administration, The University of Michigan, Ann Arbor. Formerly director of the Paton Accounting Center and chairman of the accounting faculty, he has participated in a number of research projects related to internal control and management control. He is a retired partner of Ernst & Whinney, a past president of the American Accounting Association, and currently a member of the Public Oversight Board of the AICPA's SEC Practice Section. His publications include a number of monographs and articles in leading journals.

Peter Tiessen, Ph.D., is currently an associate professor of accounting at the University of Alberta. He received a doctorate in business from the University of Minnesota in 1976. In addition to more than ten years as a university faculty member, he has served as an accountant and auditor in industry and government. He spent the 1981-82 academic year on sabbatical leave at The University of Michigan and has been closely associated with this research for The Institute of Internal Auditors since the inception of the project. His primary research interests center on control issues in organizations; and he has been published in *The Accounting Review* and *Accounting, Organizations and Society* on related topics.

Robert H. Colson, Ph.D., received his doctorate in accounting from The Ohio State University in 1980 and is currently an assistant professor of accountancy with the Weatherhead School of Management of Case Western Reserve University, Cleveland, Ohio. He has had experience in both industrial and public accounting and is the author and coauthor of a number of working papers on various topics in managerial accounting.

Contents

Foreword v
Acknowledgments vii
Special Recognition viii
About the Authors ix
List of Tables xiii
1 Introduction 1
   Purpose of This Research 1
   Nature of the Research 2
   The Questionnaires 2
   Research Seminars 4
   Effectiveness of the Research Procedures 4
   Overview of Conclusions 5
   The Current State of Internal Auditing 6
   Leadership and Resources 8
2 The Basic Issues 11
   The Focus of Internal Auditing 11
   Ultimate Responsibility 16
   Career Possibilities 22
   Scope of Internal Audit Services 25
   Potential and Program for the Future 29
3 The Directors of Internal Auditing Perspective 37
   Directors' Age, Education, Experience, and Career Objectives .. 37
   Factors Affecting Directors' Job Satisfaction 43
   Growth of Internal Audit Departments 51
   Responses to Developments Impacting Internal Auditing 53
   Variety of Internal Audit Activities 59
   Classification of Internal Audit Departments 64
   Internal Audit Relationships with Others 72
   Some Miscellaneous Matters of Interest to Internal Auditors ... 79
4 Internal Audit Staff Members' Perspective 85
   Internal Audit Staff Demographics 86
   Scope and Content of Internal Audit Staff's Tasks 91
   Work-Related Attitudes and Job Satisfaction 95
   Some Impressions from the Staff Questionnaire 109
5 Senior Management, Audit Committee Representative, and
   Independent Accountant Perspectives 113
   Representatives of Senior Management 113
   Audit Committee Members 123

Independent Accountants 135
Respondents' Final Comments 147
Appendix A: Questionnaire Responses 149
Appendix B: Discussion Paper for Research Seminars 221
Appendix C: Differences in Audit Expenditures Across Industries 241
Appendix D: Differences in the Responses of Career and
 Noncareer Internal Auditors 249
Appendix E: Influence of Nondomestic Activities on Internal Auditing....261
Appendix F: Package Mailed to Directors of Internal Auditing 267
The Institute of Internal Auditors Research Foundation: 1984-1985 269
The Institute of Internal Auditors International
 Research Committee: 1984-85 271

List of Tables

3- 1	Directors of Internal Auditing — Age and Length of Service	37
3- 2	Directors of Internal Auditing — Age Groupings	38
3- 3	Directors of Internal Auditing — Experience Groupings	38
3- 4	Directors of Internal Auditing — Educational Background	39
3- 5	Directors of Internal Auditing — Major Subject of Study	39
3- 6	Directors of Internal Auditing — Number Holding Professional Designations	40
3- 7	Directors of Internal Auditing — Memberships in Professional Organizations	40
3- 8	Directors of Internal Auditing — Experience at Entry to Audit Department	41
3- 9	Directors of Internal Auiting — Career Plans on Transferring from Internal Audit	42
3-10	Directors of Internal Auditing — Rank Ordering of Three Most Preferred Jobs	43
3-11	Directors of Internal Auditing — Growth of Internal Audit Departments	52
3-12	Directors of Internal Auditing — Respondents Grouped by Size of Audit Staff in 1982	52
3-13	Directors of Internal Auditing — Respondents Grouped by Average Internal Audit Department's Salary in 1982	53
3-14	Directors of Internal Auditing — Ten Most Common Initiatives in Response to the FCPA	53
3-15	Directors of Internal Auditing — EDP Audit Strategies	55
3-16	Directors of Internal Auditing — Estimates of Nondomestic Operations	57
3-17	Directors of Internal Auditing — Estimates of Quality of Internal Control in Domestic and Nondomestic Countries	57
3-18	Directors of Internal Auditing — Method of Performing Audits in Nondomestic Countries	58

3-19	Directors of Internal Auditing — Nature of Audit Effort	59
3-20	Directors of Internal Auditing — Purpose of Audit Effort	60
3-21	Directors of Internal Auditing — Subjects of Internal Audit Effort	61
3-22	Directors of Internal Auditing — Percentages of Time Spent on Specific Activities	62
3-23	Directors of Internal Auditing — Allocation of Internal Audit Department's Time	63
3-23A	Directors of Internal Auditing — Allocation of Available Internal Audit Department's Time by Size of Staff	63
3-24	Directors of Internal Auditing — Frequency of Internal Audits	64
3-25	Directors of Internal Auditing — Internal Audit Activities and Performance Levels	65
3-26	Directors of Internal Auditing — Respondents' Companies Grouped by Audit Activities	67
3-27	Directors of Internal Auditing — Relationship Between Internal Audit Activities and Industry Classifications	70
3-28	Directors of Internal Auditing — Relationship Between Internal Audit Activities and Company Characteristics	71
3-29	Directors of Internal Auditing — Influence of Others on Scope of Internal Audit Program	72
3-30	Directors of Internal Auditing — Line of Directors' Responsibility	72
3-31	Directors of Internal Auditing — Years of Establishment of Audit Committee	73
3-32	Directors of Internal Auditing — Reason for Establishment of Audit Committee	73
3-33	Directors of Internal Auditing — Composition of Board and Audit Committee	74
3-34	Directors of Internal Auditing — Reporting Relationship with Audit Committee	75
3-35	Directors of Internal Auditing — Views on Matters to Be Taken Directly to Audit Committee	76
3-36	Directors of Internal Auditing — Audit Committee's Interest in Internal Control	77
3-37	Directors of Internal Auditing — Most Appealing and Least Appealing Job Features	78

3-38	Directors of Internal Auditing — Appeal Index for Features of Director's Position	78
3-39	Directors of Internal Auditing — Work Relationship with Independent Auditors	79
4- 1	Internal Audit Staff Members — Numbers of Returned Questionnaires	85
4- 2	Internal Audit Staff Members — Respondents' Ages	86
4- 3	Internal Audit Staff Members — Length of Time With Current Company of Employment	87
4- 4	Internal Audit Staff Members — Length of Time in Current Position	87
4- 5	Internal Audit Staff Members — Educational Background	88
4- 6	Internal Audit Staff Members — Professional Certifications	89
4- 7	Internal Audit Staff Members — Membership in Professional Organizations	89
4- 8	Internal Audit Staff Members — Experience with Present Employers	90
4- 9	Internal Audit Staff Members — Experience with Prior Employers	90
4-10	Internal Audit Staff Members — View of Transfer to Internal Audit	90
4-11	Internal Audit Staff Members — Analysis of Time Spent on Audit Activities	93
4-12	Internal Audit Staff Members — Analysis of Time Spent on Audits in Company Units	93
4-13	Internal Audit Staff Members — Future Work Preferences	97
4-14	Internal Audit Staff Members — Attitude Toward Professional Reading	97
4-15	Internal Audit Staff Members — Reading Preferences	98
4-16	Internal Audit Staff Members — Extent of Challenge in Work Assignments	99
4-17	Internal Audit Staff Members — Opportunity to Improve Audit Expertise	100
4-18	Internal Audit Staff Members — Internal Audit Experience as a Contribution to Career Success	100
4-19	Internal Audit Staff Members — Evaluation of Job Features	105

4-20	Internal Audit Staff Members — Comparison of Internal Auditing and External Auditing	107
4-21	Internal Audit Staff Members — Relationship of Job Satisfaction and Work-Related Attitudes	108
5- 1	Representatives of Senior Management — Reasons for Growth of Internal Audit Departments	114
5- 2	Representatives of Senior Management — Reliance on Internal Auditing	114
5- 3	Representatives of Senior Management — Attention Given to Recommendations by the Internal Audit Department	116
5- 4	Representatives of Senior Management — Management's View of the Purpose of the Internal Audit Function	120
5- 5	Representatives of Senior Management — Comparative Rating of Internal Audit Department	121
5- 6	Representatives of Senior Management — Factors Inhibiting the Usefulness of Internal Auditing	121
5- 7	Representatives of Senior Management — Support for the Internal Audit Function	122
5- 8	Representatives of Senior Management — Audit Committee Interest in Internal Control	122
5- 9	Representatives of Senior Management — Relative Importance of the Internal Audit Department's Activities	123
5-10	Representatives of Senior Management — Evaluation of Internal Audit Department Relative to Other Departments	124
5-11	Representatives of Senior Management — Factors Inhibiting Internal Auditing from Becoming More Useful	124
5-12	Audit Committee Members — Frequency of Various Meetings	125
5-13	Audit Committee Members — Meetings with the Director of Internal Auditing at the Director's Request	125
5-14	Audit Committee Members — Primary Responsibility of the Director of Internal Auditing	126
5-15	Audit Committee Members — Frequency of Private Meetings with the Director of Internal Auditing	127
5-16	Audit Committee Members — Attention Given to Recommendations of Internal Audit Department	128
5-17	Audit Committee Members — Involvement of Auditors' Committee in Business Concerns	129
5-18	Audit Committee Members — Views on Internal Auditors' Independence and Authority	130

5-19	Audit Committee Members — Reliance on Internal Auditing for Adequacy of Company Control	131
5-20	Independent Accountants — Relative Importance of Internal Audit Tasks	136
5-21	Independent Accountants — Relative Importance of Internal Audit Function	136
5-22	Independent Accountants — Primary Responsibility of the Director of Internal Auditing	137
5-23	Independent Accountants — Private Meetings of the Director of Internal Auditing with the Audit Committee	138
5-24	Independent Accountants — Independence and Support for Internal Auditing	139
5-25	Independent Accountants — Treatment Accorded Recommendations of Internal Auditors	140
5-26	Independent Accountants — Reliance on Internal Audit Function for External Audit Function	142
5-27	Independent Accountants — Factors Influencing Reliance on Work of Internal Auditors	143
5-28	Independent Accountants — Time Spent in Testing and Evaluating the Work of Internal Auditors	144
5-29	Independent Accountants — Ratings of Internal Audit Department's Relative to Others in Same Company	144
5-30	Comparative Ratings of Internal Audit Departments by Representatives of Senior Management, Audit Committees, and Independent Accountants	145
5-31	Independent Accountants — Rating of Internal Audit Department with Other Internal Audit Departments	145
5-32	Independent Accountants — Work Relationships: Independent Accountants and Internal Auditors	145
5-33	Independent Accountants — Factors Inhibiting Usefulness of Internal Auditing	145
5-34	Independent Accountants — Factors Inhibiting usefulness of Internal Auditing	147
C-1	Average Number of Internal Auditors per Company	241
C-2	Distribution of Respondents by Industry	242
C-3	Average Number of Internal Auditors per 1,000 Employees	242
C-4	Average Expenditures On Internal Audit Salaries (in thousands)	243
C-5	Average Expenditures on Internal Audit Salaries per $1,000,000 of Revenue	244
C-6	Average Expenditures on External Audit Fees (in thousands)	245

C-7	Average Expenditures on External Audit Fees per $1,000,000 of Revenue	245
C-8	Average Internal Audit Salaries	246
D-1	Differences in the Attitudes of Career and Temporary Directors of Internal Auditing	252
D-2	Differences in Job Satisfaction: Career and Temporary Directors of Internal Auditing	255
D-3	Differences in the Attitudes of Career and Temporary Internal Audit Staff Members	256
D-4	Differences in Job Satisfaction: Career and Temporary Internal Audit Staff Members	259
E-1	Director's Questionnaire — Responses to Selected Questions Classified by Percentage of Nondomestic Operations	262

1

Introduction

Internal auditing, like other business activities, has felt the impact of a broad range of recent developments. These include mandatory audit committees of the board; the Foreign Corrupt Practices Act of 1977 (FCPA); adaptation of the computer to a wide variety of applications in business; increasing diversification, size, and geographical dispersion of U.S. corporations; strong foreign competition in both domestic and foreign markets; and a variety of applications of the centralized/decentralized theories of management. The extent and the nature of that impact, however, have not been readily apparent. Nor have they been the same in all companies or industries.

Purpose of This Research

Research provides a means of obtaining information. It can bring to a given topic an independent point of view in obtaining information not previously available, in organizing and analyzing that information, and in reaching both conclusions and recommendations based on it. We consider that to be our assignment.

We were asked to study recent and current developments impacting internal auditing. It was anticipated that, from such study, we might acquire information not available. We also expected to offer some suggestions on how internal auditing can most appropriately respond to such developments for its own good and for the benefit of the business community.

Research into an applied field like internal auditing is unlikely to provide a series of surprises or revelations. People working within the activity being researched know enough about it to understand that the factual information gathered by researchers is not actually "new." Research can collect only existing facts, and those facts are not likely to be unknown to perceptive people thoroughly familiar with the activity. Thus, research data often confirm what some people already "know."

But research can and should do more than that. Researchers should be able to analyze their information systematically and effectively. By organizing it logically, they may discover patterns and relationships not previously recognized. What was merely suspected becomes both known and interrelated with other information. Thus, our task as researchers in this case is to search the data so generously supplied by those who responded to our questionnaires and participated in interviews and seminars. As we identify patterns and relationships, we must consider their significance and the implications they have for the future of internal auditing.

If our analysis is reasonable, our suggestions won't seem revolutionary to those who have already pondered the same facts and relationships. The better our analysis and the more thoughtful their pondering, the closer our recommendations should be to those in the internal auditing profession who have thoughtfully and persistently studied these same issues from an entirely different point of view. The usefulness of our research lies in the support it provides to progressive thinkers in the field.

One of the developments affecting internal auditing is the effort by internal auditors to improve the profession's practices and status. Internal auditing is fortunate to have practitioners and educators who dedicate their time, talent, and energies toward improving the level of practice in their field. They work through The Institute of Internal Auditors (IIA) and other organizations to accomplish this purpose.

Out of their efforts has evolved, among other things, the *Standards for the Professional Practice of Internal Auditing*. The *Standards* provides a definition of internal auditing and criteria against which the organization, qualifications, and performance of internal auditors and internal audit departments can be measured. Because internal auditing is an evolving profession, the *Standards* is subject to continuing review and revision. Conceivably, this research and the consideration of the issues it identifies may aid in the further refinement of IIA's *Standards*.

Nature of the Research

The Paton Accounting Center has been deeply involved in research on internal control for the past few years. This research has continually involved various aspects of internal auditing. Thus, we had a large body of relevant information and considerable experience from which to draw comparisons and extrapolate trends. As with any new project, however, we are duty bound to approach it without bias or prejudgment of any kind. Our previous studies added to the amount of evidence available to us; they did not constrain our analysis or conclusions in any way.

The research program included four distinct steps:
1. Introductory interviews.
2. Questionnaires.
3. Research seminars.
4. Analysis of data.

Early in the research, members of the steering committee arranged a series of interviews with directors of internal auditing for some of the major corporations in the United States. These interviews provided us with an understanding of attitude, policy, and practice and with an opportunity to question outstanding internal auditors of long and varied experience. We found the interviews extremely important as we proceeded to other parts of the research program.

The Questionnaires

Our major device for obtaining information was a series of questionnaires mailed to companies whose internal audit representatives had indicated an interest in participating in the study. We had planned to develop separate questionnaires for directors of internal auditing, for internal audit staff members, and for members of senior management to whom the directors of internal auditing report. In discussing the content of these questionnaires with members of the steering committee, the suggestion was made to include representatives of a company's audit committee and of its independent accountants as well. Thus, we had five possible questionnaires for each company.

Our plan for distribution of questionnaires was complex. A first mailing of postcard responses was used to determine which directors within IIA's membership were interested in participating in the research project. A brief description of the work involved was included in the invitation. Each director was asked (1) to respond to an extensive questionnaire, (2) to request his immediate superior in the company organization to respond to a shorter questionnaire, and (3) to ask a member of the company's audit committee and (4) a representative of the company's independent accounting firm to do the same. In addition, he was (5) asked to select a number of his staff members, who would constitute a representative sample, to respond to another questionnaire. The burden for the director of internal auditing was not a light one.

Our mailing program provided each director with the appropriate instructions, questionnaires, and envelopes. Each person who was asked to complete a questionnaire received an addressed, stamped envelope and instructions to mail it directly to the researchers in the envelope provided. We received no responses that led us to believe this instruction was not followed.

The list of directors of internal auditing who initially agreed to cooperate with us was not as well balanced as we desired. A disproportionate number of those responding were from small companies. As a result, a second request went out to larger companies; and a better balance of large and small companies was obtained.

Respondents fell into three groups:
- From companies for which we had a full complement of questionnaires (director, staff, senior executive, audit committee, and independent accountant).
- From companies for which we had less than a complete range but as full a complement of responses as possible (for example, some companies had no audit committee; others had no independent accountant).
- From companies for which we received partial returns only.

Questionnaires	Mailed	Returned
Directors of internal auditing	524	330
Staff members	2,437	1,240
Senior management	524	266
Audit committee members	524	232
Independent accountant	524	278
Total returns	4,533	2,346
Five complete sets of responses		176
Sets as complete as structure of company permitted (missing audit committee, staff, or independent accountant)		74
Total sets		250

As a final comment on the research questionnaires, we emphasize that our access to internal auditors was through The Institute of Internal Auditors. Cooperation in completing our questionnaires was solicited through IIA staff members and was limited to IIA-member companies. We did not seek information from companies which were not represented in IIA membership. The extent of any bias in our reported data resulting from this restriction is not measureable by any means with which we are familiar.

Research Seminars

Another technique for obtaining research data used in this study is the research seminar. As we use the term, it involves bringing together a group of informed people who are interested enough in a specific subject to give up a half day to discuss the topic, make adequate preparation for the session, and participate freely and fully in the discussion. Participation is by invitation only. Well in advance of the seminar, each participant is provided with a paper prepared by the researchers. The intent of this paper is to raise issues that will elicit participants' experiences, views, and concerns.

For our purposes, exchanges among participants in which different viewpoints are expressed, specific cases illustrating why they differ with one another, and criticisms of our ideas presented in the discussion paper are all useful research data. We have found such seminars to be extremely useful for testing conclusions and for obtaining ideas and reactions that could never be obtained solely through questionnaires or interviews.

In this study, four such research seminars were held in three different cities and with different types of participants.

The fourth step in the research program was an extensive analysis of the questionnaire responses and other data. Analysis based on a variety of statistical techniques and discussions within the research group led to the conclusions and recommendations expressed in the following sections of this report.

Effectiveness of the Research Procedures

Each of the research procedures served its purpose. The introductory interviews served to acquaint us with internal auditing as it is practiced within major corporations under the direction of leading members of The Institute. That background assisted us in developing our questionnaires and in planning our seminars.

The questionnaires supplied a wide variety of information. Copies of each questionnaire are available in the appendices to this report and responses to the questions are also shown. The amount of information provided is extensive. Each questionnaire was specifically designed for the group to which it was sent, and unique kinds of information were sought from each. The director's questionnaire is especially interesting because we included a variety of questions of an experimental nature aimed at providing information that would permit us to identify significant characteristics of companies and their internal audit departments. This permitted a classification which might be relevant to recognizing reasons for different patterns of internal audit activities. The results of those questions and the analysis of responses are presented in Chapter 3.

Once the questionnaire data were received, tabulated, and a preliminary analysis completed, plans were made for the research seminars. Our primary purpose was to test the conclusions from our preliminary analysis. Through the helpful offices of The Institute, seminars were arranged in Dallas, New York, and Chicago. One included directors of internal auditing only; one included internal audit staff members only; and two included a mix of staff members, directors, independent accountants, senior executives, and others — all from different companies. Past experience has proved that a group of 18 to 25 is close to the ideal for this purpose (depending, of course, on the makeup of the group).

In one of our seminars, the attendance was well below the intended minimum; but the characteristics of the participants more than made up the difference, providing us with a spirited and varied discussion. In another meeting, no limit had been placed on the enrollment; so the number of participants exceeded 50. The sheer size of the gathering made extended interchange among the participants difficult, although the seminar was successful in providing us with the views of a large number of interested and informed directors on the issues raised in our discussion paper.

Over all, the seminars were quite successful in affording us an opportunity to expose our preliminary conclusions and obtain additional research data.

Analysis of the questionnaire responses and the seminar discussions proved difficult. The sheer quantity of information and the necessity of prioritizing equally interesting data offered major problems. In addition, the expectation that our interpretation of the accumulated evidence might provide a point of reference for long-range planning by The Institute adds an interesting yet presumptive element to our analysis. As will be evident to those who read the entire report, we have not hesitated to prioritize matters of interest revealed by our research or to make recommendations to The Institute on the basis of the information available to us. At the same time, we have followed a policy of full disclosure, making all our research data available to those who wish to make their own analyses.

Overview of Conclusions

As we reviewed the data collected through our research steps, we were impressed again and again with six significant issues which we have classified as of first importance. In a real sense, merely identifying these issues is itself a major conclusion. Each of them receives individual attention in the following pages of this report. They are listed here with brief explanations to provide an introduction to the following sections:

1. Does internal auditing have a central focus, or is it a collection of miscellaneous and unrelated services varying greatly from company to company?
2. To whom or to what do the responsibilities and the loyalties of the director

of internal auditing and the members of his[1] staff run? With the increasing interest in internal control, the responsibilities placed on audit committees, and the sheer size and the complexity of business enterprises, the services provided by internal auditors have become more useful to a wider range of interests in the corporation. Among these several interests, which takes priority? Can changing conditions or relationships influence the ranking of these priorities in certain cases?
3. What is the nature of the career possibility provided by internal auditing? Is it sufficiently attractive to assure that internal audit's personnel needs can be filled with people of adequate quality?
4. What is the appropriate scope of internal control activities within a company? Other research has noted that internal control is an ambiguous term. How should internal auditors interpret it in order to best serve those interests who look to them for service?
5. Given that internal auditing has attained a certain status, recognition, and opportunity for service in business and corporations, what lies ahead? Are there additional opportunities for growth and for service? For what objectives should internal auditing strive in the near future and long-term future?
6. How should internal auditing go about realizing the opportunities open to it, be they expanding or contracting? What should it do through its national organization or otherwise to make the best of the opportunities it faces?

This research was not originally aimed at the resolution of these specific issues, and there is an important question whether the data gathered provide adequate bases for the resolution of such policy questions. Yet our research data do suggest possible answers of these issues and unquestionably emphasize their importance. If our research does no more than draw the attention of IIA members to these issues and stimulates discussion and ultimate resolution, we will be pleased.

The Current State of Internal Auditing

This research was not initiated as a state-of-the-art study of internal auditing. Yet the variety of research methods, the nature of the information obtained, the interchanges with internal auditors, and previous research into internal control have given us considerable information about internal auditing as it now exists. Our perceptions of the current state of internal auditing undoubtedly influence our conclusions and recommendations; so in the interests of full disclosure, we have some obligation to present them.

None of the following is intended to be critical in any sense. We seek to present an objective description of certain aspects of internal auditing which we believe to be important to our conclusions. We accept the conditions as we found them as a base from which to proceed, nothing more.

Well Established But Not Well Defined

Internal auditing is a well-established and well-respected activity, but there is little indication that it is well defined or clearly directed in any overall professional sense. Other interests in business appear to think well of internal auditing. Senior executives, members of audit committees of boards of directors, and independent accountants responded to our questionnaires with relatively high ratings for internal audit departments. The services provided by internal auditors are seen as essential to corporate success, a valuable protection to shareholders and officers of the company, and a service that could be even more beneficial. Responses highly critical of specific internal audit departments were a very small minority.

We found it interesting to construct a "self-image" of internal auditing from our conversations with internal auditors and from our seminar discussions. Almost without exception, internal auditors think well of what they are doing. They find it important, challenging, educational, and even exciting. They believe that they perform at a high level of quality and achievement. Yet they are not so sure that other internal auditors do as well. Also, they do not perceive that they are highly regarded by people outside the internal auditing profession.

Departments Vary Widely

Within companies, internal audit departments exist at all stages of development, a fact to be expected but very easy to overlook. New companies are formed every day, most of them with great expectations. Not all of them succeed, of course. Those who do gradually add the departments and controls necessary to keep up with growth. Some companies have fully developed internal audit departments which have carried out a broad range of services for years. Other companies have recently hired their first internal auditor and expect him to develop both the department and its audit program. Then there are a number of companies whose internal audit departments fall at various points between these extremes.

The attitudes toward internal auditing also vary widely. Some managements have had very positive experiences with their internal audit departments and are very supportive. Others have had either no experience or perhaps even unfortunate experiences and find difficulty in determining what to expect from internal auditing and what resources must be provided if those expectations are to be met. Thus, when one generalizes about internal auditing, as we will do from time to time in this report, the possibility of exceptions should always be recognized.

Companies' Needs Differ

A company's need for an internal audit department and for the type of services that such a department should provide varies with industry characteristics, the size of the company, geographical dispersion, diversification, and decentralization. All companies have objectives they seek to obtain. They also have policies, expressed or unexpressed, within which those objectives are to be sought. To assure that officers and employees seek the company's objectives within its policies, controls of various kinds are needed. A major service of internal auditing is to determine whether those controls are adequate, in place, and functioning effectively. Companies like banks or retail stores that handle large quantities of assets having general appeal and wide usefulness face different problems of control than do companies whose products are less appealing or of an intangible nature.

As a company adds additional operating locations, its problems of control increase. As it expands into countries whose cultures vary and as it adds new products, services, and activities, its control problems increase. A company with a single product made in one location with a limited number of people and sold to a highly restricted market has minimal control problems compared with the large diversified, decentralized company offering many products in markets all over the world.

Leadership and Resources

For the reasons already discussed, internal auditing is likely to vary significantly from company to company in the kinds of activities and services provided. Internal audit activities are influenced by other factors as well. The company's need should be paramount, but in some cases the interests of the internal audit staff are also influential. Some internal auditors are well attuned to their company's needs; others are not. For example, a young person with limited experience on a company's independent accountants' staff may be hired by that company to develop its internal audit department and audit program. Such a person has little to bring to his new assignment other than recently gained knowledge and a willingness to learn. He may not be able to recognize the needs of the company and know how to meet them as they grow and change over time.

Another factor of great importance is found in the resources made available to the director of internal auditing. Without adequate personnel and other support, the best director available will be unable to provide all ther service needed and maintain quality. A combination of unqualified leadersip and limited resources is unfortunate but not known, especially in young, growing companies.

Resources available to the internal audit department come from decisions made by the company's management. Such decisions are likely to be strongly influenced by the personal experiences and knowledge of the executives concerned. A single bad experience with employee dishonesty, misunderstandings, or other breakdowns of control may do more for the flow of resources to an internal audit department than all the well-prepared budgets one can find. On the other hand, failure by an internal audit department to perform up to management's expectations, whether reasonable or not, is also likely to have an impact on the flow of resources.

Similarly, the constructiveness of the approach followed by members of the internal audit department, their attitude toward those whose work they review, and their responsiveness to requests for advice and assistance have an influence on the reception accorded them by operating and administrative employees.

Many people are able to set their own standards of performance and to hold to these whatever their conditions of work. Many others, however, require supervision and review to assist them in adhering to adequate standards. Leadership in internal auditing is just as influential as leadership in any other activity. Without adequate leadership, quality performance is unlikely, especially in an activity in which the ability to assess situational needs and to design ways to meet them is so important.

A responsibility of leadership is to provide opportunity. A director of internal auditing can provide no more opportunity to his staff members than is provided to him by senior management. Resources, opportunity, and leadership are closely related to one another and to the quality and the effectiveness of internal auditing. Our observation is that each of these tends to be company specific, a factor that adds to the variability of internal auditing from one company to another.

Within internal auditing, loyalties are likely to vary with the personal plans and opportunities of the auditors concerned. We found no strong understanding or teaching with regard to an overriding professional loyalty to an institution, position, or ideal. On a number of occasions when the subject of "whistle blowing" slipped into the conversation, the attitude of those present was neither positive nor negative. Some of those who had on occasion "blown the whistle" were bitter about the results of having done so.

Generalizing anything very significant from the previous description of the state of the art of internal auditing as we found it is difficult. We see considerable diversity in activity and quality of performance with some very strong highlights in specific situations. Differing and strongly held views about "my responsibility in my job" exist. There appears little standardization or uniformity of activity, less professional identification than one might expect, and a keen interest shown by company management in more demanding service from internal audit departments. Subsequent chapters consider these conclusions and the reasons for them in greater detail.

---

[1]Throughout this report, the pronouns he, his, etc., should be read as referring indiscriminately to both sexes.

2
The Basic Issues

This chapter discusses each of the basic issues listed in the preceding chapter. The relevant data, the nature and the implications of the issue, and our views on their resolution receive attention. Stated briefly, these issues are concerned with:
- The focus of internal auditing.
- Ultimate responsibility.
- Career possibilities.
- Scope of internal audit services.
- Potential and program for the future.

The Focus of Internal Auditing

Diversity of Activity and Point of View

The previous chapter pointed out the differences from company to company influencing internal audit departments. Given their company's goals and circumstances, executives analyze their needs for internal auditing as they see them and then devise a company-specific solution. This results in significant diversity in internal audit practice and different views of what internal auditing is and should be.

Some companies staff their internal audit department with personnel schooled in auditing theory and technique and who plan to spend all or a significant part of their careers in internal audit activities. Other companies establish only a core of personnel who see internal auditing as their chosen career field. They add to this core other employees who are "passing through" an internal audit experience as part of an executive-development program or with some other training purpose in mind. The proportion of career auditors to temporarily assigned auditors varies.

We were informed that some companies rely exclusively on employees assigned temporarily to internal auditing except for the person who heads up the internal audit function. Such a company staffs its internal audit function with people whose ambitions within the company are directed elsewhere. They are temporarily in internal auditing for a learning experience. They know that and appreciate the experience and knowledge they acquire but necessarily look beyond internal auditing to whatever they consider their real career interests to be.

It seems likely that people committed to a career in internal auditing and others who are committed only for two or three years of training will have somewhat different attitudes toward their work, membership in professional organizations, their evaluation of internal audit activities, and their responses to the kinds of questions included in our questionnaires. It also seems likely that employing companies may have different expectations with respect to the ways in which committed internal auditors and those serving in that capacity only on a temporary basis will participate in professional activities such as continuing education courses and service on professional organization committees.

We find some important differences in the nature of the assignments given to those engaged in internal auditing — whatever their long-run interests may be:
1. Some are engaged chiefly in determining whether officers and employees are performing in compliance with company rules and procedures.
2. Some are engaged primarily in financial auditing in support of the independent accountants.
3. Some are engaged primarily in operational auditing intended to improve operating economy and efficiency.
4. Some are engaged in a combination of 1, 2, and 3.

Thus, we see two important pairs of differences within the group of internal auditors responding to our questionnaires. The first of these has to do with the career interests of those responding. Internal auditors now committed to a career in internal auditing are likely to place a greater emphasis on professionalism in internal auditing than are those without such a commitment. The second has to do with the nature of the activities engaged in by internal auditors, an emphasis on compliance with company rules and procedures versus a concern for efficiency and effectiveness of operations.

The total implications of these two differences are difficult to visualize. The following diagram is an oversimplification but may make the point clearer.

	Compliance auditing	Operational auditing
Committed to internal auditing	1	2
Not committed to internal auditing	3	4

Consider the differences between two groups of internal auditors. Those classified in cell 1 are people chiefly engaged in compliance auditing who are committed to internal auditing as a career. Their range of activities and perceptions about their profession differ widely from auditors classified in cell 4 (those primarily engaged in operational auditing and not committed to internal auditing as a career).[2]

Our preliminary analysis of the questionnaire responses from directors of internal auditing found wide variations in activities performed by internal audit departments. A scrutiny of the data suggests that there are significant disparities in the activities of some internal audit departments in comparison with others. An impressive number of activities that some directors list as "always performed" within their departments are indicated by other directors as "never performed."

The official definition of internal auditing in The Institute's *Standards for the Professional Practice of Internal Auditing* reads:

> Internal auditing is an independent appraisal function established within an organization to examine and evaluate its activities as a service to the organization.

This is a broad definition which does not specify the functions of an internal auditor. Any tendency to be critical of that definition, however, is effectively quelled by the variety of responses from our questionnaires.

Because of these responses, we included a discussion of their implications in each one of our research seminars. If the activities of internal audit departments are so variable, is there any common thread that identifies internal auditing and distinguishes it from other activities necessary within a complex organization? While we received a variety of responses, we were also surprised by a widely shared attitude toward the question. A number of seminar participants apparently found the question to be insignificant. They did not regard it necessary to identify any specific activity that they had in common with all or most other internal auditors. It was more important for them that their services were in demand, that they performed them satisfactorily, and that they were making a contribution to their companies' welfare.

Others took the same general position but with somewhat different emphasis. They did not want to be "defined out" of internal auditing by a definition of the profession that was too narrow.

Importance of a Common Interest

This raises the question of whether identification of a common activity or interest is worth analyzing. The response hinges largely on one's point of view.

Members of any profession must be recognized by some common characteristics — skills, responsibilities, objectives, services, etc. Establishing such a common interest is important for several reasons:
- To assist internal auditors in banding together for mutual support, communication, and advancement.
- To help construct training programs for improvement and advancement.
- To aid in the design of appropriate research.

We believe that the ability to define internal auditing in precise terms is essential to a continually improving and more efficient type of activity. This shifts the question from "Is identification of a common interest worth doing?" to "Can internal auditing be identified?" Both questions should be answered in the affirmative.

Accordingly, we believe internal auditors would find a definition of internal auditing that provided the following guidelines very useful. A definition of internal auditing should identify:
1. What internal auditors do and what they do not do.
2. For whom they perform their service.
3. How they can serve effectively.

4. What they should be doing to qualify themselves to serve effectively.

Some of the other major issues introduced in the opening pages of this report relate directly to these quidelines and will be discussed in later sections. At this point, we will look at what internal auditors do.

Emphasis on Internal Control

Our analysis of questionnaire returns and seminar discussions indicated that, although responses to the director's questionnaire show great diversity in what internal auditors do, the diversity is not as great as it first appears. Statistical analysis of the response data finds a strong consensus that concern for and with internal control is the element that typifies internal auditing. The core activities, common to almost everything that internal auditors do, relate to some aspect of a company's internal control.[3] Once that idea becomes evident, we find that there is indeed a common thread running through the apparently diverse activities suggested by the responses to the questionnaire.

The activities engaging the attention of internal auditors can be related to internal control in one of four ways:
- Monitor the effectiveness of internal control procedures in use.
- Investigate actual or potential breakdowns of internal control.
- Assess the risk of internal control lapses and failures.
- Make recommendations for the improvement of controls and for appropriate responses to internal control risk, thereby contributing to the economical and efficient attainment of company goals within the company policy.

In a very real sense, internal auditors are experts in internal control. Their greatest service to their companies lies in assuring that controls are adequate and effective. When breakdowns occur, they make investigations to discover whether the failure is one of system deficiency or personnel fault and strive to assure that measures are taken to remedy the weakness.

Because internal auditors are also knowledgeable about accounting and other related matters, they will be called on for additional services from time to time. This is not unusual for experts in any activity. Most experts acquire skills and knowledge outside their immediate specialty, so they are sometimes called on for help with other matters. For internal auditors, the specialty is internal control.

Performance Versus Monitoring

One additional consideration is important. Internal auditors make a distinction between performing and monitoring internal control procedures. In many companies, the establishment and the performance of internal control measures are assigned to the controller's office. The controller is charged with the responsibility for developing and maintaining a system that provides for protection of assets and reliability of financial data. The internal audit department serves as a monitor of the effectiveness of the controller's system and provides assurance to senior management that management's policies are complied with.

If they are not, the audit function recommends action that will result in compliance.

Internal audit's relationship to internal control is not one of performance of control so much as identification and assessment of internal control risks, of review and improvement in control procedures, of monitoring performance and providing assurance to management, and of investigation and analysis. Our observations and discussions lead to the conclusion that there are indeed employees described as internal auditors who spend much or all of their time in the performance of internal control procedures. Whatever their designation, such employees are effectively members of the controller's department; they are not engaged in internal auditing.

To be sure, monitoring may require the repetition of certain activities. For example, to monitor the adequacy and the effectiveness of a bank-reconciliation process, it may be necessary for a member of the internal audit staff to substitute himself briefly for the person who normally does that task in order to understand and test the process. Our perception is that, in the most effective internal audit departments, monitoring has largely replaced the continuing performance of internal control procedures. In some of the new and developing internal audit departments, the performance of certain crucial internal control procedures is still retained by the internal auditors.

Importance of Internal Control as a Center of Interest

We can think of few activities within an organization that are more important to its success than maintaining control. Internal auditing provides management with genuine assurance that adequate controls are in place, that they are being performed as intended, and that any failures are investigated and remedied on a timely basis. This provides an invaluable service to company management, one that frees management from an essential concern so it can turn its attention to other matters. To perform that service well, internal auditors must have a thorough understanding of the company's activities, an ability to assess risks and balance costs with benefits, and an appreciation of economy and efficiency. Internal auditors must keep current with developments that offer assistance or threats to management control. Always alert to potential weaknesses in control, they also must have a concern for better ways to reach company objectives.

When policies fail to bring about desired objectives, internal audit should be among the first to recognize the failure and to offer alternative policies with a higher potential for success. In that sense, internal auditing offers rich opportunities for innovation and positive contributions to the company's welfare. Internal auditing should be viewed as a search for improvement as much as a search for errors and irregularities.

We believe that recent developments in the study of internal control provide increasingly important challenges for internal auditing. If internal control is accepted as the real center of interest for internal auditing, opportunities for personal career development, for service to others, and for distinguishing internal auditing from other activities become more apparent and more realistic. Internal auditing then becomes an activity closely linked with management objectives and policies.

Ultimate Responsibility

Who Relies on Internal Auditing?

Both practically and conceptually, the wide range of services provided by internal auditors should be expected to benefit a number of interests in the corporation. The board of directors, general management, operating management, and the shareholders should benefit from internal auditing. This raises an interesting question. In case of a conflict of interest among these beneficiaries, to which one is internal auditing responsible? There is some advantage in considering this question on a conceptual basis before proceeding to the research data for a more empirical view.

Management's Needs. General management has the widest range of responsibility, the greatest exposure to risk, the strongest interest in adequate control, and minimal opportunity for direct involvement in control activities. For these reasons, general management should have a keen interest in the quality, scope of service, and findings of its internal audit department. Given the direct responsibility for internal control placed on senior management by the FCPA, general management can never rest comfortably without some assurance that appropriate controls are in place and functioning. The one means of providing assurance that is readily available, competent, and sufficiently independent of operating considerations is the internal audit department.

General management also needs protection from the surprise and the embarrassment that follow wide dissemination of information about a failure to comply with governmental regulations. In addition, management cannot afford to be unaware of derelictions of duty, to fail to react promptly to deficiencies of any kind, or to be uninformed about what is happening in remote portions of the company.

The efficiency and the economy of operations are also a direct responsibility of general management — one it can delegate but never escape. Constant inquiry into the relative advantages of present and possible alternative practices and procedures is essential if the latest developments are to be reviewed for adoption. As competition at home and abroad intensifies, the search for better methods must be carried on in a variety of ways. Management requires assurance that the search is proceeding with skill and dispatch.

In all companies, the need exists for reliable data on which to make daily operating decisions. However qualified and disciplined the accounting employees may be, the possibility of error through illness, inexperience, competing demands, dereliction, and a host of other reasons is always present.

When irregularities do occur, management requires prompt investigation and appropriate action to assure that what happened once will not occur again, to provide confidence that any opportunities for recovery have not been overlooked, and to maintain or create a control environment conducive to satisfactory performance by all employees.

If an internal audit department can meet these needs, management is well served. In addition, because management can now turn its attention to positive actions without nagging worries about the effectiveness of control measures, all who have an interest in the enterprise's success are also well served.

Needs of the Board of Directors. Members of the corporate audit committee, who represent the board of directors, have much the same concerns as general management without the same immediacy of interest. Directors feel a responsibility for the company's success and for the adequacy of its control measures, but their role is one of policy rather than operation. They do not wish to be embarrassed by internal control or other breakdowns; they desire deficiencies corrected and failures investigated; they expect the same kind of assurance that management seeks. If the question of the ultimate responsibility of internal auditors is satisfactorily resolved, directors can be content with reminding management of dangers and asking if appropriate protective measures have been taken. If they do these things and are alert to any indication that control measures are not satisfactory, they have met their responsibility. Management, on the other hand, must accept operational responsibility for any deficiencies or breakdowns of control.

Operating Management's Control Needs. Operating management succeeds or fails on the quality of its operational efficiency. Cost control, quality control, and meeting production schedules constitute its primary responsibilities. Each of these calls for adequate control measures to be in place and functioning. Thus, operating management also desires satisfactory controls. It also seeks assurance that subordinates assigned to assist in obtaining the unit's goals are diligent, are performing within company policy, and are striving to achieve the unit's objectives.

When operating units become of a size and independence that they require their own treasury and accounting activities, the responsibility for maintaining adequate controls over these activities typically falls to the unit's operating management. Therefore, on a smaller scale, operating management may have the same needs as general management.

Shareholders' Needs and the Possibility of Conflicting Interests. Although they may have less direct concern, shareholders also benefit from the services of internal auditing as it serves the managerial interests previously described. Thus, we have what initially appears to be a happy harmony of needs and benefits. What is desirable and beneficial to one interest in the company is desirable and beneficial to all. But that is not the full story.

The potential for a conflict among these interests must be recognized as a continuing possibility. What if the chief executive officer or another important executive is conducting himself in ways that violate company policy or fails to seek the company's objectives? To whom do the responsibilities of the internal audit function run? To make the issue as clear as possible, let us assume that the internal audit function is the first to learn that the CEO has violated behavioral standards clearly established for his position. What does the internal auditor do?

The variations on the theme are many. The CEO may himself bring the deviation to the attention of the director of internal auditing. He may explain that, whatever the apparent violation may be, the action is taken for the ultimate good of the company and will work well in the long run. Or the CEO may refuse to discuss the subject with the director and instruct a staff member to inform him to drop the matter.

The conflict faced by the director of internal auditing is evident. He works under; reports directly or indirectly to; and looks for promotion, tenure, and compensation to the CEO. How can he be expected to maintain in his monitoring, investigating, and evaluating the attitude that the CEO is just another company employee to be reviewed, investigated, and reported if in violation of company policy?

On the other hand, if the director fails to take that position, how does he reconcile his responsibility to the owners of the company, the shareholders, the members of the board, and the audit committee who are elected to represent the owners?

Conceptually, the resolution of the conflict is clear. From the point of view of the shareholders, the CEO is just another employee, one whose position unavoidably puts him above many of the control measures used to motivate, encourage, and assist other officers and employees to seek company goals within company policies. Thus, his activities require special attention from internal auditors. If the ultimate employer of the members of the internal audit department is the body of shareholders, the internal auditors owe them first responsibility. They must report any deviations by the CEO, and the existence of the audit committee provides a ready means to facilitate such reporting.

Unquestionably, this complicates the duty of the internal audit function. When faced with an extreme case such as misuse of company funds by the CEO, the issue is clear and its resolution is apparent. But seldom is the reality as clear as the illustration. The demands of the situation are that, throughout his work and regardless of his relationship to the CEO, every internal auditor must recognize the possibility of dereliction at every level in the company and constantly be alert to any irregularity that has occurred. He must be prepared to investigate to confirm or refute his suspicions and to report his findings. For the staff member, the report goes to the director of internal auditing. From the director of internal auditing, it should proceed through appropriate channels to the CEO and also to the audit committee of the board of directors.

This puts a heavy burden on internal auditors; but without their acceptance of that burden, shareholders and directors alike are left without any defense against the rare, yet possible, event of unscrupulous or careless executive behavior.

Respondents' Views on Internal Audit Responsibility

A number of questions in our questionnaires provide responses directly relevant to the question of internal audit responsibility. Together they present a mixed picture with variation among companies. There is some advantage in reviewing the responses by type of respondent first and then summarizing the results.

Directors of Internal Auditing. Ninety-four percent of responding directors are located in corporate headquarters rather than in operating units. Their reporting responsibilities, which are frequently multiple, are at a high level organizationally. As is to be expected, for salary and promotion purposes, they report at a lower level. Question 9 with its responses follows:

To whom are you responsible for each of the following purposes? (Check as many items in each column as apply.)

	Audit Reporting Purposes (%)	Salary and Promotion Purposes (%)
Audit committee — board of directors	79.7	6.7
Chief executive officer	42.7	33.0
Chief financial officer	36.7	38.2
Controller	11.8	10.9
Treasurer	3.6	3.6
Administrative vice president	5.8	5.5
Operating unit-line management	5.2	.3
Other (specify)	11.5	15.5

The organizational level at which directors of internal auditing are placed within the company also has implications for the strength of their position. Responses to Question 10 are as follows:

What is the organizational level of the director of internal auditing in relation to that of the:

	Above (%)	Below (%)	Equal to (%)
Chief financial officer	3	85	12
Controller	16	38	46
Treasurer	11	49	40

Salary levels of directors tended to run well below the relative organizational levels.

The relationship of the director of internal auditing with the audit committee is complex and made up of a combination of practices and personalities. In the ideal situation, the director would be sufficiently familiar with the chairman of the committee to feel free to discuss any matters of possible importance. In the least desirable situation, he would view the chairman of the audit committee as a stranger with a high position in the company and with whom he could converse only on formal terms and under specified conditions. Our discussions with individual directors has led us to conclude that the latter situation exists in many companies.

The following extracted responses are especially relevant in portraying the relationship in question:

- 92 percent of responding directors have the right to take specific matters directly to the audit committee on a confidential basis.
- 22 percent have had occasion to do so.
- 46 percent have at some time received direct requests from the audit committee.
- 55 percent of the responding directors feel obligated to report such requests to other members of management if they have not already been so informed.
- Directors report in person to the audit committee anywhere from one to 12 times a year with 50 percent of the responses indicating three meetings a year.

A key question is whether the director meets with the audit committee on a regular and confidential basis without any other members of management present. The responses to this question ran 54 percent affirmative and 46 percent negative, indicating an inadequate recognition of the internal auditor's responsibility.

Another question that has implications for this relationship between the director and the audit committee about the kinds of items that would initiate direct communication is: "Which of the following matters would you take directly to the audit committee?"

Item	Would (%)	Would not (%)
1. Significant misuse of corporate assets by a corporate officer.	76	24
2. Noncompliance with capital budgeting requirements by the vice president of manufacturing.	5	95
3. A shortage in the cash receipts from a substantial branch office which the controller acknowledges but contends is not of sufficient importance to bring to the attention of the audit committee.	41	59
4. Information that leads you to believe that the chief financial officer is pressuring the controller to make some accounting changes in order to increase current earnings.	58	42
5. Failure by your superior to fund three new internal audit positions which you as director of internal audit feel are essential.	49	51
6. Reduction by your superior of funds available for internal audit training.	26	74

As noted in Chapter 3, the absence of a strong consensus in these responses reflects the developmental stage of internal auditing.

Audit Committee Members and Independent Accountants. Audit committee members and independent accountants seem to have an understanding of the internal auditors' split loyalty. To the question "The primary responsibility of the director of internal auditing is to . . . ," they responded as follows:

Response	Audit Committee (%)	Independent Accountants (%)
Audit committee	26	32

Chief executive officer	14	16
Audit committee and chief executive officer equally	39	23
Other	21	29

Members of senior management, members of audit committees, and independent accountants recognize the usefulness of internal auditors for their own purposes and also for the purposes of others. Ninety percent of the audit committee respondents stated that the director of internal auditing had an explicit invitation to bring his concerns directly to the audit committee without prior notification of company management. Twenty-eight percent stated this had occurred within the past year, and 16 percent stated it had occurred within the past five years but not the past year. A disturbing factor is the relatively low proportion of directors of internal auditing that meet regularly with members of the audit committee without other members of management being present.

The Internal Audit Environment and the Issue of Responsibility

Bringing matters directly to the audit committee is not always an easy task for the internal auditor. This is particularly true if meetings with the audit committee are infrequent and if senior management is always in attendance. In those cases, the internal auditor's only motivation to take his concerns to the audit committee may be his own conscience. In addition, his status in the organization is such that the officers responsible for financial matters — the controller, treasurer, and chief financial officer — may outrank him and receive considerably larger salaries.

The strength of his position, thus, is not conducive to the kind of alertness to possible irregularity, persistence in investigation, and forthrightness in pursuit of a satisfactory resolution of potential and actual infraction of company policy that is expected of auditors. This is not to say that internal auditors do not measure up to their most difficult and risk-laden responsibilities. We are confident that many do. The audit environment, however, is not as conducive as it might be for that desired action.

Recently, during a presentation to a large group of internal auditors in an IIA meeting, a member of the group raised the question of "whistle blowing" to report dereliction of executive duty. He had done so once, had been discharged from his position as a direct result, and was now suffering some unfortunate consequences. During the ensuing discussion, he received some sympathy; but there was also some attitude of "What did you expect?" There appeared no strong feeling within the group that, given the same conditions, all present would have done the same thing.

There is a message in this for internal auditors, for senior management, and for members of the audit committee, and for the board of directors. Unless measures are taken to strengthen the internal auditor's position and resolve, not all internal auditors will measure up to their ultimate responsibility when and if they meet it.

Career Possibilities

High Satisfaction, High Turnover

Responses to the staff questionnaire tell us that most internal auditors do not intend to stay in internal auditing. Seventy-five percent of those responding stated they did not plan to remain in internal auditing throughout their careers. When asked how long they expected to stay in internal auditing, responses ran as follows:

Length of Stay	Percentage
Less than one year	7
One to three years	54
Four to six years	31
More than six years	8

No doubt, these responses are influenced by the fact that many of those who returned our questionnaire had made their career choice outside internal auditing long before they entered their present activity. Even the majority of those internal auditors who have reached the pinnacle of their departments as directors consider themselves to be interested in internal auditing only temporarily. Sixty-two percent of the directors stated they did not plan to stay in internal auditing throughout their careers.

On the positive side, internal auditors — even many of those who consider their long-term interests elsewhere — are quite satisfied with their work, as the data in chapters 3 and 4 indicate. The staff's and director's questionnaires included a number of questions designed to determine how respondents felt about their work activities. A fair generalization is that internal auditors find their work far more satisfying than not.

When asked to list the most appealing features of their work, staff members named "intellectual challenge of work" and "variety of assignments" most frequently. The next two responses were "general work atmosphere" and "contribution to success of company." The least appealing features were "travel," "compensation," "relationship with independent accountants," and "status and prestige of position."

In social conversation, 35 percent refer to themselves as "auditors," 36 percent as "internal auditors," 10 percent as "EDP auditors," and seven percent as "accountants."

Directors of internal auditing responded to similar questions in much the same way. They find the work challenging and interesting. Again, the least appealing features include heavy travel, their relationship with independent accountants, and the general work atmosphere. There are few aspects of the work that they find very dissatisfying.

These data present an interesting set of facts. Those engaged in internal auditing find it to be an attractive, interesting, and educational experience. Yet the majority have no intention of staying with it. Even recognizing that many internal auditors had their career choices made well before they entered internal auditing, one might expect that an activity which apparently has so much work appeal might change the career choices of some or that many who entered internal auditing only for experience and understanding might be attracted to it as a career. Such does not seem to be the case.

Another consideration relevant at this point deserves attention. We were impressed by the nature, extent, and quality of service that internal auditing now provides and even more so by the service that senior management and directors would like to have from their audit staffs. Internal auditing is a skilled occupation that calls for intensive understanding of the company, familiarity with control methods, the ability to respond to conflicting loyalties, and the capacity to assess risks and match control and audit methods with them. How is such an activity to maintain itself over time while relying so substantially on participants whose work expectancy is generally less than five years?

Reasons for Short-Term Interest

In addition to the fact that many internal auditors have already chosen other careers to which they believe experience in internal auditing can make a contribution, our data reveal other reasons why internal auditing does not hold a greater proportion of its participants. First, as a group, internal auditors are viewed by senior management and by members of the audit committee as definitely superior to most of the other company employees. In response to the question "Please rate your internal audit department relative to other departments and activities in your company," responses were:

	Senior Management (%)	Member of Audit Committee (%)
Very superior	7	9
Superior	48	63
Average	43	27
Disappointing	2	1
Very disappointing	0	0

Audit staff members and directors are seen by experienced executives and board members as among the most able people in the organization. It may follow, then, that they are also among the more highly motivated and ambitious.

A second clue is found in the data cited about relative status and salary. In the company's organization chart, directors of internal auditing seldom rank above chief financial officers, controllers, or treasurers. Bright young recruits to the financial side of a company are not likely to miss this relationship. Add to this the fact that salary levels lag even more than organizational ranking, and the long-term appeal of a position in internal auditing becomes even less attractive to able and aggressive employees.

Third, some interesting indications of preference are found in questions asking staff members and directors what kind of work they plan to do when they leave the internal audit department. Because so many internal auditors come with a background in accounting, it is not surprising that the largest number plan to transfer into some accounting activity. Next is finance, and third is line management.

Now note that 86 percent of the respondents to the staff questionnaire find their work to be an excellent or a good chance to learn new things about their company and that 80 percent agree that it makes a good or an excellent contribution to their ability to succeed in almost any department of the company.

To sum up, we have a group of able young people just beginning their careers in business. They see limited opportunity for advancement within internal auditing. They find the work interesting, challenging, a great learning opportunity, and an experience that will make a contribution to their future success anywhere in the company. As a result, they are eager to get into internal auditing but also eager to get on with their career plans. As soon as they have obtained the major benefits from participation in internal audit activities, they look forward to moving on to some other activity en route to managerial status in finance or operations.

When we review questionnaire returns from directors of internal auditing, we find the same kinds of responses. The directors find the work interesting and challenging; it provides opportunities to learn about the company. Nevertheless, in spite of obvious success, they are interested in moving out of internal auditing into some other activity. Why? Although we did not ask that question directly, the answer seems obvious. Internal auditing does not provide them with the same opportunities for advancement they find elsewhere.

An important point of difference between responses from the directors and their staffs warrants mention. Directors prefer to transfer to operating management when leaving internal auditing. Operating management is closely followed by finance with accounting a distant third. We find this interesting on two counts. First, people who have come into the company with an accounting or a general business background and who have had internal audit experience now have an interest in operating management. The change in interest is itself significant. Second, after obtaining substantial internal audit experience, they consider themselves competent to move into operating management.

There is a point here that deserves special attention. Directors and staff members were queried as to the kind of work they would like to transfer to if they moved out of internal auditing but stayed with the same company and what kind of work they would seek if they left the company. In each case, operations or general management ranked high. It ranked higher, however, in response to the first of these questions. Experienced internal auditors evidently feel that their experience has given them a competitive advantage in seeking a managerial position within their company. They feel, however, that this advantage would not be quite as important if they were starting fresh in a new company.

Now we must return to the question of whether internal auditing presents an attractive career opportunity. Data indicate that a high percentage of experienced internal auditors wish to transfer to other activities. The data also give us the reason they wish to leave. Neither the top position in internal auditing, the compensation, nor the basis for advancement to general management positions are perceived as adequate. For maximum attainment of career goals, most internal auditors seek routes outside of internal auditing.

On the other hand, internal auditing is viewed by those who practice it as highly beneficial to them in their preparation for careers in operating or general management. Indeed, the nature of the work seems to suggest such a career to some who may never have considered it before. Additionally, there are many directors of internal auditing who find their activities and position sufficiently rewarding so that they are quite content. Generally, these are directors in large companies where the position is a responsible and respected one. Thus, internal auditing presents rather remarkable career opportunities, careers in internal auditing and in other company departments at an executive level. It presents more career opportunities than careers.

Scope of Internal Audit Services

Present and Anticipated Internal Audit Activities

Questionnaire data already cited establishes a wide range of activities for internal audit departments. Additional questions addressed to directors of internal auditing reveal their expectations with respect to changes in the nature of their audit activities in the near future.

Activity	Total audit time spent (%)	
	Now	In 5 years
Detection of errors and irregularities — This activity is directed at the prevention or timely discovery of errors or irregularities in processing or recording transactions.	20	15
Monitoring management control — Management control strives to obtain compliance with the applicable rules and procedures established by company policy.	27	26
Performance evaluation — This activity assesses the efficiency or the effectiveness with which company goals are attained.	14	19
Monitoring internal accounting control — Internal accounting control strives to assure that published financial statements present fairly the financial position and results of operations of the company in accordance with generally accepted accounting practice or other standards and that assets are appropriately safeguarded.	32	28
Decision-making review — This activity evaluates the effectiveness of management's operating and financial decisions.	7	12

Over the next five years, directors of internal auditing apparently expect a shift, but not a great one, from error detection and monitoring controls to performance evaluation and decision-making review. The responses suggest relatively little dissatisfaction with present activities and no expectations of great change. Within individual departments, of course, other movements may be in progress.

Senior management was asked the extent to which management now relied on the internal auditing function for a variety of services and the extent to which they felt management would like to rely on the internal audit function. Respondents replied that they would like to rely more heavily on internal auditing for every one of the functions listed (refer to Chapter 5). These included evaluating the effectiveness of management's financial and operational decisions, the efficiency, and the effectiveness with which company goals are attained and assuring compliance with all relevant governmental regulations. Rather than a shift from some services to others, management desires more of all, including some not now considered by many internal auditors to be an important part of their activities. If general management has its way, internal auditing will do what it is doing now — only better — and will also take on some new activities.

The Meaning of Internal Control

One of the troubling aspects of recognizing internal control as the focus of internal auditing is the variety of ideas conveyed by that term. Research performed by the Paton Accounting Center for the Financial Executives Research Foundation (FERF) concluded that the term was understood so differently by different interests in business activity that it should be abandoned and other terms substituted for it.[4]

The term "internal control" has been used for many years by various interests in business activity — by operating and general management, by independent accountants, and by internal auditors. Although the term was in general use, authoritative definition and discussion existed only in the literature of independent accounting. Because they found discussion of the meaning of internal control essential to establishing the boundaries of their responsibility in auditing, independent accountants had perhaps unintentionally but effectively co-opted the term. When one looked for other discussions and definitions, such were not to be found.

The first attempt at an authoritative definition of internal control appeared in a booklet published in 1949 as a special report by the Committee on Auditing Procedure of the American Institute of Accountants (now the American Institute of Certified Public Accountants). That booklet broadly defined internal control as follows:

> Internal control comprises the plan of organization and all of the coordinate methods and measures adopted within a business to safeguard its assets, check the accuracy and reliability of its accounting data, promote operational efficiency, and encourage adherence to prescribed managerial policies. This definition possibly is broader than the meaning sometimes attributed to the term. It recognizes that a "system" of internal control extends beyond those matters which relate directly to the functions of the accounting and financial departments. Such a system might include budgetary control, standard costs, periodic operating

reports, statistical analyses and the dissemination thereof, a training program designed to aid personnel in meeting their responsibilities, and an internal audit staff to provide additional assurance to management as to the adequacy of its outlined procedures and the extent to which they are being effectively carried out. It properly comprehends activities in other fields as, for example, time and motion studies which are of an engineering nature and the use of quality controls through a system of inspection which fundamentally is a production function.[5]

From the standpoint of independent auditing, for which it was first stated, this definition was soon found to contain a serious flaw. When independent accountants asserted in their audit opinion that their examination complied with generally accepted auditing standards, which required a review of internal control, they claimed a review far broader in scope than most of them actually made or felt necessary for audit purposes. Furthermore, the implied responsibility for such a review was well beyond the obligations the profession wished to accept. Hence, in a very short time, efforts were made to amend the definition. A first step was to divide internal control into two parts:

- Accounting control, which included safeguarding assets and checking the accuracy and the reliability of accounting data, the first two requirements in the definition.
- Administrative control, which included the second pair of requirements — promoting operational efficiency and encouraging adherence to prescribed managerial policies.

We then had three terms — "internal control," which included "accounting control," and "administrative control."

The independent accountants described their audit responsibilities as a review of accounting control with the privilege of extending their review to administrative control. This was true in cases where specific administrative controls might compensate for apparent weaknesses in accounting control.

But experience suggested to the accounting profession that further delimitation of the definition might be useful. In 1972, modifications in the professional literature limited the meaning of "safeguarding assets" and restricted the independent auditor's responsibility for the reliability of financial records to those used for external reporting purposes only. The 1948 definition, a broad definition that had meaning and usefulness for managers and internal accountants and auditors, had been replaced by a very specialized definition intended to serve the purposes of independent accountants acting in an audit capacity.

The FCPA introduced the term "internal accounting control." The relationship of that term to CPA literature is evident. Nonetheless, it constitutes a new term not yet well defined for any purpose.

The FERF research found that members of operating management, especially those in production, tend to think of internal control in terms of their own work. To them, the essence of internal control is found in a combination of quality control, cost control, and meeting production schedules on time. They see internal control as all the positive steps needed to assist employees in meeting quality, cost, and time standards; expectations; and budgets. The technical definition of the term developed by independent accountants for their own purposes has little meaning for operating management.

Senior management, unlike operating management, must be concerned about externally reported financial data. Senior management is also much concerned about the same matters as are their operating managers. Thus, senior management should think of internal control in the broad terms envisaged in the 1948 definition that includes accounting control and administrative control, both finance and operations.

The FERF study suggests that internal control has lost its usefulness as a meaningful term because of the different interpretations to which it is subject. That work suggests that accounting control is a suitable term for the concept developed by CPAs for their purposes and that management control is an appropriate term for the broad concept held by senior management. Thus, management control includes all measures used by management to motivate, encourage, and assist officers and employees to attain a company's goals within company policy. This is a broad concept of internal control and the one most appropriate for internal auditors intent on maximum service to management.

Internal Audit and Management Control

We have described this terminology problem at some length here only because we think it already is and will become even more important to internal auditing. When asked to indicate the extent to which they would like to rely on internal auditing for increased services, senior management indicated that it is seeking assurance on management control, not just accounting control. The implications of this conclusion for internal auditing are little short of staggering.

Consider for a moment the variety of activities and interests within the company that have some part in management control as that term was just defined.

- Security — physical protection of assets and personnel.
- Insurance — casualty-risk assessment and protection.
- Personnel — screening employees, motivation via compensation and other recognition.
- Controller's office — accounting and financial controls.
- Treasurer's office — cash control, investments, and related income.
- Production management — quality control, cost control, schedule maintenance, safety, and supervision.
- Management information systems — protection of DP facilities, equipment, software, and information such as quality control over systems under development.
- Legal department — conflicts of interest, compliance with regulations, and investigations of improper conduct.

Other illustrations might be added, but this is sufficient to make the point that management controls are necessary to minimize a wide variety of personnel failures and that responsibility for them is located in a surprisingly diverse number of departments and functions within the company. The question immediately appears: Who oversees management control to assure that overlapping is reduced to a minimum and that no important matters of control are omitted because no one has been made specifically responsible?

The responses to the senior management questionnaire suggest that management does have concern for the overall adequacy, effectiveness, and economy of management controls. Answers to the questions imply that senior management would be happy to see internal auditing expand into a number of areas that many internal auditors may not now consider to be a responsibility or an opportunity. Regulatory compliance and operational efficiency are matters of prime importance to executives. If no one takes the responsibility for establishing and reviewing control measures to assure appropriate responses to these needs, management may have serious control weaknesses of which it is unaware.

Management's need for some assurance seems clearly established by responses to the questionnaires. Internal auditing already has expertise in controls, a broad scope of activity, and the confidence of management. The opportunity is striking; the challenge is a little overwhelming. But if internal auditors, the acknowledged experts in control, do not accept the challenge of extending their expertise to the broader field of management control, some other interest surely will. We know of no other interest as well qualified.

Potential and Program for the Future

The last two issues noted in Chapter 1 can best be considered together. Given that internal auditing has reached a certain stage in its development, (1) what are its prospects for the future and (2) how can these prospects be realized most effectively? We will discuss them in that order.

Contrasting Views of Internal Auditing

Depending on how and where one spent his time, a researcher in internal auditing might come away with very different impressions. From the data we collected through our research techniques, we have obtained an overview of the activity as it is practiced in many organizations including many relatively small and developing companies. We believe it to be a fair cross section of internal audit departments as found in the United States and Canada. How should one characterize internal auditing based on this information? One possible characterization follows:

Internal auditors constitute an amorphous group of accounting and business-oriented people, most of whom consider themselves only temporarily attached to that activity and have their sights set on careers well beyond their current work. They provide a wide variety of useful and interesting services which are valued highly by management. These services could be increased and expanded if internal auditors had skills and a point of view they are now considered by management to lack.

If this is an accurate description, internal auditing faces a significant problem at best. However well regarded its services may be, it is not meeting all management's needs. If the service is truly needed, management will find another way to obtain it. The widely held belief on the part of management that internal auditors are not sufficiently management oriented presents them with a sizeable handicap in obtaining additional resources sufficient to provide for management's needs. A sharper focus on these needs and on internal auditing's ability to meet them seems in order.

A More Exemplary Model. Fortunately, the previous model is not the only one we found in practice. In our interviews and from questionnaires and discussions, we know that another model of internal auditing exists. In some companies, the internal audit department is viewed as one of considerable prestige and status. The director of internal auditing ranks high in the organization, reports directly to a senior official at the highest or second level in the company, and meets regularly with the audit committee for which special assignments are performed. His staff members are considered to be experts in internal control. They carry on a recurring review or monitoring of procedures to determine their effectiveness; they review the system or systems periodically to determine whether revision or modification is desirable; they are continually relied on to watch for new internal control risks, to assess them, and to determine on a cost-benefit basis what control procedures would be appropriate; they are asked to make investigations where actual or potential deficiencies in internal control have been discovered and to report thereon with their recommendations for future controls.

Internal auditors in such departments are often invited by unit managers and other levels of operating management to consult on a wide variety of accounting and control subjects. Because of the nature of their work and their status within the company, they have little difficulty in attracting company personnel and new recruits to serve in internal auditing and are successful in holding some of the best and brightest of these for long-term careers in internal auditing. When they are unable, for whatever reason, to hold able members of the department who decide their interests and likes are elsewhere, the departing members leave internal auditing with respect and appreciation for the experience and training they have received. Thus, internal auditing is thought and spoken well of throughout the company by people at all levels who regard highly the quality of personnel and quality of work in that department.

Such internal audit departments are considered by management to perform a valuable service. But more than that, they are considered by management to be a reservoir of talent that thinks and acts like management itself, a reservoir that can be drawn on for competent analytical, control-oriented people to meet whatever exigencies management may have at any time.

A Variety of Needs and Opportunities. It would be a mistake to assert that every internal audit department has the same opportunity to attain exemplary status or that every internal auditor would like to work in such a department. Like any other occupation, internal auditing attracts a wide variety of people with diverse talents and interests. Some companies have relatively uncomplicated operations with little opportunity for errors or irregularities. Their needs for internal auditing may be lighter than the needs of more complex companies operating on a diversified and decentralized basis. We hesitate to prescribe for all companies or all internal auditors.

At the same time, as earlier parts of this section have indicated, we are impressed by the remarkable opportunities available to internal auditors in some companies, the skilled work being performed in some internal audit departments, and the need for similar qualities of work in other companies. Hence, we now offer some general recommendations for internal auditing.

We suggest that, if internal auditing is to provide maximum service to the wide range of enterprises and organizations it serves, it needs:
- An achievable goal.
- A positive program for achieving that goal.
- A strong institute or other means to bring together the resources and talents necessary to develop and implement such a program.

An Achievable Goal

The goal of internal auditing should be to establish for itself an acknowledged, indispensable role serving general management in ways open to no other group within the company. We suggest that such a role is ready and waiting for internal auditors. They should become specialists in evaluating, monitoring, and investigating management control. Management control here is conceived as a broad term covering all that was implied in the original 1949 AICPA definition of internal control and in the more recent definition that reads: "Management control includes all measures applied by management to encourage, motivate, and assist officers and employees to seek and attain the company's goals within the company's policies."

Is such a goal achievable? We believe it is. To attain it, internal auditors must obtain:
1. An appreciation of managements' responsibilities, opportunities, constraints, and skills.
2. An understanding of the nature and the scope of management control. This includes identifiying and assessing risks, selecting cost-beneficial control measures, monitoring practices, and planning and executing investigations.
3. Familiarity with the company's goals, policies, organization, operations, and relevant industry factors such as regulation and competition.

A Program for Action

A positive program to achieve such a goal calls for a number of activities such as:

1. Defining internal auditing in understandable terms that recognize its ultimate responsibility to the owners of the enterprise and its immediate responsibility to management.
2. Recognizing and serving the needs of all internal auditors.
3. Establishing a training program adequate to qualify internal auditors to achieve the goal stated above.
4. A research program that provides a continuing flow of information to strengthen internal auditing in all aspects.

A Definition for Internal Auditing. Early in our report, we found the definition of internal auditing in the *Standards for the Professional Practice of Internal Auditing* to be something less than adequately descriptive. That definition reads:

> Internal auditing is an independent appraisal function established within an organization to examine and evaluate its activities as a service to the organization. The objective of internal auditing is to assist members of the organization in the effective discharge of their responsibilities. To this end, internal auditing furnishes them with analyses, appraisals, recommendations, counsel, and information concerning the activities reviewed.

We believe the following definition would be more informative and more useful:

> Internal auditing, which is ultimately responsible to the owners of the enterprise, is a service to senior management and other enterprise interests that includes (1) monitoring management controls; (2) anticipating, identifying, and assessing risks to enterprise assets and activities; (3) investigating actual and potential lapses of control and incidents of risk; and (4) making recommendations for improvement of control, the response to risk, and the attainment of enterprise objectives.

Note that included in this possible definition is a statement of the internal auditor's ultimate responsibility to the owners of the enterprise. This is a responsibility that most internal auditors will never have to face. Almost without exception, chief executive officers and their associates are honest, dedicated, and serve with honor and integrity. Yet for the internal auditor who must resolve the hard question of conflicting loyalties, we believe a specific reminder of that responsibility is desirable. We also believe that the forthright statement of such responsibility will strengthen internal auditing as a profession and its status in the eyes of others.

Two Classes of Internal Auditors. Our data make clear that there are at least two and possibly three classes of people serving as internal auditors. First, there are those who are committed to internal auditing as a long-term career; these are a minority. Second, there are those whose career commitment is elsewhere and who view their assignment to internal auditing as a useful but temporary experience. Finally, there are those who are undecided as to their interests and eventually place themselves in one or the other of the first two groups. For our purposes here, we need discuss only those permanently and those temporarily committed to internal auditing.

We think it is of fundamental importance that the needs of both groups be recognized and served. Because of the extent of turnover, internal auditing will always be searching for additional qualified recruits. Indeed, the data indicate that constant replacing and retraining must be an important factor in planning within the profession. When those who regard internal auditing only as a temporary assignment leave, where do they go? Most of them go elsewhere within the company. Many seek a position in management, accounting, or finance. If they leave with a good feeling for the experience and the training they received, so much the better for internal auditing. If they are impressed with the quality of work performed within internal auditing, with the high standards of review and training, and with the supervision they have experienced, internal auditing will have less difficulty in recruiting. More important, its status and prestige within the company will improve.

An interesting point here is that there is little indication that the "temporaries" and the "permanents" require different types of training. Those who look to internal auditing for a career need a great deal of management education. Those who plan to leave internal auditing often have ambitions for careers in management. They also need management education. Once the members of either group have taken whatever orientation courses are considered desirable and have obtained the necessary audit skills, it appears that immediate enrollment in management training courses would be beneficial.

It is a mistake to delay such training courses until a commitment to a career in internal auditing has been made. There are many people who enter internal auditing with a desire to leave within a few years because their career interests lie elsewhere. If they discover through training courses and experience that internal auditing is involved with management control matters across the entire company and that it looks at a wide variety of activities from the broadest possible management point of view, they may well conclude that there is no better way to prepare for a career in general management than to accumulate a longer period of experience and training in internal auditing.

Training Programs. Little need be said about training programs except that they are essential. The need for a strong management emphasis is apparent and has been stressed. Management control in the sense that it has been used in this report is a topic that has received relatively little attention in accounting and auditing literature. Some pioneering work is much needed. To some extent, the criteria for such control systems have been identified.[6] These provide a basis for selecting cases and experiences that will encourage student discussion and learning.

Because management control extends to every activity within the company, there is almost no department or activity that does not provide an opportunity for study. Those designing the training program will be well advised to remember that the intent is not to make the student an expert on purchasing, insurance, or data processing. The real intent is to consider the possible internal control risks and to determine those control measures that offer the most efficient and economical method of meeting the risk. We have a great deal to learn about management control, both in theory and practice, and probably even more about the best ways to teach it. Our expectation is that some of the greatest progress to be made on this score in the next few years will come from internal auditors.

Topics for Research. We have little doubt that, over the next few years, a large number of research subjects will be offered to The Institute of Internal Auditors Research Foundation for support. The availability of funds is an important incentive, but the opportunity to obtain research data not previously available is the greatest incentive researchers can have. To the extent that members of The Institute cooperate with researchers in responding to requests for interviews, questionnaire returns, and seminar participation, researchers will be encouraged to submit proposals.

We recognize, of course, that every request for information is an imposition, sometimes one that is impossible under the circumstances. We recognize also that the benefits to anyone from completing some questionnaires is minimal. We urge, however, that The Institute, as an official policy, encourage responding to questionnaires and other requests from researchers when and if those requests evidence adequate preparation and appear to bear on significant subjects.

We find in our research data many researchable subjects we would like to investigate further. We find it striking, for example, that next to "travel," "relationship with independent accountants" is the least appealing feature of internal auditing in the minds of directors of internal auditing. It ranks the same in the responses of internal audit staff members. Because management considers the internal audit department to be an important means of reducing external audit fees, some investigation of this attitude on the part of internal auditors seems warranted as well as interesting. A number of other leads are suggested by the data reported in the following chapters and appendices.

Institutional Support

The development of a challenging training program and the direction of ongoing research efforts do not occur spontaneously. A strong organization is essential to provide continuing guidance and leadership. The institutional needs of internal auditing appear to us to be unique.

Most groups of people drawn together by similar interests and the desire to further those interests rely on committees of members to conduct business and make policy decisions. Members who see their organization as the means to reach personal professional goals will devote considerable time over long periods before they attain positions of influence. Members who represent firms or companies are often subsidized by their partners or by their companies so that they can perform the services and gain the experience necessary to qualify them for committee chairmanships. After one has demonstrated strong interest by serving on minor committees for a number of years, a member may serve on a major committee for three years and then, through diligent effort, be selected as chairman for another three-year term. The point to be noted is the number of years required for active participation in the organization in order to make an important contribution or have significant influence.

Recall that most internal auditors anticipate getting out of internal auditing within five years and that many plan on no more than three. This greatly reduces the number who are available for extended service within any organization representing internal auditors. It also indicates that:

- Some important positions must be filled with members whose experience may have been far less than desired.
- A large segment of the internal audit population may never be represented effectively at the policy-development level.
- Companies will not wish to subsidize employees for such committee work because their service horizon is so limited. We think this creates some unusual problems for progress toward the goals discussed earlier in this section.

This set of conditions appears to place special burdens on two groups. Those internal auditors who are committed to long-term careers in internal auditing must pick up a disproportionately greater share of committee and other institutional work. Compared with the total membership, there will be fewer of them than in many other interest groups. Their burdens will be heavier, and progress may be slower. The other group to be affected is made up of the organization's staff members. Since they must substitute for member time and effort, they face the temptation to usurp decisions that should be made by members. They must also accept and discharge a responsibility to make sure that the segment of the membership not officially represented on important committees is not neglected. Perhaps ways can be found to encourage a continuing interest from "internal audit alumni" so that some of them continue their participation after transferring to other activities within their companies. For the long-run health of internal auditing, the "temporaries" must not be neglected. Finally, IIA staff members must make a special effort to keep up with developments in internal auditing and to maintain a continuing active contact with working auditors. This will ensure that their recommendations and proposals are relevant to current conditions.

---

[2]Appendix D reports the results of an analysis of responses by career and noncareer internal auditors for directors and staff members.

[3]"Internal control" is used here in the broad sense of "management control" described later in this chapter.

[4]R.K. Mautz and James Winjum, *Criteria for Management Control Systems* (New York: Financial Executives Research Foundation, 1982).

[5]American Institute of Accounts, *Internal Control, Elements of a Coordinated System and Its Importance to Management and the Independent Public Accountant: Special Report of the Committee on Auditing Procedure* (New York: American Institute of Accountants, 1949).

[6]*Ibid.* R.K. Mautz and James Winjum.

3

The Directors of Internal Auditing Perspective

As mentioned in Chapter 1, five questionnaires were used in the study. By far the longest, the Questionnaire for Directors of Internal Auditing included a wide variety of questions and produced a significant amount of research data. Three hundred and thirty useful replies were received. The mailing list was provided by The Institute of Internal Auditors and represents volunteers from its membership.

Discussion of the questionnaire responses in this chapter is organized around the following subjects:
- Directors' age, education, experience, and career objectives.
- Factors affecting directors' job satisfaction.
- Growth of internal audit departments.
- Responses to developments impacting internal audit.
- Variety of internal audit activities.
- Classification of internal audit departments.
- Internal audit relationships with others.
- Some miscellaneous matters of interest to internal auditors.

Directors' Age, Education, Experience, and Career Objectives

Age and Time in Present Position

The title "director of internal auditing" has become a general term to describe the position of the person who heads the internal audit function in U.S. and Canadian companies. We use it with that meaning throughout this report. From our questionnaire addressed to directors of internal auditing, we collected the following information about the ages of respondents and their length of service as director:

Table 3-1
Directors of Internal Auditing
Age and Length of Service

Years	Minimum	Maximum	Average
Age	24	64	41
Years of service with present employer	1	46	10
Years of service in present position	1	40	5

50 percent of the directors were less than 39 years old.
50 percent of the directors had been with their present employer for less than seven years.
48 percent of the directors had been in their present position for less than three years.

Taken alone, these data offer cause for interesting speculation. A substantial proportion of internal audit directors are relatively youthful. An equally substantial proportion have had limited experience with the company that now employs them.

When read in conjunction with other data collected during this research, this information becomes even more impressive. For example, one of the questions in the senior management questionnaire asked the directors' superiors to indicate the extent to which they would like to rely on internal audit for such matters as:
- Evaluation of the effectiveness of management's operating and financial decisions.
- Integrity of company officers and employees.
- Efficiency and effectiveness with which company goals are attained.
- Adequacy of internal control procedures.

Responses to that question show that management would like to rely on internal audit to a significant extent for these matters. In order to do that, internal audit leadership may need more experience and maturity than is evident in our response data. Similarly, in replying to a query about the factors that keep internal auditing from becoming more useful to the company, senior executives ranked "lack of managerial perspective on the part of internal auditors" as a significant reason. In fairness, we must say that one cannot expect a mature managerial perspective from people who lack general business and company-specific experience.

The following tables present some additional interesting information about the ages and experience of directors:

Table 3-2
Directors of Internal Auditing
Age Groupings

Years	Responses Number	Percentage
30 or less	38	12
31 - 40	145	44
41 - 50	80	24
51 - 60	53	16
Over 60	12	4
No response	2	—
Total	330	100

Table 3-3
Directors of Internal Auditing
Experience Groupings

Years	In present position			With present employer		
	No.	%	Cum. %	No.	%	Cum. %
1	54	16	16	32	10	10

Table 3-3 (continued)

2	60	18	34	32	10	20
3	43	13	47	29	19	29
4	28	9	56	16	5	34
5	27	8	64	27	8	42
6 — 10	65	20	84	65	20	62
11 — 15	17	5	89	40	12	74
16 — 20	4	1	90	24	7	81
21 — 30	1	.5	90	31	9	90
31 — 40	2	.5	91	20	6	96
41 — 50	0	—	91	3	1	97
No response	29	9	100	11	3	100
Total	330	100		330	100	

These data could describe a new and developing activity in which very few directors have had time to accumulate many years of experience. Although internal auditing has been an accepted part of business operations in some companies for many years, many other companies have only initiated internal audit departments recently. There are indeed a significant number of internal auditors who stay in the profession a long time, ultimately become directors, and continue in that position for the rest of their careers. However, there also are many who become directors early but do not remain in the position for very long.

Directors' Educational Qualifications

The following tables show that (1) most directors have college degrees and that (2) accounting was the most common major subject in their college work:

Table 3-4
Directors of Internal Auditing
Educational Background

	Responses	
	Number	Percentage
High school	12	4
Institute diploma	8	2
Some university study	18	5
Bachelor's degree	201	61
Master's degree	91	28
Total	330	100

Table 3-5
Directors of Internal Auditing
Major Subject of Study

	Bachelors		Masters	
	No.	%	No.	%
Accounting	180	62	31	34
General business	53	18	44	48
Engineering	4	1	1	1

Table 3-5 (continued)

Computer science	0	0	0	0
Arts/science	26	9	7	8
No major indicated	29	10	8	9
Total	292	100	91	100

A variety of professional designations were reported by respondents and are summarized as follows:

Table 3-6
Directors of Internal Auditing
Number Holding Professional Designations

	Responses	
	Number	Percentage
CPA/CA	159	48
Certified Internal Auditor	78	24
Certified Bank Auditor	17	5
Certified Information Systems Auditor	29	9
Certified Management Accountant/Registered Industrial Accountant	5	2
Certified General Accountant	3	1
Other	17	5
None	96	29

The professional organizations to which the responding directors belong are reported in the following table:

Table 3-7
Directors of Internal Auditing
Memberships in Professional Organizations

	Responses	
	Number	Percentage
The Institute of Internal Auditors	322	98
American Institute of Certified Public Accountants	134	41
The Canadian Institute of Chartered Accountants	16	5
American Accounting Association	13	4
Canadian Academic Accounting Association	0	0
National Association of Accountants	41	12
The Society of Management Accountants	2	1
Certified General Accountants Association	3	1
State CPA Society/Provincial CA Institute	102	31
Bank Administration Institute	60	18
EDP Auditors Association	49	15
Other	64	19

A variety of organizations is included under "other." The Financial Executives Institute, the Computer Security Institute, the American Institute of Banking, and industry-accounting organizations are among those mentioned most frequently.

There is little in the above data that requires comment. The high percentage of responding directors who are members of The Institute of Internal Auditors probably results from the way in which the questionnaires were distributed. Other than this, the data are informative but contain no surprises.

Sources and Backgrounds of Responding Directors

Directors came to their present positions through a number of routes and from a number of sources (see Table 3-8). A significant number entered their present employers' internal audit departments at a staff or supervisory level. However, a majority came in at a managerial level and from there moved into the director's position. Four came into their present director's position with no previous internal audit department experience in their present companies.

The number transferring into their present departments from the internal audit departments of other companies is greater than the number who transferred into their present departments from public accounting.

The most interesting figure, however, may be the number who entered their present departments at a managerial level, transferring from a nonauditing position within the same company. What does this imply for internal auditing? One possible interpretation might be that management considers experience within other departments of the company to be of considerable importance — even more important than skill in auditing.

Another possibility might be that many companies rotate new employees through a number of departments; a transfer to internal audit comes late enough in the sequence that promotion to management is in order. An opposite conclusion, given the low-average-prior-work experience of this group of directors, might be that a management position in internal auditing may not require more than a very few years' experience. Future research may provide an opportunity to explore this matter more completely.

Table 3-8
Directors of Internal Auditing
Experience at Entry to Audit Department

	Entered Staff/Supervisory Level				Entered Management Level			
	No.	Aver. Prior Exp. in Years	Aver. Total Exp. in Years	Some Audit Exp.	No.	Aver. Prior Exp. in Years	Aver. Total Exp. in Years	Some Audit Exp.
Entered with no work experience	7	0	17.7	0	-	-	-	-
Entered from an internal audit position in another company	38	10.2	18.5	13	90	12.2	17.4	45
Entered from a position in public accounting	23	5.3	12.7	23	85	8.9	16.1	85
Entered from a nonauditing position								
In present company	50	2.4	21.0	0	26	3.5	25.6	0
In another company	-	-	-	-	7	10.4	18.8	0
Total	118				208			

Four entered as directors with no internal audit experience in present company.

Table 3-8 (continued)

Two from an internal audit position in another company.
Average prior experience — 13 years
Average total experience — 16.5 years
Two from nonaudit positions in present company.
Average prior experience — 20 years
Average total experience — 20 years

Directors' Career Plans

When asked "Do you plan to remain in internal auditing throughout your career?" 121 responding directors (38 percent) answered "yes," while 200 (62 percent) answered "no."

All respondents are people who have been successful in internal auditing. They serve in the top position in the internal audit department. Yet only 38 percent plan to remain in internal auditing throughout their careers. Many present directors, indeed a majority, plan to leave internal auditing and their present positions.

Another very striking set of facts is the responses to the question about how long directors plan to stay in internal auditing.

- Less than one year — 7 (4%).
- One to three years — 108 (55%).
- Four to six years — 63 (32%).
- More than six years — 18 (9%).

Those who plan to seek careers in activities other than internal auditing have very limited horizons for service in their present positions.

An idea of the careers that those who plan to leave internal auditing consider more appealing is found in the answers to the question: "What type of work do you expect to transfer to if you leave the internal audit department?"

Table 3-9
Directors of Internal Auditing
Career Plans on Transferring from Internal Audit

	Responses	
	Number	Percentage
Accounting	38	19
Finance	59	30
Production/engineering	0	0
Marketing	0	0
Personnel	0	0
Operating management	63	32
Electronic data processing management	4	2
Administrative management	12	6
Consulting	5	2
Other	18	9
Total	199	100

The plans mentioned most commonly under "other" are "administration" and some variation of consulting. Several mentioned one or more of the listed possibilities.

Responses to a slightly different question ("If you were to look for another job, would you look for a position in . . .") also contribute to our understanding of the types of careers directors of internal auditng consider more appealing than their present positions.

Table 3-10
Directors of Internal Auditing
Rank Ordering of Three Most Preferred Jobs

	First	Second	Third
Internal auditing	111	38	41
External auditing	2	14	20
Accounting	8	38	44
General management	80	71	59
Financial management	92	81	40
Operations	12	35	45
Marketing	0	6	6
Personnel	0	4	10
Electronic data processing	5	9	18
Other	12	5	16

The activities mentioned most commonly under "other" are consulting, some aspect of systems design or administration, and self-employment.

The various routes which led present directors to their positions indicate that a wide range of activities appeals to them as alternative job possibilities. Interestingly, a significant number of them seek management positions. Many directors of internal auditing apparently see their present position as a means of advancing their careers within the company rather than as a career in itself.

Factors Affecting Directors' Job Satisfaction

How well do directors of internal auditing like their work? What aspects of company policy, organization, and procedures influence their attitudes? The information gathered through our questionnaires provided opportunities to investigate directors' attitudes and their interrelationship with company and job characteristics. Some of the questions in the questionnaire for directors of internal auditing and in the questionnaire for senior management were intended to provide information for that purpose.

Part II of the directors' questionnaire was designed to generate information about the organizational structure and management practices of respondents' companies, the respondents' attitudes toward internal audit job characteristics, and their preferences in career orientations. This included data about directors' job satisfaction which we related to company characteristics and to personal attitude responses. Thus, we tried to sort out aspects of organizational structure, management style, work-related attitudes, and career orientations that are of general concern to the directors in our sample. We also attempted to discover interrelationships among them. To our knowledge, there has been no wide-scale research effort to determine how directors of internal auditing think about their

organizational roles. Our intent was to begin identifying the dimensions of a number of organizational and personal variables as they are perceived by directors. The major research findings, which are discussed more thoroughly in the following sections, include:
- Directors generally work in environments which allow considerable discretion within audit manual frameworks, exhibit moderate centralization of decision making, encourage flexibility in achieving work results, and value persuasion and participation in management action.
- Directors receive varying degrees of support from audited organizational units. In many companies, there is ambivalence regarding whether the internal auditor is viewed as a source of constructive assistance (positive) or as a policing activity (negative).
- Directors experience significant uncertainty with respect to the clarity of their organizational roles, feel challenged by their jobs, and value their learning opportunities highly.
- Directors are generally satisfied with their jobs but have concerns about the extent of travel, their ability to advance within the company, their compensation, and their relationship with independent auditors.

In the following discussions, we have attempted to build a model of those factors most important to internal auditors' job satisfaction as indicated in the questionnaire responses. Job satisfaction is viewed as resulting from the interaction of organizational structure, job characteristics, and career-orientation variables as depicted in the following diagram:

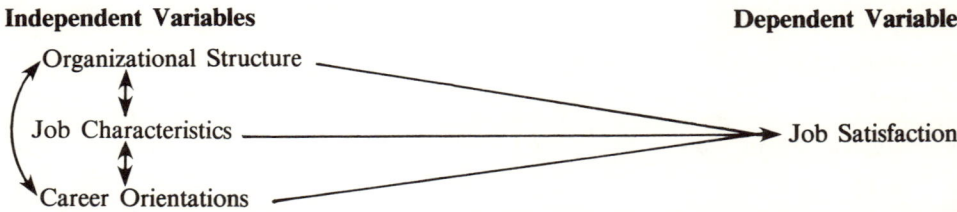

The underlying research question is: To what extent do the different mixes of independent variables impact job satisfaction? Since this line of research is just beginning for internal auditors, fine distinctions are not yet possible. However, our results indicate that job satisfaction is systematically related to organizational structure, to job characteristics, and to career-orientation variables. These relationships suggest ways for corporate managers to improve job satisfaction for their internal auditors, if necessary, and to avoid future dissatisfaction where all is now well. As this line of research develops and some of the initial relationships are tested more rigorously in future research, the theoretical model will become more specific and useful.

Perceived Organizational Structure

Organizational structure variables that could affect internal audit job satisfaction include formalization, intraorganizational support, centralization, flexibility, authority, and participation. Since these variables could be perceived differently by directors of internal auditing, we asked numerous questions about these dimensions. In addition, we used factor analysis[7] to identify those features which are most important to them.

Formalization refers to the degree to which organizational activities are standardized or codified. In a highly formal organization, everyone would be expected to observe detailed instructions in accomplishing tasks. Less formal organizations allow workers more personal initiative and creativity in fulfilling their work roles. Formalization in internal audit organizations consists of prescribing detailed audit manuals and procedures for audit assignments (A, II, 23).* Responses to this question indicate that in most internal audit organizations, auditors have freedom to exercise a high degree of initiative in performing their audits. Generally, they are not expected to follow detailed audit manuals. The data show (A, II, 59) that, although standard audit programs are widely used, they serve only as guidelines for individual auditors who create their own detailed audit procedures.

Centralization encompasses a number of dimensions related to the locus of decision-making authority within an organization. Centralized organizations tend to restrict decision making to a few top executives without allowing subordinates significant opportunity for discretionary judgment. Two aspects of centralization were found to be especially important for directors of internal auditing. The first (A, II, 3) reveals a moderate degree of centralization in decision making within internal audit departments. A small number of people make most important internal audit decisions. The second aspect (A, II, 33) indicates a lesser but still significant tendency toward centralization in the review of the directors' discretionary decisions. In sum, though the degree of centralization in internal audit organizations is not severe, there is a definite trend toward centralized decision making within internal audit departments and in the centralized review of the directors' discretionary judgments.

Organizations with flexible structures encourage workers to seek out and rely on experts in a given situation rather than to follow strictly the chain of command specified in the formal organization chart. Internal audit departments are characterized by structures that encourage flexibility in establishing communication channels (A, II, 39) and in reliance on informal, cooperative relationships which facilitate getting the job done (A, II, 8).

Organizations may permit and even foster different ways of exercising authority. In some instances, authority is exercised primarily through persuasion and education. In others, it might be exercised by commands that brook no argument and include an implicit threat. In still other organizations, the exercise of authority might be closely allied with rewarding desired performance with

---

*(A, II, 23) means Appendix A, Part II, Question 23 of the director's questionnaire. This code is used throughout this section. Readers are encouraged to refer to these questions for more information.

bonuses, recognition, or other forms of incentive. The questionnaire data support the conclusion that, at the director's level, internal audit organizations are characterized by persuasion rather than command (A, II, 25 and 47) and by offering incentives for attaining performance objectives (A, II, 24).

Organizational managements differ with respect to the amount of decision-making participation they encourage on the part of subordinates. The general tendency of internal audit departments is toward a moderate degree of participation in management actions (A, II, 29, 30, and 51). The spectrum of responses on the participation dimension was quite broad with 60 percent of the directors indicating clear participative styles, 33 percent indicating nonparticipative styles, and 7 percent undecided about the styles of management in their companies. On the whole, internal audit departments appear to exhibit a moderate degree of participation.

Intraorganizational support refers to the importance attached to the particular subgroup or activity within an organization by other organizational subgroups and activities. In the perception of the directors of internal auditing, the organizational support from audited subgroups varies according to their perception of internal audit's purpose. First, directors believe that unit managers generally look to internal audit as a source of constructive assistance (A, II, 42). Second, unit managers in a majority of companies tolerate the internal audit function as a necessary business practice (A, II, 27). Third, there is a divergence of opinion about whether unit managers tend to look on internal audit largely as a policing activity (A, II, 46). Forty-four percent agree that internal audit is perceived to be a policing activity; 48 percent disagree; and 8 percent are uncertain about the acceptance of internal audit by managers of audited units.

Perceived Job Characteristics

Job-characteristic variables for which we collected data include role clarity, job challenge, and learning opportunities. The following discussion focuses on the dimensions from Part II of the questionnaire which were identified most clearly across our entire sample for the three job-characteristic variables.

Role clarity concerns whether directors believe their organizational role is well specified. We were concerned about role clarity for two reasons: (1) because of earlier evidence suggesting that directors of internal auditing could be involved in multiple-reporting relationships (A, I, 9) and (2) because of the possible ambiguity that reporting to more than one "superior" might create. The dimensions of role clarity that stand out for directors of internal auditing concern their performance evaluation (A, II, 41) and executive expectations about internal audit performance (A, II, 53). Although many directors (53 percent) feel certain about the specific job aspects on which their performance will be evaluated, a significant minority (40 percent) are clearly uncertain about those specific job aspects that are most important. In addition, 54 percent of the respondents agree that at times executive expectations of their positions appear to conflict; 32 percent apparently find no such conficts in their situations. A relatively high percentage (14 percent) of the respondents were uncertain whether executive expectations with regard to their position appear to conflict.

One possible interpretation of this uncertainty is that the respondents actually did not sufficiently understand their roles and were unable to assess their superiors' expectations of them. The degree of role clarity for internal audit directors has dimensions that require constructive and positive management, particularly since directors with low role clarity tended to have lower scores on job satisfaction measures.

Aspects of job challenge which we investigated relate to routineness (A, III, 56), unanticipated problems (A, II, 58), the use of expertise (A, II, 60), difficult situations (A, II, 61), and time commitments (A, II, 62). The responses to most of these queries indicate that directors of internal auditing generally find their jobs to be challenging. The most important type of job challenge isolated by the statistical techniques was the absence of routineness (A, II, 56). Most of the directors (61 percent) responded that their work challenged their ability or ingenuity, while only 5 percent found their work to be routine. The remaining 34 percent described their jobs as half routine and half challenging. Overall, directors appear to find their jobs challenging.

The components of learning opportunity which were investigated included: the chance to learn new things about their company (A, II, 64) and the contribution of their internal audit experience to their ability to succeed in almost any department in their company (A, II, 65). Both components of learning opportunity were very high for directors of internal auditing. They perceive numerous opportunities to learn new things. Moreover, they believe that what they learn about the company as an internal auditor contributes positively to future management opportunities.

Perceived Career Orientation

We collected data about five aspects of directors' career orientation: their professional commitment, their commitment to organizational goals, their organizational immobility, their external orientation, and their concern for career advancement. Multiple questions about each of the five role-orientation variables permitted queries about different dimensions. In the following paragraphs, we report the results that stand out as being particularly important for directors of internal auditing.

For directors of internal auditing, professional commitment is exemplified according to three principal concerns:
- Active membership in The Institute of Internal Auditors (A, II, 17f).
- Passing the CIA exam (A, II, 17h).
- Passing the CPA/CA exam (A, II, 17i).

The first two items, which deal with specific internal audit interests, exhibited a greater concern than did the third item, which pertains more to general auditing.

Specifically, 78 percent of the respondents believe professional commitment means being active in The Institute of Internal Auditors; 8 percent view IIA activity as not being important for a professional commitment; and 14 percent are uncertain. Likewise, 63 percent of the directors believe passing the CIA exam is an important aspect of professional commitment; 13 percent view it as unimportant; 24 percent are uncertain about the CIA exam's relationship to internal audit professionalism. For the third concern, 5 percent of the respondents identified passing the CPA/CA exam as an important element of professional commitment; 28 percent were uncertain; and 21 percent found it to be unimportant for professional commitment in internal auditing.

Three concerns about professional commitment were identified in the statistical analysis as critical in the minds of directors. All of them deal with a director's relationship to professional organizations or certification. There were other aspects of professional commitment which were not highly associated statistically with the professional commitment variables. Among these was a question about compliance with professional standards in the face of a superior officer's request to the contrary (A, II, 48). Sixty-seven percent of the respondents would refuse to comply with a superior's request to perform an audit in a manner not in accord with internal audit standards. Nineteen percent would not refuse, and 14 percent are uncertain. The respondents comprising the 67 percent are not the same individuals who value the three dimensions of professional commitment identified as important in the preceding paragraph. That is, those who agreed with the importance of professional organization and certification activities generally did not agree with the importance of refusing to comply with an inappropriate audit request from a superior.

The underlying question here is normative. What should constitute the essentials of professional commitment? The questionnaire responses point to the acceptance of and conformity to professional institutions — rather than personal responsibility — as the basis for professional commitment. Is institutional conformity more or less desirable as the basis for professional commitment than a personal responsibility to stand up to a superior when professional standards are at issue? What responsibilities are appropriate for internal auditors with respect to professional commitment?

None of the features of the commitment to the company's goals stood out as being consistently important to directors of internal auditing. The item most highly associated with their responses on other dimensions of this variable was a general question related to loyalty to an employer (A, II, 26). While 68 percent agreed that their primary loyalty belongs to the employer, 22 percent and 10 percent disagreed or were uncommitted.

Although other dimensions of this variable (A, II, 11, 19, and 54) indicate, on an average, a high degree of concern for company-specific goals, the responses of particular directors are not consistent on these items. One would expect that a low-number response on Question 11 would go along with a high-number response on Question 19. For some respondents, this is indeed the case. But for many more, a low response on Question 11 is accompanied by a low or average-level response on Question 19. Because of this inconsistency, the commitment to organizational goals is not a well-specified variable. In sum, directors of internal auditing are clearly concerned with meeting organizational goals; but the components of their commitment are diverse and not well defined.

The most important aspects of directors' organizational immobility relate to their plans to pursue careers with the company for which they currently work. Most have no immediate plans to leave their current companies (A, II, 13 and 16). Sixty-two percent of the respondents would not leave their current place of employment for a company they considered to be better managed without significant salary increase (A, II, 4); 65 percent would leave their current company if offered higher pay (A, II, 34). However, a large number of the respondents who said they would not leave their company of employment in Question 4 also answered that they would not leave their company of employment in Question 34, leading to a moderately high degree of consistency between the respondents' replies to the two questions. On the whole, directors of internal auditing exhibit some organizational mobility with increases in compensation playing a major role in motivating company switches. Without an offer of significant pay increases, they appear committed to employment in their current companies.

The external orientation variable is concerned with sources of directors' professional auditing stimulation. Most directors (73 percent) responded that they find outlets within their departments to discuss professional auditing interests (A, II, 6). The amount of professional auditing stimulation received at professional meetings is far more variable (A, II, 36). This variability is also reflected with respect to professional journals (A, II, 45). Continuing education seminars of companies are not viewed as a strong source of professional auditing stimulation (A, II, 49). In summary, directors look toward their departments for professional auditing stimulation rather than to professional meetings, professional journals, or continuing education seminars of companies.

Career advancement consists primarily of concern for salary levels and promotability. The main component of promotability deals with thinking of new and better ways of performing one's task (A, III, 30). Most directors (77 percent) believe that improvements in task efficiency lead to promotions. Many of them believe that salary levels indicate one's contribution to the company (A, II, 7). Although the data do not support the idea that directors are unconcerned with salary levels, there is a clear indication that promotability issues outweigh salary issues for the directors in our study. This may reflect the fact that directors' salaries are institutionally lower than controllers' or treasurers' salaries (A, I, 11). The best hope for salary improvement appears to be promotion out of internal auditing.

Job Satisfaction

Twelve aspects of job satisfaction were investigated in Question 55. Factor analytic-techniques showed that all 12 are viewed consistently by directors of internal auditing and form important components of job satisfaction. For the most part, there is an extremely high degree of correlation among the job satisfaction concerns. Directors who are satisfied are usually satisfied in all respects, while those who are dissatisfied are dissatisfied on all counts.

The overwhelming responses of the directors were toward the "satisfied" end of the scale. Even for concern for advancement (item 4), where directors indicated the least satisfaction, 67 percent said that they were satisfied.

In a related question, we asked the directors to rank in order the three features of their work that they found most appealing and the three features that they found least appealing (see Table 3-35). Ranked in order of magnitude were:
- Intellectual challenge of work.
- Variety of assignments.
- Contribution to success of company.

Ranked as least appealing by a very large margin was "travel." Following travel, the job features indicated as least appealing were:
- Relationship with independent accountants.
- General work atmosphere.
- Compensation.

We correlated the various organizational and personable attitude variables with the job-satisfaction variable in order to assess the degree to which organizational and attitudinal factors affect job satisfaction as reflected in our data. Role clarity, challenge, and learning opportunities have strong, positive relationships with job satisfaction. Directors who indicated high levels of role clarity, challenge, and learning opportunities were also very satisfied.

Of the career-orientation variables, organizational immobility and concern for career advancement had very high correlations with job satisfaction. Directors who have made up their minds to remain with their current companies are consistently in the groups who responded "very satisfied" or "satisfied" on the job-satisfaction variable. The responses of directors on the career-advancement variable, as compared to the job-satisfaction variable, also show that directors who are most optimistic that innovation leads to promotion are satisfied with their jobs. Job satisfaction is correlated positively with commitment to organizational goals and with professional commitment at high and moderate levels respectively.

External orientation, however, has a negative relationship to job satisfaction. Directors who tend to be oriented toward groups outside their departments for internal audit stimulation tend to be less satisfied with their jobs than those who are internally oriented. On the whole, directors who are optimistic about promotions as rewards for innovations and who are committed to their companies show a very high degree of satisfaction.

Among the organizational variables, the degrees of centralization and formalization of audit decision making have no appreciable relationship to job satisfaction. Directors in flexible organizations tend to have higher job satisfaction as did those whose companies have participative management styles. Persuasive use of authority is related to high job satisfaction, while issuing orders and commands without explanation is related to lower job satisfaction. Directors whose managers do not view internal auditors as "policemen" indicated higher job satisfaction than did their counterparts in firms where internal audit is seen as a policing function.

The correlations discussed above give clues to the reasons why some directors are dissatisfied or not as satisfied as others. Principally, it appears that lack of job satisfaction is related to not having colleagues in the internal audit department with whom to share professional interests, not being an active participant in management, being viewed as an organizational policeman, and having to follow superiors' directives without receiving adequate explanation. These constitute matters — along with time spent travelling, relationship with independent accountants, general work atmosphere, and compensation — where improvements could have a positive effect on directors' job satisfaction. Improvements in job satisfaction could lead to higher quality of work and to increased interest in internal audit careers.

Growth of Internal Audit Departments

To determine the effects of developments on the growth of internal audit departments, one needs a continuing series of data revealing the size of internal audit departments over time. In this way, changes in size can be related to the developments at issue. No such data appear to be available on any systematic basis. We felt a need for such information, especially for the period in which the FCPA was promulgated and disseminated. At the same time, we were concerned lest a request for information requiring respondents to search their files, especially if such information was not readily available, might discourage respondents from returning questionnaires, thereby reducing the validity of the entire study.

We decided to ask for a minimum of such information and designed Question 20 of Part I of the director's questionnaire for that purpose. Even the limited information we requested is a burden to many respondents and may not be available for others. The information received as a result is scanty but useful. Not all respondents answered all the questions. Nevertheless, a sufficient number did respond to provide some useful indications. The tables in this section summarize the information received.

Note that imposition of the FCPA did not have any dramatic effect on the size of internal audit departments. The data in Table 3-11 show a steady growth in the size of internal audit departments but one that appears to lag behind growth in revenues and assets. Note also that internal audit growth is positive, although there is basically no change in the number of total company employees over this period and that company expenditures on internal audit salaries surpassed external audit fee expenditures during the 1978-1981 period.

Table 3-11
Directors of Internal Auditing
Growth of Internal Audit Departments*

Year**	No. of Internal Audit Positions	Total Internal Audit Salaries	External Audit Fee	No. of Company Employees	Average Internal Audit Salary	Company Size in Thousands Revenues	Assets
1974	13.3	$243,950	$289,650	19,851	$17,291	$ 850,850	$1,306,800
1977	15.5	343,840	382,920	20,389	19,805	1,123,400	1,672,000
1978	16.4	404,860	438,500	21,440	21,363	1,273,200	1,926,400
1981	18.6	600,990	527,140	21,686	26,314	1,928,900	2,731,000
1982	18.9	668,390	551,680	21,177	28,791	2,024,000	2,892,000
1983	19.5	731,850	581,490	21,431	31,115	2,229,100	3,158,800
1984	20.3	804,510	620,710	21,861	32,877	2,482,700	3,446,200

*Appendix C expands the analysis of responses to Question 20 of Part I of the director's questionnaire and supplies some interesting data on internal audit costs and independent audit fees by industry group.

**All figures except dates are averages; the averages are based on companies which provided a complete set of data for the full period; 1974 through 1981 are actual; 1982 through 1984 are respondents' estimates.

An analysis of the growth of average internal audit positions relative to company employees indicates that the greatest growth occurred during the 1974-1977 period. No spectacular increase in the size of audit staffs followed passage of the FCPA. As data explained in a subsequent section indicate, responses to it were generally of a different nature.

The reported data also include some interesting comparative information about the size of internal audit departments and about average salaries in them. The following tables group respondents' companies by size and by average internal audit salary to indicate the number having audit staffs of various sizes and different average internal audit salaries:

Table 3-12
Directors of Internal Auditing
Respondents Grouped by Size of Audit Staff in 1982

Number of Internal Audit Positions	Number of Firms	Percentage of Firms
Fewer than 10	162	50
10 - 19	64	19
20 - 29	42	13
30 - 49	28	9
50 - 99	22	7
More than 100	9	3
Total	327	100

Table 3-13
Directors of Internal Auditing
Respondents Grouped by Average Internal Audit Department's Salary in 1982

Average Internal Audit Salary	Number of Firms	Percentage of Firms
Less than $25,000	98	33
$25,000 - $29,999	74	25
$30,000 - $34,999	60	20
$35,000 - $39,999	26	8
More than $40,000	41	14
Total	299	100

Probably the most surprising information in these tables is the substantial size of the average internal audit salary in some companies.

Responses to Developments Impacting Internal Auditing

Not all the current developments impacting internal auditing could be segregated for specific inquiry and attention. In this section of our report, we present our findings on three developments:
- The FCPA.
- Increased use pf EDP.
- Increase in international operations.

Responses to the FCPA

From previous research, we knew that a variety of initiatives had been undertaken by companies when first confronted with the FCPA. In Question 31 of Part III, we listed 21 possible responses to the FCPA and added an "other" category to accept any initiatives we might have overlooked. We received a wide range of answers. Respondents were invited to check as many of the possibilities as their companies had chosen. All initiatives listed received some check marks ranging from 30 to 222. The "other" category was checked 28 times.

The ten initiatives receiving the most attention are listed in Table 3-14 below:

Table 3-14
Director of Internal Auditing
Ten Most Common Initiatives in Response to the FCPA

Initiatives	Number of Companies	Percentage of Companies
Your company took specific actions to create an increased awareness of the importance of internal controls among operating managment.	222	67
Senior management became more active in internal control concerns.	192	58
The audit committee became more active in internal control concerns.	181	55
Your company initiated a formal review of the internal control system.	180	55
Your company initiated new controls or revised existing controls.	169	51

Table 3-14 (continued)

	Number	Percentage
Documentation of internal control weaknesses and recommendations for improved controls increased in internal audit reports.	162	49
Revision or initiation of a corporate code of conduct to address issues raised by the FCPA was undertaken.	138	42
Specific actions were taken to create an increased awareness among internal auditors of the importance of detecting and minimizing fraud possibilities.	133	40
Your company developed a fully documented internal control file.	130	39
Internal audit recommendations gained increased authority.	126	38

Little comment on this list is necessary; the items speak for themselves. Almost as interesting as the previous ranking is a list of some of the possibilities that did not make the top ten. These include:

Possibilities	Number	Percentage of Respondents
Internal audit emphasis on fraud potential and detection increased.	89	27
Internal audit monitoring of management's compliance with the corporate code of conduct was initiated or increased.	118	36
The position of director of internal auditing was elevated within the company's organizational structure.	77	23
A direct reporting relationship between the board of directors and the director of internal auditing was instituted.	52	16
Internal audit resources were increased in response to the FCPA.	99	30

To some internal audit departments, the FCPA offered an opportunity for growth, increased service, and improved status. To others, it did not. One might surmise that those companies that did not elevate the position of director of internal auditing, for example, had already established that position at a satisfactorily high level. However, none of our other data is directly supportive of such an assumption. Unfortunately, the data collected do not permit us to examine other possible explanations of the different responses to the FCPA.

Increased Use of EDP

Other research conducted at the Paton Accounting Center has noted the rapid adoption of computer-based information systems for business purposes, the difficulties in maintaining control of such systems by senior management, and the fears that many senior executives have about EDP methods that they don't thoroughly understand. That research strongly suggested that there was often a substantial gap between the attitudes of data-processing managers and internal auditors. The relationship was often one that failed to reflect mutual respect, ability to appreciate the other's viewpoint or needs, or cooperation for the good of the company.

We asked directors of internal auditing to rank the quality of internal control over EDP systems in their companies relative to other activities and functions which are audited by internal auditing. The question addressed ten different aspects of the EDP system and provided the opportunity to rate each aspect as "very superior," "superior," "neither superior nor inferior," "inferior," and "very inferior." By far the heaviest concentration of evaluations fell right in the middle — "neither superior nor inferior" — with "superior" a significant leader. The two extremes were seldom selected. The responses to the next two questions of the director's questionnaire show their concern about the quality of internal control over EDP:

Question 32 of Part III

Increasing reliance on computers for information processing purposes has created a source of internal control difficulty for many companies' internal audit groups. The statements below characterize several common responses to the internal audit problems associated with assuring internal control over EDP activities. Please consider these statements and *place the number corresponding to the response which best describes your company's current EDP audit strategy in the space provided at the end of the statements.*

Please use the "other" option only if none of the statements describes the essence of your company's current response.

Question 33 of Part III

Many companies have not yet settled on a permanent response to the EDP audit problem. Which of the statements in Question 32 would best characterize your view of what EDP auditing will be like in your company in the future? Statement number _____ best describes your company's future response to the problems associated with EDP auditing.

Table 3-15
Directors of Internal Auditing
EDP Audit Strategies

		Present		Future	
		No.	%	No.	%
1.	Your company has taken no special action to assure internal control over EDP systems.	23	7	7	2
2.	Your company has a group of EDP specialists (not in the internal audit department) which has the responsibility to assure internal control over EDP systems.	23	7	9	3
3.	Your company has a group of EDP specialists in the internal audit department which works independently to assure internal control over EDP systems.	114	35	81	25
4.	Your company has a group of EDP specialists which works in teams with non-EDP internal auditors to assure internal control over EDP systems.	69	21	64	20
5.	Your company has a group of EDP specialists which advises, consults with, and trains internal auditors to assure internal control over EDP systems.	15	5	35	11
6.	All of your company's internal auditors have sufficient EDP expertise to assure internal control over EDP systems as part of their normal auditing activities.	24	7	105	33

Table 3-15 (continued)

7. Your company's internal auditors do not have special EDP expertise, nor do they need it to adequately perform their internal audit duties.	9	3	2	1
8. Other	47	15	15	5
Total	324	100	318	100

Most of the "other" responses described current efforts to provide the internal audit function with EDP expertise through training of some kind. Some borrow expertise from other departments or use outside assistance.

The emphasis on responses to 3, 4, and 6 calls for some comment. An independent group of EDP specialists, whether located in the internal audit department or elsewhere, provides assurance to internal auditing only if the two groups can effectively communicate with each other. EDP experts who are not audit trained may provide an important review function, but they cannot replace internal auditors. On the other hand, knowledgeable executives in a number of large companies have informed us that there are data-processing complexities that only a few specialists can understand. All internal auditors would benefit from EDP expertise, but it is unlikely that they could master all the technicalities of a major management information system and then remain current year after year.

The internal audit solution for the data-processing problem is not yet clear. Companies differ significantly in the complexity of their systems; technological developments occur at shocking rates of speed; means to combine in one person the talents, skills, and attitudes of auditors and EDP specialists are rare. For the immediate future, combinations of responses to 6 and either 3 or 4 appear to be a reasonable strategy. However, a director using this strategy should consider it an interim measure to be modified when more information becomes available.

To elicit from respondents some idea of the difficulties they face in maintaining internal control over their EDP systems, we included Question 35 of Part III: "Please share with us your perspective on any specific difficulties your company experiences in maintaining internal control over EDP systems." Not every respondent commented on this question. Those who did were concerned about the rapid growth of EDP within their companies and the control problems which result from that growth. They were also concerned about the neglect of internal control which accompanied rapid expansion. This concern involved those in data processing who often have no appreciation of control matters and managers who sometimes place emphasis on production and economy, disregarding control.

Several answers described the failure to document changes in EDP systems. Even when the original documentation was successful, changes to the system were not accompanied by updated documentation. Thus, either time or a personnel change could result in a system which was not really understood by its users.

Another concern is directed at the common existence of uncontrolled access to systems and the data they process. As EDP systems handle more and more information, the importance of restricting access becomes greater. Apparently, in some cases little attention is paid to classifying the data in the system and to restricting access to information that is not job related.

Lack of user awareness about EDP systems and of their limitations troubles some respondents. Those who rely on the EDP system to accept, process, store, and return their data often do not understand how this is done. As a result, they are not aware to what extent others have access to confidential data. Users are often unaware of the many errors made during data processing. They intentionally or unintentionally abdicate responsibility for control, expecting that the EDP department will attend to that problem. But too often, the data processors have neither an interest in nor an understanding of internal control. Both users and data processors too often emphasize speed and economy. This absence of concern with internal control is a continuing worry for internal auditors.

International Activities

The responses to two questions imply that the internationalization of U.S. and Canadian corporations may not be causing any serious problems for internal auditing. The percentage of companies' operationns in economically developing and underdeveloped countries is still very small. Somewhat surprisingly, the directors' evaluations of the quality of internal control in those countries are not as pessimistic as one might expect.

The following table reports the responses to a question inquiring about the extent of overseas activities (A, III, 36):

Table 3-16
Directors of Internal Auditing
Estimates of Nondomestic Operations

Location	Percentage
Domestic — United States & Canada	92
Nondomestic — Economically developed countries	5
Nondomestic — Economically developing countries	2
Nondomestic — Underdeveloped countries	1
	100

The directors' estimates of the quality of internal control in these classes of countries appears in the following summary:

Table 3-17
Directors of Internal Auditing
Estimates of Quality of Internal Control in Domestic
and Nondomestic Countries

Location	Very Poor Quality (%)	Poor Quality (%)	Neither High Nor Poor Quality (%)	High Quality (%)	Very High Quality (%)
Domestic — United States and Canada	0	4	23	60	13

Table 3-17 (continued)

Nondomestic — Economically developed countries	2	9	37	47	5
Nondomestic — Economically developing countries	5	20	58	13	4
Nondomestic — Economically underdeveloped countries	6	24	59	7	4

If the internal control in nondomestic countries is no worse than the directors' estimates and if the percentage of their companies' operations in nondomestic countries is as low as claimed. it seems unlikely that internationalization has posed any substantial problem to most internal audit departments.

The following table reports the manner in which the directors stated they performed internal audit functions in nondomestic countries:

Table 3-18
Directors of Internal Auditing
Method of Performing Audits in Nondomestic Countries*

	Nondomestic, Economically Developed Countries	Nondomestic, Economically Developing Countries	Nondomestic, Economically Underdeveloped Countries
The internal audit function is performed entirely by local audit personnel.	12	5	4
The internal audit function is performed by local audit personnel with occasional corporate audit's on-site review.	9	8	4
The internal audit function is performed by local audit personnel with regular corporate audit's on-site review.	12	15	9
The internal audit function is performed entirely by corporate audit personnel.	61	63	74
Other	6	9	9
	100	100	100

*See Appendix E for additional analysis of responses to this and related questions concerned with internal auditing of nondomestic operations.

For the most part, "other" answers were "not applicable, no internal audit participation," or "no overseas function."

Question 39 of Part III asked: "What changes, if any, do you expect to make in your audit practice for nondomestic operations over the next few years? (Please describe)." Because only a small proportion of the companies represented in the study have extensive foreign operations, the number of answers was not large. Of those responding, many plan on increased U.S. training for their nondomestic auditors. This includes creating an awareness of needed internal controls on the part of management personnel and auditors. Some directors are planning to establish regionally based auditors to cover a number of nondomestic plants and activities in various countries. Others will try to establish increased coordination with local personnel, expand their audit effort with increased growth, do more functional auditing, and give more audit attention to EDP.

Variety of Internal Audit Activities

Part III of the director's questionnaire included questions directed at discovering which aspects of possible internal audit activities receive the most attention. One question, discussed subsequently, inquired about specific audit procedures. The questions discussed here are concerned with broad classes of activities.

The Nature of Internal Audit Activities

Question 25 was concerned with the amount of time given to types of internal audit activities now performed. Question 26 used the same classification but asked directors what the distribution of time should be. Table 3-19 shows the responses:

Table 3-19
Directors of Internal Auditing
Nature of Audit Effort

Activity	Proportion of Time — Now (%)	Proportion of Time — Should Be (%)
The actual *performance* by internal auditors of internal control procedures such as bank reconciliations, test counts, account analyses, etc.	10	8
The *testing* of the extent to which the work of others *complies* with internal control requirements prescribed by company policy.	41	41
The *evaluation* of the appropriateness of internal control features currently called for by company policy.	32	34
The *initiation* of new or additional internal control features deemed necessary for new or continuing business activities.	17	17
	100	100

The range of activity indicated by the responses to these questions is impressive. There is a significant difference between performing internal control procedures in compliance with instructions and in testing the extent to which the work of others complies with internal control requirements. there is a greater difference between performing or testing and evaluating the propriety of internal control procedures now called for by company policy. The extent of judgment necessary to evaluate established company policy procedures implies considerable knowledge of the company's operations, sufficient experience to evaluate internal control risks, and judgment to make cost-benefit analyses.

Note that the directors are responding for the total audit effort of their departments. If internal auditors of little experience are participating in this type of work, as the staff-questionnaire responses suggest, they are gaining experience that we expect is relatively rare for employees of their age and experience.

The same comment is pertinent to the initiation of new or additional internal control features. A responsible manager would not like to see inexperienced personnel making decisions about the establishment of new or the elimination of present internal control practices. Yet responses indicate that a substantial proportion of audit effort is spent this way. This does not necessarily mean that new or inexperienced internal auditors are seeking such decisions but that the question should be raised all the same.

Another interesting fact is the minimal effort devoted to the actual performance of internal control procedures. We suspect that many people in business think of internal auditors as endlessly poring over business documents and checking them carefully against the records. The responses to these questions show the opposite to be true. Only a small part of their time goes to such work, and the directors expect to reduce that proportion even more.

We are impressed with the apparent fact that directors of internal auditing are well satisfied with the present distribution of the time of their staff members. A slight reduction in performance and an increase in evaluation are the only adjustments they would make.

The Purpose of Internal Audit Activities

Questions 27 and 28 of Part III are directed at the purpose of internal audit activities and the division of time among what we see as the major purposes now and five years from now. Table 3-20 shows the responses:

Table 3-20
Directors of Internal Auditing
Purpose of Audit Effort

	Allocation of Time (%)	
	Now	In 5 Years (%)
Detection of errors and irregularities. This activity is directed at the prevention or timely discovery of errors and irregularities in the processing or recording of transactions	20	15
Monitoring management control. Management control strives to obtain compliance with the applicable rules and procedures established by company policy.	27	26
Performance evaluation. This activity assesses the efficiency or the effectiveness with which company goals are attained.	14	19
Monitoring internal accounting control. Internal accounting control strives to assure that published financial statements present fairly the financial position and results of operations of the company in accordance with generally accepted accounting practice or other appropriate standards and that assets are appropriately safeguarded.	32	28
Decision-making review. This activity evaluates the effectiveness of management's operating and financial decisions.	7	12
	100	100

A comparison of the percentages of time now spent for the listed purposes and the percentages expected to be spent in five years shows small differences.

The directors expect to spend less time detecting errors and irregularities and monitoring internal control and more time in performance evaluation and decision-making review. These expectations reveal an anticipated, continued broadening of the internal audit function's scope of activity with emphasis on the more demanding tasks. Interestingly, these directions correspond with the desires of senior management and members of the board of directors as indicated in responses to other questionnaires.

Although the anticipated changes are not large, they constitute a projection of past experience. This indicates that the directors do not expect significant opposition to their expansion into what many consider to be well beyond traditional internal audit activities.

These responses also evidence substantial attention to management control which extends beyond financial activities into general operations, whatever these may be for the specific company. This means that internal auditors are already involved in control procedures for manufacturing, other forms of production, and for all corresponding support activities — purchasing, materials handling, warehousing, marketing, and the like.

Less time may be spent in the detection of errors and irregularities than many people with an interest in business might expect. Policing will probably always be some part of the internal audit function, but it appears to be a decreasing one.

Likewise, the present and the anticipated increasing attention to decision-making review may be something of a surprise. Evaluating the effectiveness of management's operating and financial decisions requires considerable expertise and judgment, an ability to put oneself in management's position and weigh the costs and the benefits of possible decisions before and after they are made. Because so many internal auditors plan to spend only a short period of time in that activity, one wonders how they will gather the necessary experience and judgment. One possible answer is that the management decisions being evaluated are at a low-management level. Another explanation might be that this kind of evaluation is made only by those who do stay in internal auditing for long periods.

Subject of Internal Audit Effort

Question 29a asked respondents to estimate the percentage of time spent by the internal audit group on audits in a number of different organizational units. Responses were as follows:

Table 3-21
Directors of Internal Auditing
Subjects of Internal Audit Effort

Subjects	Percentage of Time
Corporate headquarters staff units	22
Plants and departments	36
Dealers, agencies, and branches	11

Table 3-21 (continued)

Divisional management units	19
Outside contractors	4
Corporate senior management	3
Other	5
	100

The "other" responses included joint ventures, acquisitions, special assignments, and a variety of miscellaneous activities.

Like the other questions in this portion of the questionnaire, the impression given is one of variety. Internal auditors work in all areas of the company — in production and operations as well as in finance. We were somewhat surprised to discover the amount of time spent in corporate headquarters' staff units where one would expect internal controls to be the strongest. One might conclude that substantial amounts of time are required in those units in order to review decisions made by management on operating and financial matters. Nothing in our data confirms or denies that conclusion.

The subject of audit efforts was the substance of Question 29b. It inquired into the percentages of time spent by the internal audit group on the activities listed in the following table:

Table 3-22
Directors of Internal Auditing
Percentages of Time Spent on Specific Activities

Activity	Percentage of Time
Raw-material acquisitions	9
Sales contracts	11
Labor contracts	3
Quality controls	8
Manufacturing operations	28
Transfers between units of the company	5
Warranty claims	1
Other	35
	100

"Other" activities mentioned were full financial audits, subsidiaries, computer or EDP activities, inventory control, operational audits, and special projects.

The most interesting aspect of the responses to this question is the amount of time devoted to manufacturing operations. There can be no doubt that internal auditors have moved well outside the financial portion of the business in performing audit work. Even quality control receives a considerable amount of attention.

Usage of Available Audit Time

How time is allocated by internal audit departments often indicates which matters are given priority by department members and leaders. The responses summarized in this table may be useful in showing the number of matters that require internal audit's attention:

Table 3-23
Directors of Internal Auditing
Allocation of Internal Audit Department's Time

Activity	Percentage of Time
Chargeable audit time	62
Training	6
Noncontrollable time (e.g., vacations, holidays, illness)	9
Performance evaluations	2
Planning	6
Coordination with external auditors and regulators	5
Interface with audit committee	2
Recruiting	2
Internal audit department's administration	5
Other	1
	100

To discover whether the size of the internal audit staff had any significant influence on the allocation of internal audit time, the data in the preceding table were analyzed further as follows:

Table 3-23a
Directors of Internal Auditing
Allocation of Available Audit Department's Time by Size of Staff

Activity	Size of Internal Audit Staff (%)				
	1-10	11-25	26-50	51-99	100
Chargeable audit time	56	59	66	74	67
Training	6	7	5	4	6
Noncontrollable time	8	9	10	8	11
Performance evaluation	3	2	2	1	1
Planning	8	5	5	3	4
Coordination with external auditors and regulators	6	3	2	2	3
Audit committee	2	2	1	1	.5
Recruiting	1	1	1	1	.5
Administration	9	11	8	5	7
Other	1	1	1	1	1
	100	100	100	100	100
Number of responding companies	144	60	32	11	6

Some interesting differences appear in this analysis, but no significant patterns emerge. The small number of companies with large audit staffs makes generalization involving them somewhat risky.

Frequency of Internal Audits

Information in the following table is also useful primarily for comparison purposes. It reports responses to the question: "What is the average length of time between regularly scheduled audits of your company's departments, divisions, branches, etc. Please indicate one."

Table 3-24
Directors of Internal Auditing
Frequency of Internal Audits

Interval Between Audits	Responses Number	Percentage
Less than 1 year	30	9
1 year	87	27
1½ years	58	18
2 years	63	20
2½ years	25	8
3 years	44	14
3½ years	1	—
4 years	7	2
4½ years	0	0
5 years	4	1
More than 5 years	2	1
Total	321	100

Classification of Internal Audit Departments

Part III of the director's questionnaire was designed to address key issues related to the responsibilities of internal audit departments:

1. Whether the activities that constitute the core of internal audit responsibilities can be identified.
2. Whether the mix of internal audit activities differs greatly among companies or follows a small number of identifiable patterns.

Our interest in these questions arose from the initial discussions of the project when we were trying to specify which services internal audit departments supply to their organizations. Anecdotal evidence suggests that their duties differed substantially from company to company. In addition, internal audit standards and internal audit textbooks address the duties of internal audit departments at extremely general and abstract levels. Although the professional internal audit literature categorizes activities into financial data reliability, internal control, and operational/management audits, we were unable to find any systematic attempts to identify the mix of these activities.

We designed Part III of the director's questionnaire as a first attempt to define empirically as much of the content of internal audit activities as we could from statistical analyses of the data. These analyses are useful in identifying the activities which various groups of internal audit departments do and do not emphasize. Our findings, which we discuss at more length in the following pages, include:

- Of ten internal audit activities identified by respondents as widely performed, only the review of compliance with, and adequacy of, internal control procedures constitutes a core duty.
- There is considerable diversity of practice in terms of the nature and supply of internal audit services other than review of internal control procedures.

- Internal audit departments fall into a small number of patterns in terms of the services they provide.
- When classified into mutually exclusive groups, the internal audit departments in our study are found to engage in distinctly different mixes of activities.

Using the data in Part III from the director's questionnaires, we attempted to find response patterns which would indicate a consensus about the level of performance of various internal audit activities, separating those audit services which directors considered essential from those that are more discretionary in nature. We used factor analysis[8] to group all the questions from Part III into ten mutually exclusive factors. In descending order of relevance to the core of internal audit activities, the ten factors are:

1. Review of compliance with, and adequacy of, internal control procedures.
2. Review of expense reports.
3. Search for fraud and irregularities.
4. Investigation of compliance with corporate code of conduct.
5. Determination of, or assistance with, financial data reliability.
6. Participation in development of management information systems.
7. Performance of cost-benefit studies.
8. Review of quality controls.
9. Review of budgets and performance evaluations.
10. Special assignments.

Table 3-25 presents the distributions of responses for the questions that make up each internal audit-activity factor. These responses indicate the directors' beliefs about the relative importance of these activities. The only factor on which the respondents approach consensus deals with the review of compliance with, and adequacy of, internal control procedures. Virtually all the respondents indicated that they perform the internal control activities at the "always perform" or "normally perform, rarely omit" levels. There is no corresponding consensus on any of the other nine activities factors. In all other cases, responses indicate that significant numbers of internal audit departments supply these internal audit activities at all six performance levels.

Table 3-25
Directors of Internal Audit
Internal Audit Activities and Performance Levels

Question Number	Percentage Responding					
	NP[1]	RP[2]	OP[3]	NP-00[4]	NP-R0[5]	AP[6]
Review of compliance with, and adequacy of, internal control procedures						
4. Review compliance with established control procedures.	0	1	1	6	27	65
5. Review and comment on the adequacy of internal control procedures.	0	1	1	2	24	74
Review of expense report						
16. Audit expense reports of:						
Employees	7	9	23	14	21	26

Table 3-25 (continued)

Middle management	6	8	20	15	24	26
Senior management	7	8	18	9	21	36
Search for fraud and irregularities						
7. Count cash funds.	9	21	28	12	13	17
12. Investigate alleged shortages or other irregularities.	1	4	19	11	23	43
Investigation of compliance with corporate code of conduct						
18. Investigate regarding conformity with corporate code of conduct for:						
Employees	19	12	18	12	16	22
Middle management	19	9	18	11	19	24
Senior management	20	10	15	11	16	28
Determination of, or assistance with, financial data reliability						
1. Review the extent to which external financial statements comply with generally accepted accounting principles.	36	25	19	4	8	8
2. Review the extent to which internal financial statements comply with company accounting policies.	8	10	24	18	20	20
3. Consult with divisional and/or unit personnel on accounting matters.	2	6	32	20	27	13
Participation in development of management information systems						
14. Participate in the following phases of management information systems development:						
System specification	14	15	22	19	19	11
Design	18	16	20	19	18	9
Programming	43	20	11	11	7	7
Installation	32	16	16	17	12	7
Postinstallation testing	7	8	25	19	23	18
Performance of cost-benefit studies						
15. Make cost-benefit studies of proposed changes in:						
Operating procedures	23	26	33	9	8	2
Internal control procedures	15	19	29	12	18	7
Review of quality control						
19. Review application of product (or service) for quality controls.	27	15	25	13	14	5
Review of budgets and performance evaluations						
20. Review analysis of profit or budget variances.	15	12	32	19	15	7
21. Review procedures for developing departmental or company budgets.	27	22	29	12	6	3
22. Consult with management about proposed changes in the company's	27	28	26	8	8	3

Table 3-25 (continued)

		1	2	3	4	5	6
	organizational structure.						
23.	Review the appropriateness of performance-evaluation measures for company's divisions, departments, branches, etc.	33	24	22	11	8	2
Special assignments							
13.	Audit joint ventures or suppliers' cost statements.	31	18	21	11	13	6
17.	Review usage of company-owned aircraft.	54	6	14	5	8	13

1. Never perform
2. Rarely perform
3. Occasionally perform
4. Normally perform, occasionally omit
5. Normally perform, rarely omit
6. Always perform

The responses to Question 14 of Part III may be especially revealing about current developments. Almost one-half of those responding participate in the system-specification and design phases of management-information systems development at the "normally perform, occasionally omit" level or higher. Only about 30 percent "never perform" these roles. Sixty percent of the directors "normally perform, occasionally omit" postinstallation testing. These data show that many internal audit departments have already accepted important responsibilities in developing and testing computer-based information systems. Some of those which have not may be in companies which have not yet generally adopted computerized systems. Other research indicates that developments in this direction will continue for most companies and their internal audit departments.

Classification of Departments by Activities Performed

We used a cluster-analysis technique[9] to group the 330 internal audit departments in our sample based on their responses for the ten internal audit-duties factors. The analysis placed each company's internal audit department into one of five groups and reported the average score on the ten factors for each group. Table 3-26 summarizes the results of the cluster analysis and describes the level of each group's performance in terms of the performance scale used in Part III of the director's questionnaire:

Table 3-26
Directors of Internal Auditing
Respondents' Companies Grouped by Audit Activities

Audit Activity	Group				
	A	B	C	D	E
Review of compliance with, and adequacy of, internal control procedures	5.5	5.5	6	5.5	4
Review of expense reports	5	5	2	4	4
Search for fraud and irregularities	4	4	3	4	5

Table 3-26 (continued)

Investigation of compliance with code of corporate conduct	5	6	6	2	4
Determination of, or assistance with, financial data reliability	5	3.5	2	3.5	3.5
Participation in development of management information systems	4	5	1	3	2
Performance of cost-benefit studies	5	2	3	2	3
Review of quality controls	3	3	3	3	3
Review of budgets and performance evaluations	4	2.5	1.5	1.5	2.5
Special assignments	4	2.5	2.5	2.5	1
Number of companies	77	63	68	85	37

1. Never performed
2. Rarely performed
3. Occasionally performed
4. Normally performed but occasionally omitted
5. Normally performed and rarely omitted
6. Always performed

Each of the five groups outlined above exhibits a different profile of internal audit activities performed by group members. Groups A and B perform all activities at high levels except for review of quality controls. B does less than A with special assignments, budgets and performance evaluations, and financial data reliability. The most significant difference between groups A and B is in attention to cost-benefit studies. Group C emphasizes internal control and the code of corporate conduct, giving little attention to any other activity. Group E has no outstanding emphasis other than searching for fraud and irregularities. Group D is similar to E but is much less concerned with the code of corporate conduct.

No single group is so large that it dominates the others in terms of the number of internal audit departments within the group. The distribution of companies across groups is roughly uniform except for Group E, which has approximately one-half the membership of the other four groups.

These results support the idea that, while there is some diversity among internal audit departments, our statistical techniques were able to cluster the 330 companies into five groups whose members have very similar performance levels on the ten internal audit-activities factors. This relatively small number of groups implies a limited diversity with patterns that additional research might identify more precisely.

The statistical procedures that result in the groupings shown do not explain reasons for the existence of these groups. Two hypotheses have been suggested. One is that the five clusters represent different stages of evolutionary development. Groups A and B represent the more advanced audit departments, aggressively engaging in a variety of activities and high levels of performance and giving significant attention to operational as well as financial matters. Group C is probably the farthest behind from a developmental viewpoint and is only beginning to perform some of the operational types of activities that groups A and B now routinely perform.

A second hypothesis is that the auditing needs of commpanies differ widely. Not all companies desire operational auditing from their internal audit staffs. For some companies, the most important activities that internal auditing can ever perform are restricted to financial activities with heavy emphasis on review of expense accounts and the prevention or the search for fraud and irregularities.

We would be more comfortable with the second hypothesis if we could find some industry or other differences that distinguish companies in Group C from the other companies represented. However, our statistical analyses were unable to detect a specific effect of industry, size, and other possible explanatory variables on cluster-group membership. We recognize that there may be other possible explanations of the groups. Therefore, we expect to continue searching for a defensible rationale that accounts for these groups.

Internal Audit Activities and Company Characteristics

We were particularly alert to any relationships between the performance of internal audit activities and company-specific characteristics. This is because systematic patterns in these relationships would be useful in theorizing about the organizational role(s) appropriate for internal auditing. As reported in the preceding section, the results are weak at the cluster-group level. This is principally because of statistical problems caused by smaller than optimal group sizes. However, similar analysis relating the ten internal audit-activities factors directly to company characteristics reveal a number of very strong relationships.

Using factor-analytic techniques[10] on the responses from Part II of the senior management's questionnaire, we derived seven key company-specific characteristics that might affect the performance of internal audit activities:

1. The extent of divisionalized, multiproduct operations.
2. The competitive level of the company's markets.
3. The extent of delegation of authority.
4. The degree of vertical integration.
5. The level of asset riskiness.
6. The degree of technological complexity.
7. Management's dominant leadership style.

We added to this list company size, internal audit department's size, and the major industry of the company's operations. To obtain a set of ten company characteristics, regression analysis[11] revealed that a number of internal audit activities are influenced by company-specific characteristics. Some differences in performance levels of internal audit activities are:

- Company's size.
- Internal audit department's size.
- Major industry of company's operations.
- The extent of divisionalized, multiproduct operations.
- The degree of technological complexity.

Tables 3-27 and 3-28 summarize the relationships between company-specific characteristics and internal audit activities.

Table 3-27
Directors of Internal Auditing
Relationship Between Internal Audit Activities and Industry Classifications[1]

Internal Audit Activity	Agriculture	Mining	Construction	Manufacturing	Transportation/Communication	Trade	Finance/Insurance	Service	Government
1. Review of compliance with, and adequacy of, internal control procedures	Very low[2]	High	Average	Low	Average	Average	Average	High	High
2. Review of expense reports	(No systematic pattern)								
3. Search for fraud and irregularities	High	Low	High	Low	High	Average	Average	Low	High
4. Investigation of compliance with code of corporate conduct	Very low	High	Low	High	Average	High	Low	Low	Very low
5. Determination of, or assistance with, financial data reliability	Low	Low	High	High	Low	High	Low	Low	Low
6. Participation in development of management information systems	(No systematic pattern)								
7. Performance of cost-benefit studies	(No systematic pattern)								
8. Review of quality control	(No systematic pattern)								
9. Review of budgets and performance evaluations	Very low	High	Low	High	Average	High	Low	Very low	
10. Special assignments	High	High	High	High	High	Average	Low	High	High

[1] The responses in this table indicate industry-group averages. Thus, not every company in an industry group may be described accurately.

[2] Interpretation of low, average, and high is relative to the average score by all respondents for that internal audit activity.

Table 3-28
Directors of Internal Auditing
Relationship Between Internal Audit Activities and Company Characteristics

Internal Audit Activity	Company Size	Size of Internal Audit Department	Divisionalized Multiproduct Operations	Level of Competition	Delegation of Authority	Vertical Integration	Asset Riskiness	Technological Complexity	Leadership Style
				Company Characteristics					
1. Review of compliance with, and adequacy of, internal control procedures	No pattern	Large departments perform more than small departments.	No pattern	No pattern	No pattern	No pattern	No pattern	No pattern	Firms with more informal, participative styles perform more than others.
2. Review of expense reports	Large firms perform more than small firms.	No pattern	No pattern	No pattern	No pattern	No pattern	No pattern	No pattern	No pattern
3. Search for fraud and irregularities	Small firms perform more than large firms.	No pattern	More centralized firms with fewer products perform more than others.	Firms facing greater competition perform more than others.	No pattern	No pattern	No pattern	Firms with less complex technology perform more than others.	No pattern
4. Investigation of compliance with code of corporate conduct	Large firms perform more than small firms.	Large departments perform more than small departments.	Multiproduct, divisionalized firms perform more than others.	No pattern	No pattern	No pattern	No pattern	No pattern	No pattern
5. Determination of, or assistance with, financial data reliability	Large firms perform more than small firms.	Large departments perform more than small departments.	Multiproduct, divisionalized firms perform more than others.	Firms facing greater competition perform more than others.	Firms with less delegation perform more than others.	No pattern	No pattern	No pattern	No pattern
6. Participation in development of management information systems	No pattern	Large departments perform more than small departments.	More centralized firms with fewer products perform more than others.	No pattern	No pattern	No pattern	No pattern	No pattern	No pattern
7. Performance of cost-benefit studies	No pattern	No pattern	No pattern	No pattern	No pattern	No pattern	Firms with greater asset riskiness perform more than others.	Firms with more complex technologies perform more than others.	No pattern
8. Review of quality control	No pattern	No pattern	No pattern	No pattern	No pattern	Less vertically integrated forms perform more than other.	Firm's with less asset riskiness perform more than others.	No pattern	No pattern
9. Review of budgets and performance evaluations	No pattern	No pattern	No pattern	No pattern	No pattern	No pattern	No pattern	Firms with less complex technologies perform more than others.	No pattern
10. Special Assignments	Large firms perform more than small firms.	Large departments perform more than small departments.	Multiproduct, divisionalized firms perform more than other.	Firms facing greater competition perform more than others.	Firms with greater delegation perform more than other.	No pattern	No pattern	Firms with less complex technologies perform more than other.	No pattern

Internal Audit Relationships with Others

Question 22 of Part I was a general inquiry into the extent to which others interested in the company's accounting and auditing activities influence the scope of the internal audit department's audit program. By far the single greatest influence on that program is reported to be the director of internal auditing, although many directors reported that others also have significant to very substantial influence. The responses to this question are summarized in the following table:

Table 3-29
Directors of Internal Auditing
Influence of Others on Scope of Internal Audit Program

	Very Substantial Influence	Substantial Influence	Significant Influence	Some Influence	No Influence
Director of internal auditing	271	46	5	4	0
Controller	9	27	52	143	76
Chief financial officer	29	48	69	133	32
Corporate audit committee	37	55	72	123	19
Chief executive officer	38	49	67	130	36
External CPA/CA	15	35	95	156	18
Operating management	3	19	65	168	61
Other	10	9	7	11	5

"Other" included reference to audit staff, president and chief operating officer, regulatory authorities, and others.

Question 9 of Part I addresses the issue of responsibility. It reads: "To whom are you responsible for each of the following purposes? (Check as many items in each column as apply.)" The responses were:

Table 3-30
Directors of Internal Auditing
Line of Directors' Responsibility

	For Audit-Reporting Purposes		For Salary & Promotion Purposes	
	No.	%	No.	%
Audit committee/board of directors	263	80	22	7
Chief executive officer	141	43	109	33
Chief financial officer	121	37	126	38
Controller	39	12	36	11
Treasurer	12	4	12	4
Administrative vice president	19	6	18	6
Operating unit line management	17	5	1	—
Other	38	12	51	15

The number of responses indicates that many directors have multiple responsibilities. Mentioned under "other" are executive vice president, vice president and CEO, various corporate officers, chairman of the board, secretary of the audit committee, and president. We inquired about responsibility for salary and promotion purposes as well as about audit-reporting purposes because we surmised that effective responsibility was more likely to relate to the former than to the latter. We have no doubt that many internal auditors would report their findings to the highest level possible regardless of the resulting effect on their personal careers. On the other hand, there may be instances where career considerations may impair judgment, resulting in a situation that is not in the best interest of the company.

Relationship with Corporate Audit Committee

A number of questions provided information about the respondents' relationships with their companies' corporate audit committees. As the following data show, many corporate audit committees are still quite new; and ultimate relationships are still developing. Question 24 of Part I: "In what year was your company's audit committee established?"

Table 3-31
Directors of Internal Auditing
Years of Establishment of Audit Committee

Year	Percentage
1970-1973	4
1974-1976	48
1977-1978	3
1979	5

Reasons given for the establishment of an audit committee were given in response to Question 25 of Part I: "If your audit committee was established within the past ten years, please check the statement below which best describes your understanding of the reason for its establishment."

Table 3-32
Directors of Internal Auditing
Reason for Establishment of Audit Committee

Reason	Number	Percentage
We added a committee in direct response to a specific recommendation from the SEC.	13	6
We added a committee because of the requirements of the New York Stock Exchange.	22	9
We added a committee because of the FCPA.	17	7
We added a committee as a natural development of our subcommittee's structure for our board of directors.	132	57
Other	50	21
Total	234	100

A variety of reasons appear under "other" with "recommendation of external auditor" appearing most frequently followed by regulatory requirements and recommendations from others.

Information about the number of members on the board of directors and the audit committee as well as the composition of each was provided by Question 26 of Part I.

Table 3-33
Directors of Internal Auditing
Composition of Board and Audit Committee

	Average of Responses		
Board of Directors	1974	1978	1983
Inside members (current management or officers)	3.75	3.46	3.20
External members having no affiliation with the company other than directorship responsibility	8.80	8.90	9.20
External members having some affiliation with the company (company counsel, former management, officers of affiliated companies, or major suppliers, etc.)	1.77	1.70	1.88
Other	.30	.46	.48
Total	14.62	14.52	14.76
Audit Committee			
Inside members (current management or officers)	.25	.30	.25
External members having no affiliation with the company other than directorship responsibility	3.50	3.50	3.68
External members having some affiliation with the company (company counsel, former management, officers of affiliated companies, or major suppliers, etc.)	.35	.40	.40
Ex officio members	.10	.10	.15
Other	.10	.10	.15
Total	4.30	4.40	4.58

In both cases, almost all the entries described under "other" could have been included under another of the listed categories. During the period covered in the preceding table, considerable emphasis has been directed at increasing the number of outside members on the board of directors. Some of those who support such a development might be surprised at the number of outside members already on boards. At the same time, there is little indication of any significant shift to more outside members.

Literature on the subject of audit committees usually advises that these committees should be composed solely of outside directors. According to these data, however, such is not the case. Given the participation of inside members, external members with some affiliation, and ex officio members, the actual as well as the perceived independence of that committee may be questioned.

Several questions relating to the relationship between the internal audit function and the corporate audit committee are included in Question 27 of Part I. The first of these has to do with the reporting relationship. "To what extent do members of the audit committee receive the reports issued by the internal audit department?"

Table 3-34
Directors of Internal Audit
Reporting Relationship with Audit Committee

	Responses	
	Number	Percentage
All audit reports go to the audit committee.	59	20
Report summaries are furnished to the audit committee on a regular basis.	151	51
Oral reports only are made to the audit committee on a regular basis.	33	11
Report summaries and/or oral reports are made to the audit committee on an irregular basis.	47	16
No reports are made to the audit committee.	5	2
Total	295	100

In a large company with many operating units, the internal audit department might issue so many detailed audit reports that members of the audit committee would be overwhelmed with the sheer volume. Other audit committee members might not consider reports to be their responsibility. It does seem, however, that, if the board of directors has any substantive appreciation of the work of the internal auditors, it would expect to hear from them on a regular basis in terms that would assure that significant findings are reported.

Responses to the question "How often does the director of internal auditing report in person to the audit committee?" showed that the average number of times per year for all respondents to this questionnaire is 3.8. For 50 percent of respondents, the number is 3.0. This is a higher rate of appearance before the audit committee than we had anticipated and a very encouraging bit of information.

On the other hand, when the responding directors were asked "Does the director of internal auditing regularly meet with the audit committee without any other members of management present?" the response was less encouraging. Fifty-four percent responded affirmatively and 46 percent negatively. Will the members of the audit committee or the director of internal auditing speak as freely to one another in the presence of senior management as they would in private? We think not. We would not wish to serve on an audit committee that did not meet at least once a year with the company's director of internal auditing privately without other members of management present. The data reveal that members of 46 percent of the audit committees represented by respondents to this questionnaire do not agree with us on that score.

Another indication of the closeness of the relationship between the director of internal auditing and the audit committee is found in the extent to which the audit committee calls on the director and his staff to undertake special assignments. Respondents note that 46 percent of them do receive such requests; 54 percent do not. Of those who do receive such requests, 50 percent received at least one assignment within the last year. The mean for the number received by that same group within the last year was 1.8 assignments.

Directors who receive such requests have mixed feelings about reporting to other members of management. Fifty-five percent of them "feel obligated to report such requests to other members of management if they have not already been informed." Forty-five percent feel no such obligation. The difference between these two responses could be explained in a number of ways. For some companies, it may be that the practice of the audit committee asking for assistance from the internal audit group is of such long standing that it has become ordinary. In other cases, it may be that the internal auditors are demonstrating a commendable degree of independence. It is also possible that some of those who reported might feel differently if the request were for sensitive rather than mundane information. Nevertheless, the fact that as many as 45 percent of those who do receive such assignments from the audit committee feel no obligation to report those requests to other members of management is evidence of a healthy relationship between the audit committee and the internal audit function.

In a strong but not overwhelming majority of cases, the audit committee asks the director of internal auditing for his opinion about the work of the independent accountants who perform the annual audit; 62 percent reported that they are asked, and 38 percent reported that they are not.

A very important matter relating to the strength of the dirctor's position in the company is included in Question 27f of Part I: "Does the director of internal auditing have the right to take specific matters directly to the audit committee on a confidential basis?" Ninety-two percent of respondents affirmed that right. Only eight percent reported that they did not. When asked if they had ever done so, 22 percent of those responding to the preceding question in the affirmative stated that they had done so. Seventy-eight percent reported that they had never had occasion to do so.

The final part of Question 27 of Part I was directed to the kinds of matters that respondents would take directly to the audit committee. The items listed in the question and the respondents' answers appear in the following table:

Table 3-35
Directors of Internal Auditing
Views on Matters to Be Taken Directly to Audit Committee

		Would		Would Not	
		Number	Percentage	Number	Percentage
1.	Significant misuse of corporate assets by a corporate officer.	208	76	67	24
2.	Noncompliance with capital-budgeting requirements by the vice president of manufacturing.	13	5	239	95
3.	A shortage in the cash receipts from a substantial branch office which the controller acknowledges but contends is not of sufficient importance to bring to the attention of the audit committee.	111	41	159	59

Table 3-35 (continued)

4. Information that leads you to believe that chief financial officer is pressuring the controller to make some accounting changes in order to increase earnings. 156 58 115 42
5. Failure by your superior to fund three new internal audit positions which you as director of internal audit feel are essential. 134 49 141 51
6. Reduction by your superior of funds available for internal audit training. 72 26 203 74

The differences of opinion evident in these responses are striking. Perhaps the most important issue raised here concerns possible reasons for the absence of any strong consensus. We think it likely that the absence of adequate emphasis on responsibility in internal audit literature and training programs lies at the root of these differences. Professionals with similar backgrounds and training should have a greater agreement than appears here.

A final question, related to the relationship between internal audit and the audit committee, queried the directors with respect to the interest of the audit committee in matters of internal control (Question 28 of Part I): "In your opinion, how actively is the audit committee interested in the internal control concerns of your company? (Check one.)"

Table 3-36
Directors of Internal Auditing
Audit Committee's Interest in Internal Control

	Number	Percentage
Very actively	109	35.0
Actively	132	43.0
Neither actively nor passively	48	16.0
Passively	11	3.5
Very passively	8	2.5
Total	308	100

These responses suggest significant interest on the part of the audit committees with regard to the internal control concerns of their companies.

Internal Audit Relationship with Independent Accountants

Only one question directly addressed the relationship between internal auditors and the independent accountants. We failed to anticipate the extent and the nature of the reaction that internal auditors apparently have to this relationship. It may be well to note that reaction here before reporting on the work relationship between these two classes of auditors.

Question 67 of Part II of the director's questionnaire requests respondents to rank from a list of job features the three factors that they find most appealing and the three that they find least appealing. Responses are reported in Table 3-37:

Table 3-37
Directors of Internal Auditing
Most Appealing and Least Appealing Job Features

	Most Appealing			Least Appealing		
	1	2	3	1	2	3
Travel	2	7	25	96	27	45
Intellectual challenge of work	89	64	41	9	6	7
Variety of assignments	74	82	46	2	9	4
Status and prestige of position	26	27	33	20	33	19
Contribution to success of company	74	73	49	3	13	9
Compensation	10	16	39	17	34	36
Authority accompanying auditor's position	13	18	18	21	28	26
Association with other internal auditors	1	2	10	15	23	25
Relationship with independent accountants	0	4	6	30	48	35
General work atmosphere	17	10	24	24	31	31
Other						

"Other" items included personal likes and dislikes and displayed no discernible pattern.

These data have been converted to an "appeal index" in the following table:

Table 3-38
Directors of Internal Auditing
Appeal Index for Features of Director's Position

Job Feature	Appeal Index*		Difference
	Most	Least	
Travel	5	39	(34)
Intellectual challenge of work	44	13	31
Variety of assignments	44	3	41
Status and prestige of position	17	15	2
Contribution to success of company	42	4	38
Compensation	10	16	(6)
Authority accompanying auditor's position	9	15	(6)
Association with other internal auditors	1	12	(11)
Relationship with independent accountants	1	22	(21)
General work atmosphere	10	17	(7)

$$*I = \left[\frac{3\ (\#1) + 2\ (\#2) + \#3}{3\ (330)} \right] 100$$

Next to travel, "relationship with independent accountants" ranks well ahead of any other "least appealing" feature. Responses to this question should be kept in mind as one reads the responses to the following question.

Question 30 of Part I asks: "Which of the following statements best describes your internal audit department's work relationship with your company's independent auditors? (Please check one.)"

Table 3-39
Directors of Internal Auditing
Work Relationship with Independent Auditors

	Responses Number	Percentage
Members of the internal audit department serve as assistants to the independent auditors, preparing schedules, account analyses, trial balances, etc., in connection with the annual audit.	38	12
Members of the internal audit department perform audit work in conformity with an audit program provided by the independent auditors.	48	15
Members of the internal audit department participate with the independent auditors in planning the total audit program which is then divided between the independent and internal audit groups for independent performance.	121	37
Members of the internal audit department utilize work done by the independent auditors and extend it where it is not completely appropriate for internal audit purposes.	11	3
The internal and independent auditors perform their duties independently of one another.	30	9
Other	78	24
Total	326	100

The numerous comments under "other" consisted of minor modifications of or comments on the listed items. Many described various methods of coordination and communication, and some combined two or more of those listed.

Some Miscellaneous Matters of Interest to Internal Auditors

Recognizing that our questionnaire might have omitted matters of interest to some of our respondents, we added some questions. We commenced this short series of questions with inquiries about past and anticipated contributions made by their internal audit departments.

Question 40 of Part III asked: "What, in your opinion, is the most important contribution that your internal audit department has provided for your company over the last few years? (Please describe.)"

Several respondents answered in specific terms dealing with various forms of cost saving, instances of hidden dangers revealed, recoveries effected, and similar matters. Most responses were more general. Many mentioned an increased awareness of the nature and the importance of internal control and internal auditing. Others described the assurance that internal audit gave to executives concerning the existence of effective internal control procedures. Some described their improved monitoring systems and the effect this had on company morale.

Also mentioned was analytical audit information that goes beyond monitoring present procedures and into the discovery of internal control needs and the analysis of risks. Some comments apparently reflected success in improving financial and production practices and procedures.

An independent evaluation of internal accounting and administrative controls was noted by a number of respondents. Establishing a rapport with operating personnel and an internal audit function were also mentioned. For some companies, internal auditing is still new and faces problems that established departments resolved long ago.

An unavoidable conclusion drawn from the variety of answers to this question is that cost control and bottom-line effects are of interest to many internal auditors. They see themselves contributing directly to the company's profit goals, and they take considerable pride in doing so. Some selected responses to Question 40 follow:

Objective monitoring of controls and operations at decentralized profit centers.

Analytical audit report information. Analyzing and forecasting trends and making comparisons with previously extracted information through audit software and programs.

Internal audit has forced the company to document its operating and accounting procedures and organize/construct them in a sound, orderly, and logical manner.

Evaluation of existing operating systems and recommendation for improving internal control in these systems and coordination of public audit on a worldwide basis have been carried out.

Developing ability of auditors to assess relationship between controls, operations, and productivity.

An awareness of the importance of internal controls and operating efficiency.

Control sensitivity, source of staff for special projects and requests, and source of personnel for financial and line management positions.

Obtained better rapport with operating personnel by making them more aware of the need and the benefits of effective internal controls

Excellent future employees.

The team of trained, quality control-oriented people to work on problems after they occur.

Training for the future financial managers of the company.

Awareness of controls and the impact of controls on the bottom line through increased efficiency and loss control.

Detection of employee embezzlement; verification of financial record.

Detecting and documenting a fidelity claim which resulted in an insurance recovery of over $300,000.

Enables management to feel more comfortable with acquisition candidates prior to closing the deal; supplies organization with quality mid-level management personnel.

Acceptance as an extension of management.

An understanding and perception of internal control in the broad sense by management and an awareness that accounting control is only a subset of internal control and is the responsibility of all management, not just financial.

Board-level commitment to a high level of controls has been a result of close working relationships between examining committee and the audit department.

The emphasis was on the future in Question 41 of Part III: "What is the most important contribution that you expect your internal audit department to provide for your company over the next few years? (Please describe.)" Directors' responses to this question formed an identifiable pattern. There was considerable emphasis on increasing productivity, on changing the internal audit emphasis from financial matters to efficiency of operations, and from monitoring internal control to the evaluation of management performance and financial decisions. Some mentioned minimizing the cost of the external audit. Also mentioned was the desirability of educating management to the importance of control and the role that internal audit can play in that regard.

To illustrate the nature of the responses, a few selected answers to Question 41 follow:

Provide a training service for management trainees.

Awareness of good business practices and of internal control helps solve problems before they get out of hand and keeps departments on their toes.

Monitor system of control and make constructive suggestions for profit improvement and efficiency. Also provide trained management personnel to fill necessary positions within the corporate structure.

Development of management.

Improved efficiencies of the audit function through risk analysis.

DP controls over distributed and minicomputer systems.

Increased operational auditing reviews, special projects, cost-benefit analysis.

Move from internal controls to management-performance evaluation and financial decisions.

Active involvement in systems development to ensure that all new systems or changes in existing systems have adequate internal controls and are efficient.

Compliance testing established internal control networks and identification of opportunities to assist management in discharging its responsibilities of development and use of an internal control evaluations and documentation methodology which has promoted a control-conscious environment that contributes to more reliable financial data; better safeguarding of assets; operating efficiencies; adherence to policies; and the prevention, detection, correction of errors/irregularities.

Utilizing a task-force approach to operational reviews to cross several department areas should improve cost reduction/performance redundancy more effectively.

We were also interested in potential changes in internal auditing and added Question 42 to obtain directors' views: "Please describe any significant changes or developments that you believe will occur in your internal audit function over the next few years." Perhaps the most common reply was increasing computer competence on the part of all internal auditors. Some went so far as to suggest the EDP audit function would disappear as a specialty because all internal auditors would be able to deal with any computer problems that might arise.

Associated with such competence was the expectation that advanced auditing skills would be developed and used to make internal auditors more efficient. Some alluded to mini- and microcomputers in this connection. As with Question 41, there was considerable emphasis on productivity reviews and on the evaluation of management performance. Some expect a considerable increase in the status and prestige of internal auditing. Again, some selected answers may provide the flavor of the questionnaire returns:

> Less financial and more operational audits. More women at managerial level.
>
> Overall quality of personnel should improve. Use of modern techniques, such as regression analysis, use of automated versus manual audit procedures to increase significantly.
>
> We plan to add an engineer to our staff to aid in the review of construction projects.
>
> Evaluation of operating management's performance and monitoring accounting and EDP controls plus serving as a training ground for other areas of the company.
>
> Employment of other than financial employees in the department.
>
> Reputation for quality work will improve. Spending your first five years in the internal audit department will be perceived as a good career decision.
>
> Small well-qualified group, not so much accounting oriented.
>
> The attest function in the audit effort will tend to decrease with more knowledgeable auditors and auditees and the evaluation and consulting role of the auditor will increase with more emphasis on improved efficiencies and productivity.
>
> More use of EDP softwarre, more formal risk analysts and cost versus benefits of controls, greater cooperation between internal auditors, management, and external auditors.
>
> Expanded audit coverage will evolve in the operational and/or management audit areas, and financial audits as known today will change dramatically as a result of expanding computer applications.
>
> Few in number, greater in EDP knowledge, more sophisticated techniques, stability, enhanced recognition of our contribution.
>
> Shift from strictly operational auditing to comprehensive auditing.
>
> EDP development will enable auditors to harness the power of the computer in ways practically unimaginable today. Powerful software and computer networks will enable auditors via terminals to audit a broad range of functions and data faster and with more reliable results than is now possible.
>
> No dramatic changes are on the horizon. A trend away from checking and validating toward performance evaluation will gain greater momentum. Also, use of the computer as an audit tool will grow as younger staff with significantly better EDP skills move into internal auditing.

---

[7]The discussion throughout this section is based on a confirmatory-factor analysis by using the IISREL V statistical package. The dimensions highlighted and discussed for each of the organizational

structure, job-characteristic, career-orientation, and-job satisfaction variables are those identified as statistically significant by this analysis. Complete details regarding this analysis are available from the authors.

[8]Descriptive-factor analysis with oblique rotation of the factors was used for this analysis, retaining only those factors meeting standard statistical retention rules. The ten retained factors accounted for 67 percent of the total variance. Complete details regarding this analysis are available from the authors.

[9]A two-stage-clustering algorithm was applied. In stage 1, a complete linkage-hierarchical-algorithm-generated cluster centroids were used as starting seeds for Jancy's K-means nonhierarchical algorithm in stage 2. A point-biserial-goodness-of-it statistic was used to identify significant cluster structures existing in the data. Complete details of our analysis are available from the authors.

[10]Descriptive-factor analysis with oblique rotation of the factors was used for this analysis, retaining only those factors meeting standard statistical retention rules. The seven retained factors accounted for 43 percent of the total variance. Complete details regarding this analysis are available from the authors.

[11]Ordinary-least-squares regression techniques were used, and all variables where a relationship is indicated in the text or in Tables 3-27 and 3-28 represent significance levels of at least .05. R^2 statistics indicated adequate fits and residual analysis revealed no serious departures from normality. Complete details of our analysis may be found in R. H. Colson and P. Tiessen, "The Relationship Between Industry, Organizational Context, and the Nature of Internal Audit Activities," unpublished working paper, The University of Michigan, 1983. This paper is available upon request.

4

Internal Audit Staff Members' Perspective

We received 1,240 usable responses to the staff questionnaire from internal auditors representing 336 companies. The number of questionnaires from each company depended to some extent on the size of the staff, but there is no direct correlation between the two. Some companies with large audit staffs are underrepresented, whereas companies with small audit staffs are overrepresented. Table 4-1, which shows the number of companies whose staff members returned one or more questionnaires, accounts for the number of questionnaires returned. From more than 70 percent of the participating companies, we received three or more questionnaires directly from staff members. The median number of questionnaires returned for a company was four.

Table 4-1
Internal Audit Staff Members
Numbers of Returned Questionnaires

Number of Completed Questionnaires	Number of Companies Returning this Number of Questionnaires	Total Questionnaires
1	44	44
2	52	104
3	71	213
4	96	384
5	23	115
6	19	114
7	9	63
8	10	80
9	4	36
10	3	30
11	2	22
12	0	0
13	1	13
14	0	0
15	2	30
	336	1,248
Unusable Questionnaires		8
Total Usable Questionnaires		1,240

The content of the staff questionnaire was designed to collect data to construct a profile of internal audit staff members. Areas of concern included demographic items such as age, tenure with the company, educational background, work

experience, and professional items such as staff members' perception of the scope and the content of their jobs, career orientation, and job satisfaction. The data analysis reported in the following pages centers on these dominant themes:
- Internal audit staff tend to be young and relatively new to company and internal auditing.
- Most have had some work experience in other companies.
- Most are intent on a career in management rather than in internal auditing.
- Few are certified internal auditors or express interest in certification.
- Most have accounting or financial education or work experience.
- Most are generalists, dealing with all the phases of internal audit activities performed by their departments.
- Some spend three-fourths of their time on financial audit activities and one-fourth on operational/management audits.
- Most tend to be committed to personal advancement rather than to a specific career in internal auditing or with their present companies.
- Most view internal auditing as a short-range training program and stepping stone to a management position.
- Most are reasonably satisfied with their jobs.

Internal Audit Staff Demographics

The profile of internal audit staff members depicted by the data is primarily one of young people in their twenties and early thirties who are relatively new to internal auditing. Table 4-2 details the age groups into which the respondents fall. Note that 50 percent of the staff members are 30 years of age or younger. Most staff members are between 26 and 30 years old, comprising 33 percent of the entire sample. Almost three quarters are less than 35 years old. The respondents' ages range from 20 to 66 years. The average age is 32.3; the median age is 30.

Table 4-2
Internal Audit Staff Members
Respondents' Ages

Age Years	Responses Number	Percentage	Cumulative Percentage
20-25	232	19	19
26-30	411	33	52
31-35	257	21	73
36-40	153	12	85
41-45	72	6	91
46-50	50	4	95
Over 50	63	—	100
No response	2	0	
Total	1,240	100	

Range 20 to 66
Mean — 32.3
Median — 30

Tables 4-3 and 4-4 track the length of time the staff members have spent with their current companies and in their internal audit staff positions. Almost half have been with their companies for fewer than two years. Three-quarters of them have been in internal auditing for less than two years. The average tenure with the current company is almost six years, while the average staff member has spent only two years in internal auditing. Most are young and relatively new to internal auditing.

A frequent response to the final question addressed to staff members ("We are interested in any comments you may wish to make about internal auditing in general or your present work activities. Please add any thoughts you may wish to express.") concerned the short period of time respondents had spent in internal auditing and the difficulties in evaluating internal audit as a potential career. One respondent put it, "As I have only been with the present company for one month, I have not had the opportunity to evaluate the company, my position, and how I fit into the rest of the organization."

Table 4-3
Internal Audit Staff Members
Length of Time With Current Company of Employment

Years	Responses Number	Percentage	Cumulative Percentage
Less than 1	86	7	7
1- 2	445	36	43
3- 5	309	25	68
6-10	191	15	83
11-20	146	12	95
Over 20	60	5	100
No responses	3	—	
Total	1,240	100	

Table 4-4
Internal Audit Staff Members
Length of Time in Current Position

Years	Responses Number	Percentage	Cumulative Percentage
Less than 1	193	16	16
1- 2	721	58	74
3- 5	220	18	92
6-10	71	6	98
11-20	21	2	100
Over 20	5	—	
No response	9	—	
Total	1,240	100	

Range — 1 to 36
Median — 1

The dimensions of the educational backgrounds of the staff respondents are outlined in Table 4-5. Eighty-six percent have received bachelor's degrees. The majority are in accounting (65 percent). Eighteen percent have master's degrees or higher. The majority of graduate degrees (55 percent) are in business areas and are usually MBAs. In the area of education, two important and related points were evident in the research seminars and in responses to the questionnaire's open-ended questions. First, an internal auditor needs a broader educational background than a typical four-year accounting degree. One respondent expressed this concern very aptly, "I feel that the internal auditor with a financial background has got to learn to be more of a generalist. The profession needs to develop means to teach and motivate its members to think of business as integrations of several disciplines and that the potential for contribution is in all areas, not just accounting and internal financial controls."

Second, staff members interested in education beyond the bachelor's degree perceive that a general degree, particularly the MBA, is best suited for their purposes. No doubt they value a general graduate business degree for two reasons — because broad knowledge increases their effectiveness in internal auditing and because it enhances opportunities for a promotion into financial management. Several respondents found out-of-town travel to be the least appealing aspect of their jobs because it made it impossible to pursue graduate degrees in business management.

Table 4-5
Internal Audit Staff Members
Educational Background

	Responses		Major Field of Study					
			Accounting	Business	Engineering	Computer Science	Arts/Science	None Stated
	No.	%						
Bachelor's Degree	1061	86	630	176	12	10	145	88
Percentage			65	18	1	1	15	
Master's Degree	225	18	63	124	1	7	20	10
Percentage			30	58	—	3	9	
No College Degree	177	14	—	—	—	—	—	—

Tables 4-6 and 4-7 summarize the responses to the professional certification and professional membership questions. Twenty-four percent of the respondents hold CPA or CA certificates, while 10 percent hold CIAs. However, in this same group of people, 37 percent are members of The Institute of Internal Auditors, while 16 percent are members of CPA or CA professional organizations.

Table 4-6
Internal Audit Staff Members
Professional Certifications

Certificate	Responses Number	Percentage
CPA/CA	301	24
CIA	124	10
CISA	81	7
All Other	120	41

Table 4-7
Internal Audit Staff Members
Membership in Professional Organizations

Organization	Responses Number	Percentage
The Institute of Internal Auditors	456	37
American Institute of CPAs/Canadian Institute of Chartered Accountants	195	16
National Association of Accountants	79	6
EDP Auditors Association	148	12
Bank Administration Institute	88	7
State CPA Society/Provincial CA Institute	186	15
All Other	236	19

Many of the staff respondents expressed a variety of concerns about the CIA program, including a perception of relatively "low prestige," lack of "a sufficient disciplined body of knowledge on which to base a four-part examination," and a practice-versus-theory conflict.

In addition, staff members worry about the effect of CIA certification on their careers. As discussed at length in a later section, most internal audit staff members view their experience in internal auditing as a stepping stone to a management position in another area of the company. They worry that possession of the CIA may lower their promotability in the eyes of senior management because the CIA designation implies a commitment to a narrow field (internal auditing) rather than to general management. When research seminars participants were asked why so few staff members have CIA designations, two responses were common. First, many have not been internal auditors long enough to gain certification. Second, and more important, the majority of internal audit staff members view their internal audit tenure as short-lived. Therefore, additional effort beyond their jobs is more profitably spent in MBA programs where they learn skills for the positions to which they hope to be promoted.

Of the 1,216 respondents who gave information regarding their work experience, 507 (42 percent) indicated that they had work experience with their current company prior to transferring to internal auditing. Sixteen percent of these had transferred from some type of accounting work and typically received background experience with their present employers. The staff-experience history is detailed in Table 4-8, which shows the number of respondents who claim work experience in their present companies and the average amount of experience in each category.

Table 4-8
Internal Audit Staff Members
Experience With Present Employers

	Responses		Average Years of Experience
	Number	Percentage	
Internal audit	1216	98	3.6
Accounting	197	16	4.2
Finance	40	3	3.5
Production/engineering	21	2	3.5
Marketing	17	1	4.4
Personnel	13	1	2.8
EDP	80	7	4.9
Other	144	12	4.2

Table 4-9 highlights the work experience of internal audit staff members with prior employers. Eight hundred fifty-nine staff members (71 percent) have had some work experience with other companies before joining their present companies. External auditing, internal auditing, and accounting constitute the most common types of experience with prior employers.

Table 4-9
Internal Audit Staff Members
Experience With Prior Employers

	Responses		Average Years of Experience
	Number	Percentage	
Internal audit	297	24	3.8
External audit	322	26	3.5
Accounting	275	22	3.5
Finance	65	5	2.8
Production/engineering	20	2	4.2
Marketing	34	4	2.5
Personnel	16	2	3.0
EDP	92	7	5.2
Other	212	17	3.7

As the following responses indicate, employees transferred into the internal audit department from other departments seem to view the transfer as a positive factor in their personal careers.

Table 4-10
Internal Audit Staff Members
View of Transfer to Internal Audit

Did you view your transfer to the internal audit department as:

	Yes	No
A promotion	250	114
A lateral move	131	144
Part of a training program	128	139
Opportunity leading to a management career	249	54
A "dead end"	6	230
Other	24	34

Table 4-10 (continued)

Was your transfer to the internal audit department accompanied by:		
Salary improvement	295	122
An increase in title or rank	212	169

From these data emerges a profile of internal audit staff members. It consists of the following general characteristics:

- Young.
- Relatively new to internal auditing.
- Accounting or general business educational background.
- Several years of experience with another employer.
- Some experience with current employer prior to joining the internal audit department.
- Not particularly motivated to take the CIA examination.

Scope and Content of Internal Audit Staff's Tasks

Eighty-five percent of the respondents indicated that their respective position is part of a corporate headquarters' staff unit, while 15 percent said they were located in an operating unit. Those audit staff members located in operating units listed their reporting responsibilities as follows:

	No.	%	No.	%	No.	%
Corporate director of internal auditing	105	56	116	56	117	60
Other executive at corporate headquarters	5	3	20	9	13	7
Operating unit management	78	41	72	35	63	33

Understanding Job

In general, staff members believe that they have a satisfactory understanding of the nature of their job assignments. Most have seen a formal job description. Of those who have not, the majority believe they have a good understanding of its scope from other sources. Their responses are:

	Percentage	
	Yes	No
Have you seen a formal job description of your position?	76	24
If not, do you feel that other means have given you a good understanding of the scope of your job?	90	10

Respondents also believe that their job descriptions correspond to their usual activities, although there are some exceptions. In response to the question "To what extent does your understanding of the scope of your job describe your actual activities?" answers were:

	Number	Percentage
Entirely describes your actual activities	302	25
Almost entirely describes your actual activities	712	58
Describes about half of your actual activities	190	15
Describes your actual activities hardly at all	23	2
Fails to describe any of your actual activities	5	—
Total	1,232	100

As might be expected, internal audit staff members, like other employees, are asked to perform tasks that are not strictly included in what they consider to be their job descriptions. This troubles some but does not bother others. The questions directed at these matters and the answers follow:

How often are you requested to perform tasks not included in your understanding of the scope of your job?

	Number	Percentage
Every assignment	12	1
Most assignments	58	5
About half of the assignments	110	9
Only a few assignments	733	59
Never requested to perform tasks not included in my understanding of the scope of my job	318	26
Total	1,231	100

To what extent are you bothered by requests that you perform tasks not included in your understanding of the scope of your job?

	Number	Percentage
Makes my job almost intolerable	3	—
Bothers me considerably	30	2
Bothers me somewhat	131	11
Bothers me only a little	252	21
Doesn't bother me at all	530	44
Never requested to perform tasks not included in my understanding of the scope of my job	267	22
Total	1,213	100

Nature of Work Assignments

Questions 15, 16, and 17 of Part I of the staff's questionnaire were designed to gather information about how internal audit staff members spend their time in the field. Responses to question 17 ("Indicate the percentage of your time spent auditing the following types of activities.") were not particularly useful because our respondents did not view their work assignments as falling in the activity categories we formulated. Rather, they tended to place very high percentages in the "other" category and then described their activities as "financial auditing" or "operational auditing" or in terms of the options given them in questions 15 ("What percentage of your time is spent on each of the following audit activities?") and 16 ("Where in the company do you spend most of your audit time?")

The responses to questions 15 and 16 are enlightening with respect to the large variations evident in the responses. A respondent could fill in percentages at will. The only restrictions were that the percentages must reflect the individual's experience and must total 100 percent. Because of this, the responses were indications of the variety and the depth of activity an internal auditor experiences. Tables 4-11 and 4-12 present the analyses of time spent on types of audit activities and of the location in the company where these audit duties are performed.

Table 4-11
Internal Audit Staff Members
Analysis of Time Spent on Audit Activities

Audit Activity	Percentage of Time Spent on Audit Activity								
	0	1-10	11-20	21-30	31-40	41-50	51-75	76-100	Avg.
Detection of Errors and Irregularities	103*	357	248	202	116	103	77	34	25
	8	29	20	17	9	8	6	3	
Monitoring Management Control	77	222	283	300	146	106	80	26	27
	6	18	23	24	12	9	6	2	
Performance Evaluation	332	508	216	122	32	22	5	3	12
	27	41	17	10	3	2	—	—	
Monitoring Internal Accounting Control	142	263	229	219	154	103	89	41	27
	11	22	19	18	12	8	7	3	
Decision-Making Review	424	574	158	45	18	9	10	2	9
	34	46	13	4	1	1	1	—	
									100

*Top numbers of each pair indicates the number of responses; bottom numbers indicate the percentage of responses.

Table 4-12
Internal Audit Staff Members
Analysis of Time Spent on Audits in Company Units

Company Unit	Percentage of Time Spent on Audit Activity								
	0	1-10	11-20	21-30	31-40	41-50	51-75	76-100	Avg.
Corporate Headquarters' Staff	253*	247	145	114	66	96	146	173	33
	20	20	12	9	5	8	12	14	
Plants and Departments	239	99	109	113	105	122	197	256	42
	19	8	9	9	8	10	16	21	
Dealers, Agencies, and Branches	836	178	71	55	30	23	24	23	8
	67	15	6	4	2	2	2	2	
Divisional Management	635	294	118	70	35	32	30	26	11
	51	24	10	6	3	2	2	2	
Outside Contractor	988	186	24	21	4	6	7	4	3
	80	15	2	2	—	—	1	—	
Corporate Senior Management	887	299	31	17	2	2	0	2	3
	72	24	3	1	—	—	—	—	
									100

*Top numbers of each pair indicate number of responses; bottom numbers indicate the percentage of responses.

Two conclusions emerge from a study of the data in Table 4-11. The first is that audit staff members participate in the full range of audit activities. Very few internal audit staff members spend the major portion of their time performing only one type of audit activity. This can be inferred from the small number who indicated they spend 76-100 percent of their time on a particular audit duty. Most staff members spend some time working on all five internal audit activities. The majority of the respondents spend at least some time working on decision-making reviews and performance evaluations. Thus, internal audit staff members engage in diverse types of activity without narrow specialization. This is probably one of the reasons why so many view their internal audit experience favorably. The profile of internal audit activities that can be derived from Table 4-11 indicates that an internal auditor, at whatever staff level, spends a significant portion of time in five different types of internal audit activities rather than specializing in one or two.

The second conclusion is substantiated by the averages in the last column of Table 4-11. On an average, internal audit staff members spend a little more than one-half of their time on the traditional activities of detecting errors and irregularities (25 percent) and monitoring internal accounting control (27 percent). An additional 27 percent of their time is spent on monitoring management control. This leaves 21 percent of their time for performance evaluations and decision-making reviews. Very few staff members, however, spend more than 20 percent of their time on these activities. This work, which is probably the most interesting, is shared among many rather than being reserved for only a few.

Percentages in the "average" column of Table 4-12 must be read with caution. Some respondents may have answered in terms of where they spent their time rather than in terms of the activities receiving audit attention. Internal auditors based in corporate headquarters might spend significant amounts of time preparing or writing up the results of work performed at plants, departments, and division headquarters. Experienced directors point out that it is very unlikely that any corporate headquarters' staff would receive as much as 33 percent of an internal audit department's attention.

We are not surprised at the small amount of audit attention given to corporate senior management. Senior management performs relatively few transactions. Although these may be important, the examinations should take relatively little time. The number of transactions and events occurring elsewhere, compared to the volume at the pinnacle of corporate authority, should reduce the audit effort at corporate headquarters to a small amount.

In summarizing the scope and the content of internal audit tasks, the following points from the data analysis stand out:
- Ninety-five percent of an internal audit staff is connected to a headquarters staff.
- Little confusion exists about staff job assignments.
- Internal audit staff members are seldom requested to perform activities outside

their understanding of the scope of their job and are not greatly troubled when this occurs.
- Most staff members get broad experience.
- Traditional aspects of fraud and irregularities detection and internal accounting control comprise the majority of internal audit staff's work time.
- Less than one-fourth of internal audit time is spent on performance evaluations and decision-making reviews, yet most staff members share this work to some extent.
- One-third of internal audit staff's time is spent in the examination of corporate headquarters' staff.

Work-Related Attitudes and Job Satisfaction

In an effort to discern attitudinal issues such as staff members' job involvement, career orientation, perception of the work environment, and job satisfaction, we asked a substantial number of questions at the end of part I, II, and III of the staff's questionnaire. The responses to these questions were then analyzed through factor analytic methods. These methods identified those questions with like responses as well as the pattern of responses from the respondent population as a whole. These questions then become the key factors in understanding respondents' attitudes on the various attitudinal variables relating to the questions. In this discussion of the analysis, only those questions identified by the statistical techniques will receive specific attention. This does not mean that responses to the other questions were ignored or were not important. Rather, they did not fit the pattern overall resonse as well as those that are mentioned specifically.

Our discussion of the resonse analysis in the following paragraph divides into three main sections:
- Career interests of staff members.
- Attitude profiles of staff members.
- Job satisfaction of staff members.

Career Interests of Staff Members

Most internal audit staff members (75 percent) do not plan to make a career of internal auditing. This was indicated in Question 14 of Part I. The most frequent response to the open-ended question from the staff's questionnaire indicates that the respondents view internal auditing as a good training position for a future career in management. Many said they had taken their position in internal auditing with the understanding that they would move to management in a short period of time. Following are some relevant questionnaire responses:

> Internal audit is a good department in which to gain experience close to a management point of view. If a person wants to gain management status, I feel he must use the internal audit department as a short-term experience and move on. Career critics don't make that many friends no matter how helpful they appear.

> I believe internal audit is the most effective management training program my company has to offer.
>
> Internal audit positions are excellent for training employees in company operating procedures and for future management positions.
>
> Internal auditing is a training school for future controllers and managers that pays for itself in errors found, controls improved, and personnel trained and exposed to all facets of the company.
>
> Internal audit is usually a jumping-off point to another job within the firm. It's a good experience for two to four years, providing exposures to different operations.

These five comments represent many times that number from respondents who outline the value of internal audit as a training ground for future managers.

Still, a considerable number (25 percent) indicate a desire to remain in internal audit throughout their careers. One respondent summarized this alternative perspective with the following statement:

> Many corporations view internal audit only as a training ground for potential upper and middle managers. While I agree that internal auditing provides excellent exposure to all levels and types of activities within a corporation, I strongly believe that there is an important place for career auditors who would establish the professionalism required to maintain interest and credibility in internal auditing.

Several staff respondents suggest that they would be interested in internal audit careers but did not see a viable career path within their company — either in terms of available positions or in salary increases commensurate with their experience and self-perceived value to the company. Members of this group feel they must leave internal auditing for other departments of the company where there are more opportunities for promotion in order to pursue a company management position.

Of the respondents who indicated plans to transfer to another management group, 61 percent expect to do so within three years (A, I, 14a),* implying a short tenure in internal auditing. All the staff members who expect to leave internal audit knew where they would like to transfer. Table 4-13 details the type of work internal audit staff members expect to do when they leave the internal audit department.

Accounting and financial management attract most staff members. Line management and various aspects of EDP follow. Very few plan on becoming part of marketing or production managements. A considerable number expect to transfer to general corporate management positions. The variety of interests represented is evidence that internal audit can function as a training position for a wide number of functional and general management areas.

---

*(A, I, 14a) means Appendix A, Part I, Question 14a of the staff's questionnaire. This code is used throughout this section. Readers are encouraged to refer to these questions for more information.

Table 4-13
Internal Audit Staff Members
Future Work Preferences

Type of Work	Responses Number	Percentage	Cumulative Percentage
Accounting	266	29	29
Finance	246	27	56
Production/engineering	9	1	57
Marketing	18	2	59
Personnel	9	1	60
Line management	147	16	76
EDP	80	9	85
Other*	140	15	100
Total	915	100	

*The responses to "other" occurring most frequently were "administrative management," general management," and "consulting."

In related questions (A, I, 19 and 20), we analyzed reading preferences in an attempt to assess the degree of interest that internal auditors have in functional areas. Ninety-three percent agree that regular reading of professional and business publications is necessary to keep up with current professional developments (A, I, 19); 97 percent are willing to devote at least some of their personal time to such reading (see Table 4-14). Forty-two percent do their professional reading either entirely or mostly on their own time. Table 4-15 summarizes the results from Part I, Question 20, which attempted to assess the reading preference of internal auditors in professional, business, and personal areas. The responses in the personal reading category were used as a benchmark against which to compare the responses in external audit, internal audit, accounting, and general business subjects. The internal audit and general business subjects correspond to the external audit and accounting areas. The percentages of "frequent" and "very frequent" responses are higher for the internal audit/general business periodicals than for the accounting/external audit publications. This reinforces the possibility that internal auditors want to keep abreast of general business affairs in preparation for a transfer to a management position. Note that 57 percent of the respondents indicate they engage in personal reading either "frequently" or "very frequently" and that 38 percent responded at these levels for the internal audit/general business items. A far lower number responded at these levels of frequency for the external audit/accounting publications.

Table 4-14
Internal Audit Staff Members
Attitude Toward Professional Reading

Do you consider regular reading of professional and business publications necessary to keep up with current developments in your profession?

	Number	Percentage
Yes	1,147	93
No	92	7

Table 4-14 (continued)

If yes, indicate the extent to which such reading is done on your personal time.

	Responses	
	Number	Percentage
Entirely on my own time	101	9
Mostly on my own time	381	33
Half on my own time and half on company time	357	31
Mostly on company time	277	24
Entirely on company time	31	3
Total	1,147	100

Table 4-15
Internal Audit Staff Members Reading Preferences

Professional	Very Infrequently	Infrequently	Neither Frequently nor Infrequently	Frequently	Very Frequently
External Audit	56*	13	12	10	9
Internal Audit	28	20	14	21	17
Business Related					
Accounting	61	18	12	7	2
General	21	22	20	22	15
Personal Reading	18	12	13	18	39

*Numbers in this table express percentages.

Attitude Profiles of Staff Members

Parts II and III of the staff's questionnaire were designed to capture information about different dimensions of attitudes related to:
- Job characteristics.
- Career orientation.
- Organizational characteristics.
- Job satisfaction (discussed in a separate section).

Each of these four categories is composed of several variables with a number of dimensions. The following paragraphs report the results of statistical analyses[12] which identified: (1) the important dimensions of each variable for internal audit staff members, (2) the average staff's responses on these variables, and (3) the association of the first three attitudinal categories with job satisfaction.

Job Characteristics

Three variables make up the job characteristics profile:
- Role clarity.
- Job challenge.

- Learning opportunities.

Role clarity deals with conflicts, misunderstandings, and ambiguity that might exist for staff members in performing their internal auditing assignments. Job challenge is the degree to which internal audit staff feel their tasks are either routine and hum-drum or interesting and demanding. Learning opportunities refers to the potential for acquiring new knowledge in the work environment.

Role Clarity. Two aspects of role clarity were identified as being important for staff members. One deals with the fact that staff members feel confident about the criteria used to evaluate their performance (A, II, 41). The other focuses on apparent conflict in instructions from their superiors (A, II, 53). For both aspects, the average of the responses tended toward neutrality on role clarity.

With respect to performance evaluation, slightly more than half of the respondents (59 percent) are certain about the specific job aspects on which their performance will be evaluated. Thirty-two percent are uncertain, and 9 percent are neither certain nor uncertain. On the other hand, the majority find a lack of role clarity because of conflicting instructions from their superiors. Fifty-six percent responded that there are times when instructions from superiors conflict with one another; 31 percent indicated disagreement with this view; and 13 percent neither agreed nor disagreed. On the whole, role clarity is neither weak nor strong in the viewpoint of internal audit staffs.

Job Challenge. The only aspect of job challenge identified as "important" deals with routineness (A, III, 1). Responses are summarized in Table 4-16. Forty-seven percent find that their jobs usually challenge their ability or ingenuity; 12 percent find them mostly routine, and 41 percent find them about half routine and half challenging.

Table 4-16
Internal Audit Staff Members
Extent of Challenge in Work Assignments

Do you find your work to be routine, or is it a real challenge to your ability or ingenuity? Your work is:

	Responses	
	Number	Percentage
Almost always a challenge to your ability or ingenuity	113	9
Usually challenging	471	38
About half routine and half challenging	508	41
Usually routine	125	10
Almost always routine	19	2
Total	1,236	100

Learning Opportunities. In general, staff members find opportunities for learning in their jobs. Three questions in Part III of the questionnaire inquire about these. The results are reported in Tables 4-17 and 4-18.

Table 4-17
Internal Audit Staff Members
Opportunity to Improve Audit Expertise

In connection with your job, how much chance do you get to improve your audit expertise (learn new things about your company)?

	Improve Your Audit Expertise		Learn New Things About Your Company	
	No.	%	No.	%
Very little or no chance	27	2	6	—
Little chance	91	7	20	2
Some chance	352	29	144	12
A good chance	601	49	618	50
An excellent chance	166	13	449	36
Total	1,237	100	1,237	100

Table 4-18
Internal Audit Staff Members
Internal Audit Experience as a Contribution to Career Success

How much will your internal audit experience contribute to your ability to succeed in almost any department of your company?

	Number	Percentage
Very little or no contribution	12	1
Little contribution	29	2
Some contribution	210	17
A good contribution	606	49
An excellent contribution	376	31
Total	1,233	100

From these responses, it appears that internal audit experience is valued most highly for its general contribution to an understanding of the company rather than for specific audit experience. However, the contribution to both areas is good.

Career Orientation

Responses provided information on five variables relating to career orientation:
- Professional commitment.
- Organizational goals.
- Organizational immobility.
- External orientation.
- Concern for career advancement.

Professional commitment measures the degree of loyalty internal audit staff members have to their profession. This commitment is embodied in standards, certification, professional societies, and professional responsibilities. Commitment to organizational goals concerns the extent to which staff members adopt company profitability or efficiency goals as their own. Organizational immobility is an index indicating whether employees consider themselves committed to a career in their company or willing to move to another company. External orientation deals with professional stimulation which respondents receive outside their internal audit department. Concern for career advancement measures their pursuit of promotions and other rewards.

Professional Commitment. This centers around active membership in The Institute of Internal Auditors and passing the CIA and CPA examinations. Questionnaire responses reveal no concensus about commitment to any of these. Although 50 percent of the respondents believe passing the CIA examination is something that is important for professional commitment, 25 percent think it unimportant. Another 25 percent are uncertain about its importance (A, II, 17h). Only 42 percent think activity in The Institute of Internal Auditors is important for professional commitment, while 25 percent believe it to be unimportant, and 33 percent are uncertain (A, II, 17f). Forty-four percent believe passing the CPA examination is important (A, II, 17i). The staff responses isolate the same components of professional commitment as did the responses from directors of internal auditing. However, directors tend to think that these components are more important to professional commitment than do staff members. As might be expected, directors are more committed to internal auditing than are their staff members.

Organizational Goals. A commitment to organizational goals is not consistently identified by internal audit staff members. (Directors were also inconsistent on this variable.) The only aspect showing systematic importance in the responses dealt with the responsibility to assure the efficient company operation beyond the performance of assigned internal audit duties (A, II, 21). Eighty-eight percent of the respondents believe, many of them strongly, that internal auditors have the responsibility to assure the efficient operation of the company beyond the adequate performance of assigned internal audit duties. Thus, while staff members associate responsibility for efficiency with a commitment to company goals, directors identified general company loyalty as the most important aspect of commitment to organizational goals.

Organizational Immobility. The indicators of organizational immobility that stood out as important are the intention of pursuing a career with the current company (A, II, 13 and 16) and concerns with compensation (A, II, 4 and 34). Most staff members see themselves pursuing a career with the present company but would be willing to change companies if their moves were accompanied by significant salary increases. In their narrative comments, several respondents expressed disappointment over their current compensation compared with salary levels in other departments and the type of service they provide.

External Orientation. As a group, staff members do not appear to be externally oriented. The salient aspects of external orientation relate to professional meetings (A, II, 36) and professional journals (A, II, 45). Although the distribution of responses indicates some disagreement about the lack of value of professional meetings and journals, the indication is that staff members do not receive substantial professional stimulation outside their companies.

Concern for Career Advancement. Both staff members and directors found the same two aspects of concern for advancement to be important: salaries (A, II, 7) and promotions (A, II, 30). Interestingly, 46 percent of the staff indicates that salary levels are not a general indication of one's contribution; 41 percent think they are; and 13 percent are undecided.

Staff members are more generally optimistic about promotability. Sixty-three percent believe innovations encourage promotion; 15 percent believe otherwise; 22 percent are undecided. The concern for career advancement reflects what appear to be the facts of life for internal audit staffs. Salary improvement comes with promotion to a management position outside the internal audit department rather than from recognition of contributions made within the department.

In summary, the career-orientation profile of internal audit staffs which emerges from the data analysis shows the following characteristics:
- Not strongly committed to the internal audit profession.
- Very committed to participation for company-efficiency goals.
- Concerned about their promotability over other aspects of career advancement.
- Planning to continue their careers with their current employers (not in internal auditing) unless lured away by an offer of significantly more money from a "better managed company."

Organizational Characteristics

The research questionnaire collected data reflecting respondents' views pertinent to six organizational variables that might affect audit employees' attitudes:
- Formalization of work patterns.
- Centralization of decision making.
- Organizational responsiveness to internal auditing.
- Flexibility of management.
- Authority.
- Participation.

The statistical analysis was unable to find consistent response patterns that might define the dimensions of flexibility for staff members. A discussion of the key dimensions of the other five variables follows:

Formalization of Work Patterns. In their responses to a question about initiative in developing audit programs (A, II, 1), staff respondents indicated that they do not think internal auditing is excessively formalized. Most (92 percent) agree that they are encouraged to use their initiative. One respondent elaborated on his response in these words, "Standard audit programs give us very general guidelines within which we are expected to develop a specific audit program to deal with the situations we find in the field."

Centralization of Decision Making. Two opposite aspects of centralization were identified as being important to staff members. Although 70 percent agree that a small number of people make most internal audit decisions (A, II, 3), 92 percent agree that their work calls for frequent exercise of discretionary judgment

(A, II, 5). The apparent conflict in these responses may be explained by the nature of auditing. Even if some key decisions — about units to be audited, for example — are centralized, many other decisions unavoidably must be made at the audit site by those performing the work.

Organizational Responsiveness to Internal Auditing. Two questions deal with resopndents' perceptions about how internal auditing is viewed by audited departments. Sixty-seven percent believe managers of audited departments "look on internal audit as a source of constructive assistance" (A, II, 42), while 55 percent believe internal auditing is "viewed largely as a policing activity" (A, II, 46). Some of the comments for this quesiton are quoted below:

> The most unpleasant part of internal auditing is reporting on the mistakes of other people. I feel like an outsider, a necessary evil. Interestingly, I did not feel this way as an external auditor. I did my job and left.
>
> An area which upsets me is the constant enemy relationship that occurs on every audit. I don't like feeling like a policeman.
>
> I do not like the image of a policeman and don't know how to shake it even though we stress the benefits of an audit.

In light of such responses, it appears that, although managers of audited departments do look on internal audit as a source of constructive assistance, they still maintain the "we-they" posture that makes many internal auditors feel like policemen rather than part of the company.

Authority. The exercise of authority in internal audit departments was investigated with questions about explaining changes to affected employees and the use of incentives to attain objectives. A variety of experiences are reported regarding how changes are explained and justified (A, II, 47). Forty-two percent think their companies fail to satisfactorily explain changes to those affected. Twelve percent are undecided, and 46 percent think their companies do a good job of explaining changes. Second, 39 percent perceive their companies to offer incentives in order to attain objectives; 46 percent do not; and 15 percent are unclear about this (A, II, 24). Many who feel their companies do a poor job of explaining changes responded that they offer incentives to attain objectives. This suggests that companies are perceived by internal audit staffs to use either verbal persuasion or incentive programs — but not both — in their exercise of authority.

Participation. From the staff's point of view, internal auditors rate their companies about "average" on participation. The questions that relate to this variable deal with participation in planning and implementing changes (A, II, 2) and full discussion of issues (A, II, 51). Responses to both indicate a variety of approaches to participation. Forty-seven percent think their departments foster participation in planning and implementing changes; 39 percent think their departments do not encourage participation; and 14 percent are uncertain. Forty-six percent agree that their departments have participation on the full discussion of issues, while 33 percent disagree, and 21 percent are uncertain. There is no identifiable general tendency toward either participation or nonparticipation in the management of internal auditing departments as viewed by the responding staff members. They identified "participation in planning and implementation of changes" and "full discussion of issues" as the subjects of strongest interest on the participation variable.

Of the six organizational variables, responses were insufficient to draw a conclusion concerning flexibility of management. For the others, key factors may be summarized as follows:

Variable	Focus of Concern
Formalization of work patterns	Freedom to modify audit programs
Centralization of decision making	Participation in important audit decisions
Organizational responsiveness to internal auditing	"Policeman" image of internal auditors
Authority	Use of both persuasion and rewards to achieve objectives.
Participation	Explanation of changes; discussion of issues

Job Satisfaction

Twelve aspects of job satisfaction[13] (A, II, 55) are closely related. For most respondents, satisfaction on one dimension indicates satisfaction at a similar level on the others. Four aspects of job satisfaction stand out in the statistical analysis as being of particular concern to staff members:

- Make full use of your knowledge and skills.
- Learn new knowledge and skills.
- Advance within the company.
- Improve your technical expertise.

If staff members are satisfied with these four aspects of the work, the data show they will also be satisfied on the other dimensions. The responses follow:

	Percentages		
	Satisfied	Neither	Dissatisfied
Make full use of knowledge and skills	83	3	14
Learn new knowledge and skills	80	4	15
Advance within the company	59	12	29
Improve your technical competence	74	8	18

This profile shows a group that is, on the whole, reasonably well satisfied. One exception is that some respondents are not satisfied with opportunities to advance within the company. This feature was identified earlier as of critical importance to internal audit staff members because they view their futures in terms of advancement within the company but often not within the internal audit department. The fact that 41 percent of the respondents are clearly dissatisfied or uncertain on this dimension of job satisfaction should be of concern to company and departmental management. Several respondents addressed this dimension of job satisfaction in responding to an open-ended question illustrated by the following comment:

> When I became associated with the internal audit group, I was hoping that senior management looked on the department as a grooming area for future managers. As my first year reached its completion, I realized that this was not happening within the company. Since internal auditing becomes both tedious and repetitious after a number of years, the auditors don't have a goal to work toward. Without a clear path out of internal audit, the future looks bleak. Many

respondents value internal audit experience as training for future management positions. However, the data suggest that many are disappointed when their expectation of a promotion into management is not fulfilled.

In order to understand respondents' job satisfaction more thoroughly, we asked them to rank from a list of ten the three most appealing and the three least appealing job features. Table 4-19 reports these ten job features with an index for each, showing its importance on the most appealing and least appealing scales. The higher the index, the more appealing or unappealing internal audit staff find the job features.

Table 4-19
Internal Audit Staff Members
Evaluation of Job Features

Job Features	Indices of Job Features*	
	Most Appealing	Least Appealing
Travel	12	31
Intellectual challenge of work	45	6
Variety of assignments	54	3
Status and prestige	9	21
Contribution of success of company	17	8
Compensation	16	21
Authority accompanying auditor's position	8	20
Association with other internal auditors	6	7
Relationship with independent accountants	1	26
General work atmosphere	17	17

*Higher indices reflect higher scores on the most appealing or least appealing dimensions. These are constructed indices based on the number of internal audit staff members' ranking each feature first, second, or third; they are not numbers of respondents. If every respondent ranked a job feature "first," the index would be 100.

$$S = \frac{3(\#1) + 2(\#2) + (\#3)}{3(1240)}$$

The most appealing job aspects for internal audit staff members are the "variety of assignments" and the "intellectual challenge of work." Note, too, that the indices for these two job features on the least appealing dimension are extremely small, indicating a high degree of agreement across all respondents. Almost all internal audit staff members apparently like the variety of assignments and intellectual challenge of their work.

Although "travel" rates the highest index on the least appealing dimension, there are a significant number of internal audit staff who find travel appealing. From the narrative comments, two reasons why travel is least appealing are evident. The first relates to the length of time on the job. Although we have no systematic data to support this idea, several comments in the narrative responses and in the research seminars imply that travel does appeal to people when they first enter internal auditing. After a year or two, however, the novelty and excitement wear off; and they begin to tire of travel.

The second reason concerns one's ability to maintain social relationships when travelling a great deal. Married people — or staff members interested in developing social, professional, or educational relationships that demand time spent consistently in one place — complain more about internal audit travel than do others. Travel unavoidably increases the difficulty of going to school or of completing a certification process. All these complaints point to people who are older and more interested in establishing roots. If substantial travel is an unavoidable requirement of internal audit work, then travel will have a direct impact on the age of internal audit staff members, their length of time in internal audit, and their choice of internal audit as a long-term career.

The difference between the least appealing and most appealing dimension for "status and prestige" indicates that a significant proportion of the respondents are not satisfied with their stature within the organization. This impression is reinforced by their perceptions of how managers of audited departments react to recommendations from internal audit (A, III, 10). Forty-one percent responded that managers go along with internal audit suggestions less than half the time. Eight percent either had no means to convey suggestions or never make suggestions. Forty-eight percent have managers who go along with suggestions three-fourths of the time, while only three percent concur all the time.

Another dimension of status and prestige was identified by a respondent in the following comment:

> Although I find auditing interesting and challenging, I do not feel it is held in very high esteem by line and corporate management. Quite frankly, I do not see this changing much despite what we say to ourselves about being consultants to assist management. Understanding and acceptance of internal audit by line management may never be possible.

It is important to consider such feelings of low status and prestige, particularly in light of the general praise of internal audit that was expressed by respondents to the senior management questionnaire. (See Chapter 5.) There seems to be a failure of communication between the internal audit staff and general management on this matter. One respondent suggested that management only gives "lip service" to internal audit as a "necessary but nonproduct overhead item." On the other hand, the impression received from the senior management and audit committee representatives is that they are generally supportive and pleased with the services of internal auditing and would like more. Nonetheless, the perception of low status and prestige is real, and senior management would do well to consider means of improving those perceptions.

The most surprising result from the indices of job features (Table 4-19) is the number of respondents who find their relationship with independent accountants to be the least appealing feature of their jobs. A supportable explanation of this response will require additional research data.

Internal audit staff members believe the task of an internal auditor is different from that of an external auditor (A, I, 18).

Table 4-20
Internal Audit Staff Members
Comparison of Internal Auditing and External Auditing

To what extent do you consider the task of an internal auditor to be different from that of an external auditor?

	Responses	
	Number	Percentage
Entirely different	112	9
Mostly different	521	42
Half the same and half different	434	35
Mostly the same	166	14
Entirely the same	1	—
Total	1,234	100

Fifty-one percent of the staff believe their jobs are mostly or entirely different from the job of an external auditor. Only 14 percent think it is mostly or entirely the same. Regardless of their beliefs about how different their jobs are from those of external auditors, many internal auditors spend some portion of time working on aspects of the external auditor's annual audit. Very few like the experience. The staff respondents wrote at length about their relationship with external auditors. The following quotes indicate that an important cause of this disaffection stems from their perceptions of external auditors' attitudes toward internal auditors:

> I resent the use of our department as "go-fors" for the external auditor. We are of equal caliber and should be treated as such.
>
> The biggest problem that I have to deal with, both professionally and emotionally trying, is the public auditor. They have no outside interest and expect me to eat, sleep, and live auditing for them. I have to work with them four or five months a year, and it is pure hell.

In some companies, of course, the relationship between external and internal auditors works very smoothly. In others, friction is created by two groups concerned about the same activities and information but from different perspectives and with different goals. It is natural that an internal auditor, who may feel he can make an important contribution by concentrating on productivity implications, would be frustrated if he is assigned menial work related to the financial account balances. Staff members in the research seminars also mentioned that external auditors sometimes failed to acknowledge the source of material included in their management letters — even though this information was based on findings and recommendations from internal audit working papers. We find it interesting that past attention to this relationship has been focused on how external auditors auditors can rely on internal auditors and still satisfy standards of independence. An important research contribution would be a more thorough assessment of the work relationships and attitudes of these two professions. A project sponsored jointly by the two professional groups is desirable.

Three key themes emerge from this discussion of internal audit staff members' job satisfaction:

- Generally, internal audit staff members are well satisfied with most dimensions of their jobs.
- They are especially satisfied with the variety and intellectual challenge of their work.
- They have important concerns about promotability, relationships with external auditors, travel, and compensation.

The Relationship Between Job Satisfaction and Work-Related Attitudes.

Using standard correlational methods, we analyzed the relationship between the job-satisfaction variables and the work-related attitude variables to detect any patterns of association among them. In several cases, we found that high satisfaction scores were related to scores on the work-related attitude variables. These relationships, which are summarized in Table 4-21, can be useful in assessing the effects that work-related variables have on job satisfaction.

Table 4-21
Internal Audit Staff Members
Relationship of Job Satisfaction and Work-Related Attitudes

Work-Related Attitude Variable	Job Satisfaction
Career Orientation	
Professional commitment	Slightly positive
Commitment to organizational goals	Positive
Organizational immobility	Positive
External orientation	Negative
Career advancement	Positive
Job Characteristics	
Role clarity	Very positive
Challenge	Positive
Learning opportunities	Very positive
Organizational Variables	
Formalization	Slightly positive
Centralization	Very negative
Flexibility	None
Open communication	Positive
Authority usage	Positive
Participation	Positive

The relationship in the right-hand column accompanies a high score on the variable in the left-hand column. For example, a high degree of professional commitment has a slightly positive relationship with job satisfaction; a high degree of external orientation has a negative relationship with job satisfaction.

Most of the work-related attitude variables have a positive relationship with job satisfaction. The most important relationships appear to be between job satisfaction and role clarity, learning opportunities, organizational responsiveness, and centralization. Staff respondents with high scores on role clarity, learning opportunities, and organizational responsiveness also had high scores on job satisfaction. Respondents from highly centralized work environments had consistently low scores on job satisfaction than did those from decentralized work environments.

Some Impressions from the Staff Questionnaire

We have collected and analyzed a substantial amount of data related to a variety of internal audit variables. These data have important implications for internal audit staff members' attitudes and job satisfaction. From the data analyses, we have formed certain impressions about staff members based on a number of recurring themes.

Most internal audit staff members are attracted to a company where they believe they can develop a management career. Internal audit experience serves as a means of entry and a very useful background. Except for a significant minority who plan to be career internal auditors, most intend to stay in internal audit for only a few years. For the majority who view internal auditing as a valuable but temporary experience, progress toward future management careers is of prime importance. Those who do not have graduate degrees, especially those in large companies, dislike travel because it makes graduate study difficult. The increasing emphasis on graduate degrees will no doubt intensify their feelings about travel.

There are very few internal audit specialties outside of EDP. Most staff members perform a variety of investigation, review, and decision-making tasks throughout their companies. Thus, most internal auditors are generalists rather than specialists. In the case of EDP auditors, many feel misunderstood and unappreciated by internal audit generalists. This problem is especially acute with respect to pay and grade levels for EDP auditors.

Internal audit staff members are attracted to alternative and diverse career paths when they enter the internal audit department. One path is for those who plan to remain internal auditors; the other is for those who are only passing through internal audit enroute to a management career in finance, accounting, or administration. It seems likely that the two groups view their internal audit experience differently. The latter group desires exposure to company-operating departments and to general management concerns. The former may be more interested in the development of conventional audit expertise. It is our conclusion that much the same kind of training may serve both groups well. The difference between internal audit and external audit is repeatedly noted. While internal auditors are primarily concerned with the fairness of financial statements, internal auditors focus on the company's profitability, its efficiency, the protection of management from criticism and embarrassment, and the effectiveness of management controls in the broadest sense.

Representatives of management and the audit committee indicate that they value such services and would like to see internal auditing continue to expand its range of interests into other aspects of the company's operations. This suggests that a strong educational emphasis on such matters as risk analysis, management control procedures, company goals and policies, decision-making methodology, and performance evaluation would serve staff members who plan to move into management positions and those who seek internal auditing careers.

The fact that the majority of internal auditors expect to remain in that position no more than three to five years poses some interesting problems for directors of internal auditing. Should everyone who is now an internal auditor be a member of a professional institute even though many have no intention of pursuing a career in auditing? What should be the requirements for membership? What should be the organization's purpose? Should The Institute of Internal Auditors be oriented toward long-term internal auditors or toward short-term internal auditors? Answers to these questions are not easy, but how they are answered will have critical effects on the future of internal auditing.

Two of the dominant problems internal audit staff members identified in their work are their relationship with external auditors and their status and prestige in their companies. They feel that external auditors look on them condescendingly and have a narrow scope of interests. Internally, they often feel and believe they are treated as corporate policemen who cause difficulties for audited departments. They would much prefer to be welcomed as friendly experts offering constructive assistance. The causes of these two problems emerge from the historical development of internal auditing and from audit services that are indispensable for some companies. These attitudes will be difficult to change. Yet progress as a profession will require effective improvement in organizational stature and relationships with external auditors. Otherwise, it will become increasingly difficult to attract qualified recruits. Initiatives in these areas should be undertaken promptly and vigorously. These may call for imaginative and innovative approaches not in keeping with internal auditing's present self-image. However, the success of such efforts will influence the future quality of internal auditing professionals and services.

We looked for quotations from internal audit staff members that capture the spirit of our conclusions about their attitudes. We close this chapter with some excerpts:

> I don't feel like I belong to a team in the operating units I audit. I feel like a headquarters' policeman and look forward to getting back into operations some day.
>
> One of our primary objectives is to train the future financial managers of the company. Our auditors are not career oriented but are placed back into operating components after about three years.
>
> I feel that internal auditing is not highly regarded as a profession but is seen more as a stepping stone to other management positions. We should place more emphasis on presenting internal auditing as a profession.
>
> I do not believe our company personnel fully comprehend what internal auditing is all about, nor do people I associate with socially. We appear to be the "silent" profession.
>
> Auditing involves being there after the fact, never being involved in making something important happen, only reviewing the work others have done.
>
> Internal auditing is a stressful occupation. We need more training and education in dealing with and controlling stress.

[12] The discussion throughout this section is based on a confirmatory factor analysis with the LISREL V statistical package. The dimensions highlighted and discussed for each of the job characteristic, career orientation, organizational characteristics, and job satisfaction variables are those identified as statistically significant by this analysis. Complete details regarding this analysis are available from the authors.

[13] The aspects evaluated include the opportunities available to make full use of your knowledge and skills, learn new knowledge and skills, earn a satisfactory salary, advance within the company, improve your technical competence, associate with personnel senior to your position, build your professional reputation, work on difficult and challenging problems, make constructive suggestions, be in the company of people you like, enjoy your work, and influence company policy.

5

Senior Management, Audit Committee Representative, and Independent Accountant Perspectives

In this chapter, we present the results of the questionnaires sent to those who do not participate directly in internal auditing but who work closely with internal auditors and are likely to have an informed opinion on the nature and quality of the work that they do. The results of each questionnaire are presented in a separate section of the chapter.

Representatives of Senior Management

The questionnaires sent to representatives of senior management had two purposes. First, it was intended to gather information that would reflect senior management's view of the nature, quality, and usefulness of internal audit activities within the companies they represented. Second, it obtained considerable information about the respondents' companies. The latter information was used to classify responding companies according to groups whose members used similar patterns of internal audit services. Our purpose was exploratory. We sought some basis for categorizing companies in terms of fundamental characteristics and tendencies that might give us a clue as to why internal audit departments differ so widely from one another in the nature and the scope of their activities.

Growth of Internal Auditing

The internal audit departments of a majority of the responding companies have grown in size in recent years. To the question "Has your internal audit department grown in size over the last five years?" 82 percent responded affirmatively and only 18 percent negatively. The reason for such growth are reported in the following table:

Table 5-1
Representatives of Senior Management
Reasons for Growth of Internal Audit Departments

Please rank order the three most significant causes of growth of internal auditing in your company (use "1" as most significant).

	Causes of Growth		
	First	Second	Third
Compliance obligations imposed by the FCPA and similar requirements	11	37	36
Desire by senior management to improve control	131	34	14
Recommendation of audit committee	7	33	29
Need to reduce errors and irregularities	3	27	29
Attempt to reduce external audit fees	10	37	45
Other	35	12	11

The most common explanation of an "other" response was a statement about an increase in the size of the company. There were also a number of references to the increased use of computers within the business and the resulting necessity of staffing up to provide adequate audit expertise.

Management Reliance on Internal Auditing

To discover the extent to which members of senior management rely on the work of the internal audit department and whether they want to increase that reliance, we asked the question in the following table. We asked it with respect to present activities and in terms of whether they would like to rely more on their internal auditors.

Table 5-2
Representatives of Senior Management
Reliance on Internal Auditing

Please indicate the extent to which senior management currently relies on (would like to rely on) the work of the internal audit function with regard to each of the following items. Please use the following scale:

	Extent of Reliance						
	None	Very Low	Low	Neither Low nor High	High	Very High	Total
Reliability of company's financial data:							
1. Reported externally	9/5	12/7	13/10	30/26	25/32	11/20	0/1
2. Used internally only	5/3	13/7	11/10	25/22	29/30	16/27	0/1
Evaluation of the effectiveness of management's:							
1. Operating decisions	14/7	19/10	16/15	25/27	21/28	5/12	0/1
2. Financial decisions	14/8	16/9	19/14	30/26	17/30	4/12	0/1
Integrity of company officers and employees	1/1	3/2	6/3	22/18	33/31	1/38	3/7

Table 5-2 (continued)

Efficiency and effectiveness with which company goals are attained	11/7	9/7	20/12	37/27	18/29	5/17	0/1
Compliance with established rules and procedures	0/1	0/0	2/0	4/2	32/23	56/61	5/12
Adequacy of internal control procedures	0/0	0/0	0/0	2/1	21/11	63/69	14/18
Monitoring the application of internal control procedures	0/0	0/0	1/0	3/2	21/13	59/64	16/21
Detection of errors and irregularities	0/0	3/1	4/4	16/11	37/28	34/44	5/11
Assuring company's compliance with all relevant government regulations	3/2	7/4	15/6	22/19	32/29	19/34	3/5

In each pair, the first figure represents current reliance; second figure represents extent to which senior management would like to rely on the work of the internal audit function. All the figures represent percentages of responses.

For almost every work description in the question, management would prefer to rely on internal auditing more than they do now. In view of the wide range of services listed, the responses indicating the extent to which management would like to rely on internal auditing impress us as very complimentary. The data show that management appears to be satisfied with present services and is interested in greater reliance.

To determine why senior management felt that present internal auditing services do not provide the extent of reliance that management would prefer, we included Question 5 of Part I: "Please describe briefly the major reasons for any differences between the extent of senior management's current reliance on internal audit work and senior management's desired level of reliance."

For the most part, responses fell into three groups. A common type of answer explained that the internal audit department was either new and still developing, was too small to meet its present workload, or did not have a sufficient budget and other resources to do everything that management would like it to do. The tone of these responses was not one of criticism because the limitations described were externally imposed on the internal audit department.

A second and less frequent comment concerned the lack of management expertise within the internal audit department. In some cases, this was linked with the fact that the department had only recently been organized.

A third class of responses stated that there were no significant differences in the extent of present reliance on the work of internal auditors and the reliance that management would like to have.

A few of the responses to Question 5 follow to provide some flavor of senior management's comments:

> In five years, the internal audit department has grown substantially in size and competence with some margin of additional growth needed to reach goals.
> Need for increased management expertise on internal audit staff.

Principal difference is in the areas of financial reporting and financial decisions. Emphasis has been directed toward operating environment and related procedures and controls. As these areas come under better control, emphasis will shift more toward financial areas.

Legal problems involved with discovery process by federal agencies restricts ability of internal audit to be as incisive as we would like.

Would like to see more acceptance of internal audit as a resource to provide independent, objective views of business operations.

We would like them to be able to spend more time on compliance issues and controls, but up to now there are just too many other things for them to do.

Greater emphasis on the evaluation of effectiveness of operating/financial decisions is called for. This will require an expansion of the skill base within the internal audit group.

Internal audit department's assignment is to concentrate on operating divisions, not headquarters' functions.

Experience and expertise in planning and conducting operational audits (as opposed to financial audits) needs to be improved. Performance of operational audits is a relatively recent undertaking.

To obtain some impression of the status of internal auditing within the company, we included a question designed to discover what attention is given to recommendations made by the internal audit department as a result of its examinations. Table 5-3 includes the question and reports the results.

Table 5-3
Representatives of Senior Management
Attention Given to Recommendations by the Internal Audit Department

Which of the following statements best describes the attention given to recommendations by the internal audit department of your company? (Check one.)

	Responses Number	Percentage
Recommendations by the internal audit department are a matter of record, but there needs to be no internal audit follow-up on their implementation until the following audit.	8	3
Recommendations by the internal audit department must be answered in writing within a stated time.	136	51
Recommendations made by the internal audit department are maintained in an open file until settled by implementation or mutual agreement.	81	31
Recommendations by the internal audit department must be complied with unless factually in error.	13	
Other	27	10
Total	265	100

Most of the responses under "other" represent modifications of the possibilities listed. The modifications are necessary to correspond more closely to the respondents' circumstances. Many described arbitration or appeal procedures to be followed when the internal audit recommendations were not acceptable to the operating management. Some of those responses are:

> Recommendations made by the internal audit department are normally answered in writing within a stated period of time, and recommendations are adopted in most cases.
>
> Internal audit findings are expected to be corrected, but responsibility for corrective action is left to local management. Failure to correct a serious deficiency before the next audit would be considered unsatisfactory performance.
>
> Recommendations are considered in light of cost-benefit factors and are expected to be implemented unless cost is considered out of line with benefit or an alternative solution is chosen.

Overall, the responses to this question lead directly to the conclusion that internal audit departments are highly respected within the majority of companies. Nothing in the responses gives any impression of disregard for their recommendations. Differences between auditors and auditees are to be expected. In most cases, internal auditors will discuss their findings and recommendations with the operating management before their report is submitted in final form. Even so, differences of opinion will still exist; and some appeal or arbitration procedure may be required. The important conclusion from these responses is that no one takes such recommendations lightly. This speaks well for the acceptance of internal auditing as an important activity within the company.

Contributions of Internal Audit Departments

Three open-ended questions were included to provide respondents an opportunity to express their views on the services of their internal audit departments. The first of these inquired about past important contributions by internal auditing; the second concerned anticipated contributions by internal audit; and the third asked about special problems in maintaining internal control.

Question 7 of Part I is: "What is the most important contribution that your internal audit department has provided for your company over the last few years?"

Many responses described improvements in internal control systems, success in informing others in the company of the importance of internal control, and the assurance to management that policies and rules were being complied with. Other responses described specific findings or services which the respondents felt were of special importance to the company that year. A selection of typical responses follows:

> Suggestions for constructive change in procedures or organization.
>
> Made all departments more aware of benefits of rigorous adherence to procedures, and these same departments are pleased.
>
> Improving operating controls has saved the company large amounts of money.
>
> Input to senior management decisions has been increasingly valuable.
>
> Have expanded auditing into sensitive areas, resulting in critical review of existing policies and procedures (or lack thereof) and constructive change in many cases.

Identified a defalcation in the purchasing department. In operational audits, disclosed up to $5 million in savings. Helped reduce external audit fees by improved coordination.

Decreased likelihood of internal embezzlement and fraud.

Internal auditing has allowed us to grow, both internally and externally, in a context where senior management feels that controls are in place and operational.

Continuing professional advancement is close to if not equal to the state of the art in audit programs and professionalism. This is particularly important in the EDP area.

Assuring that the accounts and records and operating results reported by company components are stated accurately and that effective internal controls are in place. Intensive training for approximately 200 young, aggressive, intelligent personnel from whom the future financial managers of the company will be drawn.

Creating a favorable acceptance of internal auditing within the company. The department lacked professionalism and credibility when organized and now maintains a very high level of both.

Impressing on operating management the full range of responsibilities and the assistance that can be given by operating as well as financial audits.

Examination of control over operating procedures. Whenever we sustain a loss, we find that internal audit was not brought in at early stages of developing a system or product. We now require this.

Provided top management and the board with an increasing level of assurance that adequate controls are in place and that financial and operational policies are being followed.

Focused emphasis on improving audit results in departments and branches through comparative ratings and audit awards. Provided in-depth analyses of operating problems in weak division with follow-up reviews to check implementation of corrective procedures.

Question 8 of Part I was similar in purpose but dealt with expectations: "What is the most important contribution that you expect your internal audit department to provide for your company over the few years?"

Anticipated contributions from internal audit departments in the next few years are very much like those received in the recent past. Senior management is looking for strengthened internal controls, improvements in efficiency and profitability, and help with a variety of specific problems. Some of the responses follow:

Suggestions for constructive change in procedures or organization.

Further develop their personnel for career path transfers into other departments.

Helps establish consistent and proper policies among parent and subsidiaries. Assurance that policies are being adhered to.

Holds down audit fees by increasing compliance with controls established.

Identifying internal control weaknesses and constructively recommending solutions with increased emphasis on operations as distinguished from transaction systems.

>Control and evaluation of capital expenditures.

>A continued training program for middle and upper managers.

>Continues to serve as the corporate conscience by overseeing the implementation of adequate controls in new systems.

>Developing and executing plans that contribute to the company's profit and growth by appraising and reporting on the adequacy and the compliance with the company's internal control system and by consulting on management's administrative practices.

>More operational audits will help managers do a more productive job. I would hope the auditors would raise operational issues which the manager would implement without pressure from above.

>In addition to a continuation of complying with policies and procedures and detection of problems, the evaluation of operating/financial decisions after the fact.

Question 9 of Part I was included to discover the extent to which representatives of senior management were concerned about specific internal control problems: "If there are any particular areas or activities within your company for which you experience unusual difficulty in achieving and maintaining what you consider to be an adequate level of internal control, please describe them briefly."

As might be expected, computers and EDP are a concern to a great many corporate executives, and these were mentioned most frequently. More surprising is the wide range of business activities which senior managers consider to present special problems of control. The following selected responses are illustrative:

>External contracting and EDP.

>Number of authorized check signers in the field due to nature of business. Developing control through bank-controlled disbursement account.

>Computerized data processing. Advanced technologies tend to outpace ability to train personnel to maintain their skills.

>The geographic diversity of field operations and the variety of supervisory personnel in the field make consistency and compatability difficult to achieve. This requires monitoring by not only internal auditing but also financial management.

>Construction activity. This has historically not been a large share of our business activity. Over the past several years, it has grown in importance; however, our audit expertise in this area has not grown accordingly.

>Company operates a series of oil-field supply stores. Personnel at a store may be as few as three people. They buy, sell, invoice, collect, etc. The control problems are obvious and fraud continues.

>A very difficult area is computer systems employing on-line capabilities. Ensuring the integrity of the basic systems and safeguarding sensitive data are a challenge without causing a degradation of economics and efficiencies.

>Quality in oral and written contacts with customers.

>Purchasing such services as market research, artwork, and the like.

>EDP security. (a) Data processing does not give job top priority. (b)

Standards are constantly rising. (c) Trained personnel are high turnover people. (d) The job is difficult.

Inventory control. Because of the nature of our business, we require significant systems and procedures to maintain the level of comfort.

Payment of claims for damages in shipment of household goods.

Documentation exceptions on lending papers.

Field auditing of natural gas-drilling operations.

Purchase of software from software houses.

Field locations where lack of staff has prevented adequate reviews.

Trust-division activities have been difficult to bring under adequate control in the trust-operating area.

Annually, we discover more than 1,000 instances of significant fraud and theft with an exposure before tax, insurance, and recovery of more than $5 million. This should be reduced.

Traditionally, it is difficult to give attention and support to marketing operations.

Management's Evaluation of Internal Auditing

There is little question about the positive way that management regards the internal audit function. In one of our seminars, a director of internal auditing described the primary task of internal auditing as that of protecting the senior management from embarrassment. We included a question to discover how management viewed internal auditing. The results show clearly that management views internal auditing as a protection and as a service.

Table 5-4
Representatives of Senior Management
Management's View of the Purpose of the Internal Audit Function

For each of the following statements, indicate senior management's view of the importance of the internal audit function in your company as:

	Percentages				
	Unimportant	Very Unimportant	Neither Important Nor Unimportant	Important	Very Important
A management training program	6	15	34	37	9
A protection to management	0	1	7	50	42
An essential activity for business success	1	3	21	53	22
A resource to assist the audit committee	1	2	10	40	47
A career for loyal but not innovative employees	59	21	19	1	0
A means for reducing external audit fees	3	9	20	57	11
An investigative arm for the company's audit committee	3	6	29	43	19
An investigative arm for senior management	0	3	13	55	29
Consultants to management at all levels for improving operating efficiency	3	11	26	45	14

A heavy emphasis on the importance of those activities which directly serve management is readily apparent. Our greatest surprise was in the relatively light consideration of internal auditing as a valuable management training program. Throughout the responses from staff members, the benefits of internal auditing as a preparation for other positions within the company, but outside internal auditing, were repeatedly emphasized. Additionally, in the narrative responses about the contribution (past and anticipated) of the internal audit department, its usefulness as a training experience was mentioned many times.

Internal audit personnel also receive high grades from senior management when compared with other personnel in the company. Question 11 of Part I and the responses follow:

Table 5-5
Representatives of Senior Management
Comparative Rating of Internal Audit Department

Please rate your internal audit department relative to other departments and activities in your company.

	Responses Number	Percentage
Very superior	18	7
Superior	127	48
Average	113	43
Disappointing	6	2
Very disappointing	0	0
Total	264	100

Unquestionably, most senior management respondents find internal auditing highly useful. The several suggestions that internal auditing is changing and that an increasing variety of services is expected led us to inquire about those factors that inhibit internal auditing from being more useful than it now is. Question 12 of Part I and the responses are summarized in Table 5-6.

Table 5-6
Representatives of Senior Management
Factors Inhibiting the Usefulness of Internal Auditing

What factors do you think most inhibit internal auditing from becoming more useful in your company than it now is? (Check as many items as apply.)

	Responses Number	Percentage
Narrow point of view of internal auditors	48	18
Inadequate appreciation by your company of internal audit capabilities	109	41
The company's historical experience with internal auditing	73	27
Limited ability of internal auditors	41	15
Lack of managerial perspective on the part of internal auditors	77	29
Inadequate supply of qualified internal audit personnel	61	23
Inadequate incentives for good people to become internal auditors in this company	54	20
Inadequate programs to keep internal auditors informed of current developments in auditing	9	3
Other	26	10

Note that the largest percentage of respondents checked "Inadequate appreaciation by your company of internal audit capabilities." This is followed closely by "The company's historical experience with internal auditing." At a time when internal auditing is changing so dramatically, historical experience is not a very good guide to future possibilities. Yet in the view of some senior managements, internal auditing may face some difficulty in overcoming its past image.

It is interesting that few respondents questioned the ability of internal auditors, although a substantial number noted their lack of managerial perspective. The combination of these two responses suggests that management training for internal audit personnel might be highly useful — both for those involved and for the future status of internal auditing.

We received a considerable variety of "other" responses, but the most common involved the difficulty of keeping good people long enough for them to be well trained and productive. Inexperience, newness of the function, insufficient resources, and a widely held view that internal audit is not a career function were also mentioned.

Respondents indicated that senior management actively supports the internal audit function. This is evident from Table 5-7.

Table 5-7
Representatives of Senior Management
Support for the Internal Audit Function

In your opinion, how actively does senior management in your company support the internal audit function?

	Responses	
	Number	Percentage
Very actively	100	38
Actively	121	45
Neither actively nor passively	36	14
Passively	9	3
Very passively	0	0
Total	266	100

In a similar fashion, members of the audit committee are considered to be actively interested in internal control.

Table 5-8
Representatives of Senior Management
Audit Committee Interest in Internal Control

In your opinion, how actively is the audit committee interested in the internal control concerns in your company?

	Responses	
	Number	Percentage
Very actively	129	49
Actively	111	43

Table 5-8 (continued)

Neither actively nor passively	15	6
Passively	5	2
Very passively	1	0
Total	261	100

Audit Committee Members

The Institute's advisory committee proposed that we include a questionnaire directed to audit committee chairmen and other representatives. In recent years, audit committees have not only grown in number and importance but have also tended to work more closely with internal auditors and with the independent accountants. Indeed, suggestions have been made that the internal audit department should work for and report to the audit committee. Use of this questionnaire, therefore, provided us with an opportunity to acquire data relevant to the relationships between internal audit departments and audit committees as well as other useful information. Two hundred and thirty-two audit committee members or chairmen responded to this questionnaire.

Relative Importance of Internal Audit Assignments

The first question concerned the importance of aspects of the audit department's assignments. Responses show a stronger interest in internal control and in the prevention or reduction of improprieties and irregularities than in detection and correction of unintentional errors. The results follow in Table 5-9.

Table 5-9
Audit Committee Members
Relative Importance of the Internal Audit Department's Activities

Percentage

	Very Unimportant	Unimportant	Neither Important Nor Unimportant	Important	Very Important
Detection and correction of unintentional errors	5	9	20	55	11
Prevention or reduction of improprieties and irregularities	4	0	2	30	64
Improvement of internal control	2	0	0	25	73
Assistance to independent CPAs in performance of annual audit	3	1	14	62	20
An investigative arm for the company's audit committee	5	6	18	44	27
An investigative arm for senior management	3	6	17	45	29
Monitoring the performance of internal control procedures	2	0	1	38	58

One unavoidable conclusion from these data is that, with few exceptions, members of corporate audit committees find the work of internal audit departments important and appear to have a generally favorable impression of them. Question 13 of the audit committee's questionnaire requested a rating of the internal audit department relative to other departments in the company. Table 5-10 reports the results.

Table 5-10
Audit Committee Members
Evaluation of Audit Department Relative to Other Departments

Please rate your internal audit department relative to other departments and activities in your company. (Check one.)

	Responses	
	No.	%
Very superior	21	9
Superior	142	63
Average	62	27
Disappointing	1	1
Very disappointing	0	0
Total	226	100

This question was followed immediately by one addressed to the perceived limitations of audit departments. The question and responses appear in Table 5-11.

Table 5-11
Audit Committee Members
Factors Inhibiting Internal Auditing from Becoming More Useful

What factors do you think most inhibit internal auditing from becoming more useful in your company than it is now? (Check as many items as apply.)

	Responses	
	No.	%
Narrow point of view of internal auditors	20	9
Inadequate appreciation by your company of internal audit capabilities	59	25
The company's historical experience with internal auditing	30	13
Limited ability of internal auditors	17	7
Lack of managerial perspective on the part of internal auditors	40	17
Inadequate supply of qualified internal audit personnel	67	29
Inadequate incentives for good people to become internal auditors in this company	41	18
Inadequate programs to keep internal auditors informed of current development in auditing	5	2
Other	30	13

In these responses, there is little criticism of the ability of internal auditors or of present training programs to keep them informed of current developments in auditing. There is considerable implied criticism of the way internal auditors are employed and treated. "Inadequate appreciation by your company of internal audit capabilities" heads the list. There seems to be some significant feeling on the part of audit committee members that their internal audit departments are competent to do far more than they are called on to do. There is also a feeling that more internal auditors are needed but that their companies are unwilling to offer the kinds of incentives necessary to obtain qualified people for that department.

Responses under the "other" category were widely divergent. Several comments indicated that there were no constraints impeding their internal audit departments and that they were doing excellent work for the companies. Some remarked that their departments were still new and developing necessary skills and personnel; some noted personality difficulties. The difficulty of holding competent people in the department and budget constraints were also mentioned.

One could almost write a paper on "how to improve your internal audit department" based on the answers to this question. It appears that audit committee representatives responding to this questionnaire are very supportive of the function and of internal auditors' abilities.

Responsibilities and Status of the Internal Audit Department

Several questions were directed to the reporting relationships of the internal audit department. The following summary shows that the audit committee meets with the internal auditor on the average of four times a year.

Table 5-12
Audit Committee Members
Frequency of Various Meetings

	Average Times per Year
Full Board of Directors	9
Audit Committee	4
Audit Committee with External CPA/CA	3
Audit Committee with Internal Auditor	4
Audit Committee with Corporate Management	4

When asked "Does the director of internal auditing have an explicit invitation to bring any concerns he may have directly to the audit committee without prior notification of company management?" 90 percent of the respondents answered affirmatively and only 10 percent negatively. This was followed by a question inquiring how frequently the director of internal auditing had to bring such concerns to the audit committee. Table 5-13 reports the results.

Table 5-13
Audit Committee Members
Meetings with the Director of Internal Auditing at the Director's Request

Does the director of internal auditing have an explicit invitation to bring any concerns he may have directly to the audit committee without prior notification of company management?

Yes	206 (90 percent)	No	24 (10 percent)

Table 5-13 (continued)

If yes, how recently has this occurred?

	Responses Number	Percentage
Within the past year	57	28
Within the past five years but not the past year	32	16
Never to your knowledge	101	49
Other	16	7
Total	206	100

What these data cannot tell us is the number of times that directors of internal auditing had concerns that should have been taken to audit committees and for some reason were not. Nevertheless, a high percentage of directors have the invitation, and a substantial number have taken advantage of it.

Question 7 directly addressed the primary reporting responsibility of the director of internal auditing. The responses show considerable differences of opinion and a difficult assignment for the director.

Table 5-14
Audit Committee Members
Primary Responsibility of the Director of Internal Auditing

The primary responsibility of the director of internal auditing in this company is to: (Check one.)

	Response Number	Percentage
The company's audit committee	60	26
The company's chief executive officer	32	14
The audit committee and the chief executive officer equally	87	39
Other	47	21
Total	226	100

An analysis of the "other" responses finds the chief financial officer as the one to whom the director of internal auditing has frequent responsibility. Others mentioned were the board of directors and a number of combinations of audit committee and board of directors with administrative or financial officers. Some comments worthy of attention follow:

> The director reports to the vice president and controller, but he has a dual responsibility in that he has a responsibility to go directly to top management and/or to the audit committee if the situation requires it.

> He reports to the chief financial officer. He is responsible first to management and then to the board of directors through the audit committee if there are irregularities which are not adequately recognized by or involve the management.

> Chief financial officer. Very surprised that this is not shown as a separate box. Most companies follow this procedure. Not showing separately could influence the accuracy of one of the most important aspects of this survey.

To be truly effective, there should be a solid line of reporting to the audit committee and a direct line to company management.

As to responsibility reporting and supervision on a day-to-day basis, this is through the chief financial officer and his office.

To the chief executive, to the chief financial officer, and to the audit committee independently as required.

One must sympathize with a person who has so many bosses. The position of the director of internal auditing does indeed present some interesting possibilities. For almost all his work, his responsibility might be to the chief financial officer or someone he designates. For the rare but possible question involving any member of management superior to the director's position, the director must have both opportunity and acknowledged responsibility to carry such matters to the board of directors, either through the audit committee or directly. In the final analysis, the only control measure to which the senior management is subject is the board of directors. However, the board is not in a position to be informed about matters with which it must properly be concerned. Here, the director of internal auditing plays an absolutely vital role. If he has no responsibility to report beyond senior management, senior management is all but exempted from internal control.

To discover how often the audit committee members think they should meet privately with the director of internal auditing, we included Question 8 in the questionnaire. Responses are reported in Table 5-15.

Table 5-15
Audit Committee Members
Frequency of Private Meetings with the Director of Internal Auditing

The audit committee should meet with the director of internal auditing with no other member of management present: (Check one.)

	Responses	
	Number	Percentage
Annually	65	28
Semiannually	71	31
Quarterly	49	21
Monthly	5	2
Never	6	3
Other	33	15
Total	229	100

The six "never" answers raise some interesting conjectures as to why audit committee members would respond this way. Unfortunately, we have no data to explain that question.

Many of the "other" responses indicate a close relationship between the chairman of the audit committee and the director of internal auditing. They note that the chairman met frequently with the director, in some cases as often as monthly. Others point out that the director always had access to the committee if he needed it. Still other respondents do not formalize the relationship with a fixed number of meetings a year but noted that the number should depend on what the director is discovering through his examination. The director should not hesitate to meet with the board as many times as he deems necessary. In a few cases, respondents answered that, unless provision was made for regular and private meetings, such meetings would not take place. Some wanted to see the director privately every time the audit committee met.

Another aspect of the status of the internal audit department concerrns how its recommendations are treated following an examination. Table 5-16 reports the result.

Table 5-16
Audit Committee Members
Attention Given to Recommendations of Internal Audit Department

Which of the following statements best describes the attention given to recommendations of the internal audit department? (Check one.)

	Responses No.	%
Recommendations by the internal audit department are a matter of record, but there need be no internal audit follow-up on their implementation until the following audit.	1	0
Recommendations made by the internal audit department must be answered in writing within a stated time.	117	53
Recommendations made by the internal audit department are maintained in an open file until settled by implementation or mutual agreement.	73	33
Recommendations by the internal audit department must be complied with unless factually in error.	21	10
Other	10	4
Total	222	100

Respondents to this questionnaire apparently believe that audit committee recommendations are given rigorous attention. The "other" responses represented modifications of one or another of those listed. There was one exception that read: "Number 2 does not work in practice; operations people do not seem to have time."

Audit Committee Activities

The opportunity to inquire about the extent of audit committee participation in a variety of activities was too great to let pass. Hence, we included questions about its involvement in a number of subjects of direct interest to internal auditing. Table 5-17 includes the items and the responses to them:

Table 5-17
Audit Committee Members
Involvement of Audit Committee in Business Concerns

	Percentage				
	Very Strongly Involved	Strongly Involved	Neither Strongly nor Weakly Involved	Weakly Involved	Very Weakly Involved
The reliability of externally reported financial data.	29	36	23	8	4
The reliability of financial data used only internally.	7	29	39	16	9
The evaluation of the effectiveness of management's operating decisions.	4	17	41	21	17
The evaluation of the effectiveness of management's financial decisions.	7	26	38	16	13
Monitoring the integrity of officers and employees.	18	43	26	7	6
The efficiency and the effectiveness with which company goals are attained.	6	24	40	17	13
The adequacy of internal control.	56	35	6	2	1
Assuring compliance with established company rules and procedures.	27	49	16	5	3
Monitoring the application of internal control procedures.	31	46	15	6	2
Detection of errors and irregularities.	14	44	29	7	6
Assuring company compliance with all relevant government regulations	18	35	27	13	7
Resource allocation to internal auditing.	15	47	25	8	5
Detection of fraud.	26	41	22	6	5

The extent of alleged involvement in internal control adequacy and of its monitoring is impressive. Compliance with company rules and procedures follows in the same vein, although it is not emphasized quite as much. Concern for irregularities and the detection of fraud also receive more attention than the evaluation of financial or operational management decisions. Anyone reading these responses is likely to conclude that the responding audit committee members are much aware of the responsibilities for internal control imposed on management by the FCPA.

Question 9 is a combination of inquiries about audit committee members' views regarding the internal audit department's independence and authority. Table 5-18 presents the respondents' views.

Table 5-18
Audit Committee Members
Views on Internal Audit Independence and Authority

	Percentage				
	Strongly Agree	Agree	Neither Agree nor Disagree	Disagree	Strongly Disagree
The audit committee has a direct impact on the amount of resources allocated to the internal audit function.	29	46	17	5	3
Internal audit possesses sufficient independence to fulfill its function.	43	50	5	2	0
Internal audit receives adequate support from management.	44	51	4	2	0
A periodic oral report from the director of internal auditing is all that the audit committee needs from him unless unusual occurrences take place.	6	26	7	38	23
The audit committee should have access to the director of internal auditing for special assignments:					
With management's consent	25	41	10	14	11
Without management's consent	37	34	7	15	6
The director of internal auditing should have authority to bring matters directly to the audit committee without notification to management when he deems this is necessary.	68	29	1	1	1

Note the interesting difference in the responses to the fourth item — reporting by the director of internal auditing to the audit committee. Some feel that a periodic oral report is sufficient unless unusual conditions exist. Others desire something more than that. Judging from other responses in this questionnaire and in the seminars, some audit committee members believe that frequent contact with the director is necessary in order to offset the daily influence of management. They wish to establish a relationship with the director in order that he will not hesitate to bring appropriate matters to their attention. No doubt, those who feel this way take the opportunity to point out to the director from time to time that his basic allegiance runs to the shareholders through the audit committee and board of directors.

There is little question about audit committee members' feelings with respect to giving special assignments to internal audit departments. Apparently, they need to occasionally get beyond the information provided to them by management and consider the internal audit department as a "friendly" resource.

Internal Audit Service to Audit Committee

Several questions taken together give the perspective of audit committee members on the importance and the nature of the service provided to audit committees by the internal audit department. Question 5 inquired about the extent of reliance by the audit committee on the work of the internal auditors. Audit committee members' views are expressed in Table 5-19.

Table 5-19
Audit Committee Members
Reliance on Internal Auditing for Adequacy of Company Control

	Extent of Reliance (Percentage)						
	None	Very Low	Low	Neither High nor Low	High	Very High	Total
The reliability of externally reported financial data.	5	6	8	22	36	20	3
The reliability of data used only internally.	3	9	12	24	27	20	5
The evaluation of the effectiveness of management's operating decisions.	13	13	13	36	16	6	2
The evaluation of the effectiveness of mangement's financial decisions.	11	9	12	40	16	8	3
Monitoring the integrity of officers and employees.	1	6	6	16	29	34	8
The efficiency and the effectiveness with which company goals are attained.	12	10	13	38	16	9	3
The adequacy of internal control.	1	1	0	3	22	52	21
Assuring compliance with established company rules and procedures.	1	3	2	7	28	48	11
Monitoring the application of internal control procedures.	1	1	0	3	23	51	21
Detection of errors and irregularities.	0	2	2	8	35	40	12
Assuring company compliance with all relevant government regulations.	4	4	7	22	30	26	7
Detection of fraud.	1	2	2	10	29	38	19

The extent to which audit committee members rely on internal auditing to assure the adequacy of company control over many of these items should be somewhat sobering. It is a considerable responsibility. This is especially true of such matters as compliance with all relevant government regulations.

The following question was an open-ended request: "If you would like to be able to place greater reliance on your company's internal audit function for any of the items on Question 5 or any other activities, please describe them below:"

The limited number of responses to this invitation suggests that not many audit committee respondents are sufficiently dissatisfied to comment on the present quality of the internal audit departments' work. The following are representative comments:

More attention to financial reports used only internally but which are the basis for major management decisions.

The active consideration of the subjects listed in questions 4 and 5 and the extent to which the audit committee will rely on internal audit will vary depending upon the particular circumstances at any given time. The audit committee is not a management-operating group. It is a committee of the board of directors assigned to monitor and review (a) the results of the annual audit, (b) the proposed financial statements for the annual report to the stockholders, (c) the accounting policies of the company, (d) the adequacy of the company's system of internal controls and internal audit procedures, (e) the policy on business ethics and compliance therewith, and (f) any matters requiring special attention of the auditors. The internal audit department, because of its basic duties, becomes a key element in the work of the audit committee, but so also are the financial management and the external auditors. To try to classify the items of the prior two questions is an impossible exercise. They are all important, yet not all the time. The audit department's duties cover part of substantially all the business concerns mentioned, so it has an important part to play in the audit committee's coverage of its responsibilities.

More emphasis on achieving results based on goals established by management.

The key concern is the total independence and autonomy of internal auditing. It needs to be written into legislation that an internal auditor reports directly to the audit committee concerning irregularities without fear of reprisals.

We are a closely knit working board. We are close to management, both the top and second levels. As a result, we have more direct firsthand knowledge of the affairs of the company.

The audit committee can place reliance as it wishes on internal auditing. We monitor closely the staffing of this function, both as to the number of personnel and also their qualifications.

Anticipate use of internal auditing as an independent source of information in helping the committee to understand certain operating problems.

Contributions of Internal Audit Departments

Question 11 asked respondents to list important contributions made by their internal audit departments over the last few years. The most frequent responses mentioned improvements in internal control, concerning actual procedures and appreciation of its importance. A selection of other responses follows:

Strengthening internal financial controls in response to management's and board of directors' concerns stimulated by the FCPA.

Establishment of internal controls to increase assurance of compliance regarding SEC requirements and policies.

Cost control and recovery together with increasing the reliability of systems and procedures.

Increased the level of control and of understanding the need for control. Also, increased communication between management, auditors, and audit committee.

Expressed concern over computer-operating deficiencies: backup capabilities. Concern expressed was greater than that shown by operating management. Audit committee supported internal audit and turned out to be right. Matter has been corrected.

Excellent effort in investigating serious irregularity. Recovered very large amount while avoiding potentially serious situations. Maintained good pressure on line management to ensure control environment.

Assurance that the bank trustees have information that does not have to be offered through management.

It has kept the entire organization on its toes and also established an excellent system of controls.

Warehouse security. Discovered a major item of fraud. Strengthened accounting procedures amounting to tens of thousands of dollars.

While Question 11 inquired about contributions made by the internal audit function over the last few years, Question 12 asked about contributions anticipated in the near future: "What is the most important contribution that you expect your internal audit department to provide for your company over the next few years?"

As usual with this type of question on this project, most of the comments referred to strengthening, encouraging, or monitoring internal control. However, other matters were also mentioned. Some selected responses follow:

We have embarked on a program to have key executives in each area of the organization serve at least a one-year apprenticeship in the internal auditing department. We feel this will improve the historical image of the function as well as enhance its future acceptance in all areas.

Company is high volume and very low profit margin. Inventory and receivables control are vital, particularly in a decentralized operation; and conformity is needed. This is the primary area in which we expect internal audit to help us and to keep us updated on efficiency and reliability of computer operations.

See to it that management has at its disposal the tools necessary to carry on its job with the greatest efficiency and effectiveness and is equipped to make the most rewarding decisions promptly.

Constantly look for improvement and efficiency for the audit committee and management. Includes weaknesses that come to their attention in the operational areas.

Internal audit has and continues to create a control environment, will add operational auditing to its contribution, and will start generating a cash flow through audit of outside suppliers.

To sense the critical areas of weakness and lack of adequate control and to pressure management to improve. Internal audit group through audit committee exerts a strong interanl pressure for improvement.

Only by serving on an audit committee can you realize the importance of a good internal audit staff and the contribution it makes to the stability of our industry.

Most respondents considered Question 15 unnecessary and gave cursory responses. The question asked: "Are there any important areas or activities where internal audit could be more useful to the audit committee." Most of the limited number of responses were quite complimentary of their present internal audit departments.

Question 16, which asked for additional comments, turned out to be more productive. A surprising number of respondents were moved to add comments, many of which indicated considerable thought and strong feelings. Only a few are included here.

> With growing pressure from the government and the public on the audit committee and the board of directors to be accountable for the integrity and controls of an organization's management, I think the job description and management skills of the head of internal auditing need to be revised. This individual must be an excellent communicator and have the confidence of the board of directors and the company's management. It requires someone with the excellent interpersonal skills — a strong, confident leader who is respected by the company personnel.

> The company has had an internal audit function about five years. Present employees have been with company about one year. The previous holder of the position did not remain in internal audit function long enough to be really familiar with company. In a smaller company, it may be difficult to employ and retain competent internal audit personnel.

> Your questionnaire overlooks the importance of relationship between the chairman of the audit committee, the head of the internal audit committee, and the head of the internal audit department — a critical factor in my experience.

> In my view, the head of internal auditing should be a member of the company's operating committee. In this way, he would have a broader perspective of the company's objectives and anticipate potential control and financial problems.

> The function of internal auditing, relative to the audit committee, depends on the true reading of the capabilities and the goals of senior management. Since senior management tends to perpetuate itself, it tends to minimize its deficiencies and cover up its errors until too late. To help the audit committee guard against these situations to the benefit of the company and its shareholders, it must rely on the internal audit function, which must cast aside all subjectivity and perform its duties as objectively as possible.

> The audit committee must be forceful enough to convince the directors and the management that it is the watchdog group responsible for the proper operation of the business and to see that shareholders' interests are properly served and satisfied.

> In my view, the function of the internal audit division of any major company should become an increasingly important part of management's working control and planning arsenal. If management concurs in this belief, a constant in-house acknowledgment of the duties and responsibility of this arm should be made to all sectors of the company. A properly run internal audit division enhances communication and depth of management and, in the long run, serves to economize with reference to the expense of independent external auditors.

> The EDP audit function and its requirement of specialized training and

knowledge are often not understood in its full dimension by persons of the usual generation that supplies top management and directors/audit committees. The younger people who have grown up with computers do not yet have these positions in most companies.

This is a regulated public utility and we are audited frequently by state and federal regulatory bodies — strong emphasis on prevention of fraud, of safeguarding materials and supplies, etc. Even a slight loss would greatly upset rate payers. Stockholders in general don't care. I serve as chairman of two other audit committees, and each committee sees its function differently because the business is different.

This is a suggestion for research. Determine what companies have written policy and procedure for internal auditors. Determine budgeting relationship to external auditing. Make a study of data and determine the extent to which internal auditing has gained or declined over the past ten years. From this, develop a prototype policy which might be useful to corporations which do not rely heavily on internal auditing.

There is an implication that internal auditing should second-guess the financial decisions of management. If the internal auditor has such a capability, experience, and perspective, he or she would not be an internal auditor. The internal auditor is a sheriff or policeman but not a superior diety. Don't try to inflate the position at the expense of the board or senior management. The internal auditor must serve senior management as well as the board.

Independent Accountants

The questionnaire for independent accountants provided an opportunity to obbtain views on internal auditing from a group completely outside the companies where the internal auditors were employed. Questionnaires included many of the same topics as those sent to senior management and members of the audit committee. We present our findings under the following headings:
- Relative importance of internal audit tasks.
- Responsibility and status of the internal audit department.
- Contributions of internal auditing.
- Reliance on the work of internal auditors by independent accountants.

Relative Importance of Internal Audit Tasks

In general, independent accountants rate the tasks of internal auditing in Table 5-20 highly, and it is difficult to find any that are not considered important. The emphasis is heaviest on "improvement of internal control" and 'monitoring the performance of internal control," and least on "an investigative arm for the audit committee," "detection and correction of unintentional errors," and "an investigative arm for senior management."

Table 5-20
Independent Accountants
Relative Importance of Internal Audit Tasks

Internal audit departments perform a variety of assignments that can be summarized under the purposes listed below. Using the response scale provided, please rate the degree of importance of each of the following internal audit purposes to this company.

	Very Unimportant	Unimportant	Percentage Neither Important Nor Unimportant	Important	Very Important
Detection and correction of unintentional errors.	2	10	24	52	12
Prevention or reduction of improprieties and irregularities.	0	1	9	53	36
Improvement of internal control.	0	1	5	34	60
Assistance to independent CPA in performance of annual audit.	2	4	17	55	23
An investigative arm for the company's audit committee.	3	8	37	39	13
An investigative arm for senior management.	1	7	19	54	19
Monitoring the performance of internal control procedures.	0	1	5	35	58
Other	0	0	3	44	53

The explanation of "other" answers were varied with operational auditing, cost savings, special assignments, evaluations of internal control, and similar possibilities receiving mention.

Question 2 was also directed at the importance of the internal audit department's activities to the company, but the substance of the question dealt more with how the company used it. Table 5-21 presents the responses and the question.

Table 5-21
Independent Accountants
Relative Importance of Internal Audit Functions

For each of the following statements, indicate your view of the importance of the internal audit function in this company as:

	Very Unimportant	Unimportant	Percentage Neither Important Nor Unimportant	Important	Very Important
A management training program.	10	23	39	25	3
A protection to management.	1	5	18	62	14
An essential activity for business success.	7	14	38	34	8
A resource to assist the audit committee.	3	6	22	50	19
A career for loyal but not innovative employees.	45	27	23	4	1
A means of reducing external audit fees.	4	10	23	52	11
A means for ensuring compliance with government regulations.	7	14	3	40	5
An aid for evaluating the efficiency and the effectiveness of management performance.	5	14	31	43	7
Other.	0	0	1	1	98

Those functions that rank the highest are in order:
- A protection to management.
- A resource to assist the audit committee.
- A means of reducing external audit fees.

Also of considerable importance are:
- An aid for evaluating the efficiency and the effectiveness of management performance.
- A means for ensuring compliance with government regulations.

These imply that the internal audit department has undertaken, evidently at company request, a rather broad range of duties.

The small number of responses in the "other" category were varied. There was some emphasis on improving internal control and in involving management in a better understanding of the importance of internal control. Use of the department for special projets and as a tool for management to use in various ways was also mentioned. One response that struck home was "a career for innovative employees."

Responsibility and Status of the Internal Audit Department

In responding to a question about the primary reporting responsibility of the director of internal auditing, responding accountants tried to be precise, using the "other" option. The most common response under "other" was the chief financial officer. Table 5-22 reports the results of Question 3.

Table 5-22
Independent Accountants
Primary Responsibility of the Director of Internal Auditing

The primary responsibility of the director of internal auditing in this company is to:

	Responses	
	Number	Percentage
The company's audit committee	89	32
The company's chief executive officer	43	16
The audit committee and chief executive officer equally	64	23
Other	81	29
Total	277	100

A few answers explaining the respondents choice of "other" follows:

The audit committee and CEO. Organizationally, the director of internal auditing is on a par with the chief accounting officer. I believe sufficient independence exists to make the reporting to the CEO appropriate in this instance.

Although audit committee reporting is important, the main reporting is to the vice president of finance and administration who is separate from the chief accounting officer.

Senior vice president of finance and administration. Internal auditing has direct access to the audit committee through the manager of the internal audit division who is secretary of the audit committee.

An operational controller who, in turn, reports to the chief executive officer.

Executive vice president, administration — his (director of internal audit) superior for administrative and personnel matters and the senior financial officer.

Senior vice president and secretary-treasurer who is a member of the board of directors. (The audit committee consists of three nonemployee members of board.)

The comptroller, although the director of internal auditing has direct access to the audit committee if necessary.

One possible conclusion from these responses is that many companies place the internal auditor in a very difficult role. He reports directly to the person ultimately responsible for the accounting and financial affairs that he audits. Even if the auditor is assured that he has access to the audit committee, should access become necessary, the natural tendency would be to clear matters with his immediate superior. In most cases, such a decision presents no problem. However, when it does present a problem — for example, a matter that conceivably should go to the audit committee but might not — what will the director of internal auditing do? If the chairman of the audit committee has established the right kind of relationship with the auditor, the results may be entirely satisfactory. If, on the other hand, the director of internal auditing has never conversed with the audit committee chairman outside committee meetings, there may be a real reluctance to trouble him with problems that possibly could be resolved elsewhere. Thus, we must conclude that the specifics of a given set of conditions will have a great deal to do with how such relationsihip work out when and if the need for true independence arises.

This raises the question of how often the auditor meets with the audit committee. Table 5-23 reports the findings on that matter.

Table 5-23
Independent Accountants
Private Meetings of the Director of Internal Auditing
with the Audit Committee

The company's audit committee meets with the director of internal auditing with no other members of management present:

	Responses	
	Number	Percentage
Annually	52	20
Semiannually	47	18
Quarterly	63	24
Monthly	8	3
Never	47	18
Other	45	17
Total	262	100

Responses listed under "other" varied. Many were on an "as-needed" basis. For some, the audit committee apparently felt its responsibilities were for the external audit only. At the other extreme, in a few cases the internal auditor was always present when the audit committee met. In several cases, there were no such meetings. A conclusion from this set of data might be that there are either fewer private meetings with the audit committee than the respondents to our other questionnaires believe or that the responding accountants are not informed of some meetings that take place.

Question 5 brought together a number of points related to the independence and strength of internal auditing. The question and results follow:

Table 5-24
Independent Accountants
Independence and Support for Internal Auditing

Please indicate the extent to which you agree or disagree with each of the items below as applied to this company, using the following scale:

	Strongly Agree	Agree	Percentage Neither Agree nor Disagree	Disagree	Strongly Disagree
Internal audit possesses sufficient independence to fulfill its function.	39	50	6	5	0
Internal audit receives adequate support from management.	28	55	8	7	1
The audit committee has access to the director of internal auditing for special assignments:					
With management's consent	26	44	19	8	3
Without management's consent	20	37	28	12	3
The director of internal auditing has authority to bring matters directly to the audit committee without notification to management when he deems this is necessary.	32	41	13	9	5

As should be expected, there are always companies in which the internal audit department has not been sufficiently accepted and cannot fully and freely function as it should. Overall, however, this evaluation by independent accountants, who should be as alert to the problems of independence and status as any group can be, is a strong vote of approval for the status of internal auditing in the majority of companies on which they were reporting.

Similar conclusions result from reviewing independent accountants' responses to the question about the treatment accorded recommendations made by internal auditors as a result of their examinations.

Table 5-25
Independent Accountants
Treatment Accorded Recommendations of Internal Auditors

Which of the following statements best describes the attention given to recommendations by the internal audit department in this company?

	Responses Number	Percentage
Recommendations by the internal audit department are a matter of record, but there needs to be no internal audit follow-up on their implementation until the following audit.	23	8
Recommendations made by the internal audit department must be answered in writing within a stated time.	168	61
Recommendations made by the internal audit department are maintained in an open file until settled by implementation or mutual agreement.	56	21
Recommendations by the internal audit department must be complied with unless factually in error.	11	4
Other	16	6
Total	274	100

Contributions of Internal Auditing

We asked respondents about the past and anticipated contributions made by the internal audit department in question 7 "What is the most important contribution this internal audit department has provided for this company over the last few years?" and question 8 "What is the most important contribution that this company should expect from its internal audit department over the next few years?"

In response to Question 7, the majority of comments concerned some aspect of internal control — documentation of the present system, improvement of some kind, monitoring, improving the control environment, and educating management about the importance of internal control. There seems little question that independent accountants view the internal audit department as extremely important to the company's internal control system.

Another response, not as frequent but more common than anticipated from these respondents, dealt with effecting decreases in the cost of the external audit. Other than these, the responses varied considerably. A few are included here:

> Viewed as a competent department which performs thorough audits to encourage compliance with company policies and controls. Reviews of vendors' contracts in construction and coal purchase area have resulted in significant cash savings.
>
> Fraud/irregularity investigations performed at the request of management have resulted in strong procedures in this area.
>
> Investigations into the existence of potential illegal payments and other similar exposure areas. Assistance with the review of security controls on a new computer system.
>
> Assurances to the audit committee of the board of directors as to the

propriety of the operating procedures followed by management and the integrity of management.

A comfort level to management and the audit committee that internal control procedures are adequate and are being complied with in a very widespread and decentralized operation.

Bringing operational inefficiencies and noncompliance with company procedures to the attention of senior management. Also, increased involvement in the EDP audit function.

Providing input into the development of necessary internal controls in new systems implemented by the company. Maintaining a high profile throughout the entire company which makes all departments aware that their work will be examined.

The internal audit department has served as a continuing contact with the many operating locations, almost as representatives of top-corporate management. In this role, they also serve as information gatherers for top-corporate management and the audit committee.

The company is unique in that a significant portion of its assets are managed by outside third parties. Internal audit plays a significant role in monitoring these third parties to determine if they are protecting the company's assets adequately. They also play a significant role in systems monitoring.

They possess a knowledge of the total operations few people in the company have. They have been very helpful in incorporating controls up front in systems being developed.

Assistance and oversight regarding controls during implementation of a major new system. Documentation of systems and evaluation of strengths and weaknesses in systems through identification of control points.

The timely identification of weaknesses in internal control or circumvention of internal control which could have resulted in material error of financial statement information.

Evaluation of documentation of accounting systems prepared by divisional accounting staffs. Internal audit reviewed the documentation and rejected several as unacceptable. These were then redone by the divisional accounting staffs.

Respondents' comments to question 8 "What is the most important contribution the company should expect in the near future?" were most frequently couched in terms of continuing what the department currently does well. Only a few offered anything in the way of new suggestions, so only a few are included here:

Assistance in strengthening controls while reducing costs of controls by innovative approaches at the same time.

The department should become more involved in operational auditing techniques, particularly for expense control purposes.

The internal audit department is to change from financial to operational auditing, and its most important contributions should be the timely monitoring of the company's present reorganization and the evaluation of controls within the new computer software packages which are being implemented.

The company should look to the internal auditor for in-house consulting in EDP, financial, strategic, and other areas. This will be a needed addition to audit functions, and the two areas should enhance each other.

To enable the company to gain a better understanding of its foreign operations and internal control improvements needed as such operations expand.

Holding down independent audit costs, testing functioning of controls, reviewing and testing EDP operations, plus assistance for special studies (i.e., operational audits).

The internal audit department in this company is very strong and highly respected and is a major factor in the oversight of the strong internal controls which exist in this company. I am sure this standard of excellence will continue, and I believe this is the most important contribution to be expected over the next few years. I believe this will also be achieved on a more cost-efficient basis as a result of more risk analysis and specific tailoring of audit procedures.

Reliance on the Work of Internal Auditors by Independent Accountants

A number of questions were directed at the acceptance by independent accountants of the work of internal auditors and the accountants' evaluations of the quality of services of internal audit departments in general. Table 5-26 presents the results of a question about reliance for audit purposes.

Table 5-26
Independent Accountants
Reliance on Internal Audit Function for External Audit Purposes

Please rate the degree to which you rely on the work of this company's internal audit function in audit matters related to forming your audit opinion.

	Responses	
	Number	Percentage
Very high reliance	46	17
High reliance	133	49
Neither high nor low reliance	56	20
Low reliance	23	8
Very low reliance	8	3
No reliance	8	3
Total	274	100

In our opinion, this is a remarkably high rating of the work of internal auditors by a group that might be considered to be their severest critics. Recall the fact that relationships with independent auditors was indicated in the responses of staff members and directors as an unattractive feature, second only to travel. If independent accountants think so highly of the work of internal auditors, why do internal auditors feel so unhappy about their work with them? The inconsistency here requires additional research.

Question 10 followed the line of inquiry established in Question 9 by seeking information on the factors that make up independent accountant's opinions about internal audit work. Partly because independent accountants indicated so high reliance on the work of internal auditors, there is little in these responses that helps us to distinguish the reasons for high versus low reliance.

Table 5-27
Independent Accountants
Factors Influencing Reliance on Work of Internal Auditors

Please indicate the manner and extent to which each of the following items has influenced your judgment regarding the degree of reliance to be placed on this company's internal audit work, using the scale provided:

	Percentage				
	Very Positive Influence	Positive Influence	Neither Positive nor Negative Influence	Negative Influence	Very Negative Influence
The position of the person or group to whom the director of internal auditing reports.	23	48	22	6	1
The responsibilities assigned by written policy to internal audit.	9	39	49	2	1
The professional competence of the internal audit staff.	33	48	12	7	1
The extent of control and supervision of work within the internal audit department.	23	51	17	8	1
The degree to which internal audit has access to company records, documentation, and personnel.	39	46	14	.5	.5
The quality of internal audit program.	19	50	24	6	1
The quality of internal audit work papers.	15	50	26	9	0
The extent of internal audit coverage.	23	51	19	6	1
The nature, frequency, and response to reports issued by internal audit.	17	50	26	6	1
Knowledge of company operations, processes, and procedures exhibited by internal audit personnel.	27	55	15	3	0
Knowledge of trends and techniques in auditing exhibited by internal audit personnel.	7	35	45	12	1
The existence of a continuing education program for internal audit personnel.	10	38	42	9	1

Because independent accountants rate internal audit work so highly, these data are useful mostly in giving us an idea of the general factors that influence the opinions of independent auditors. We are surprised by the large number that found these factors neither a positive nor a negative influence, and we are unable to account for such a response on factors like the quality of internal audit programs and audit work papers.

Respondents were also requested to indicate the amount of their audit time spent in evaluating and testing internal audit work. The question and its answers are in Table 5-28.

Table 5-28
Independent Accountants
Time Spent in Testing and Evaluating the Work of Internal Auditors

What percentage of your audit time budget is spent evaluating and testing the work of this company's internal audit function?

	Response Number	Percentage
Less than 5 percent	121	44
More than 5 percent but less than 15 percent	117	42
More than 15 percent but less than 25 percent	30	11
More than 25 percent by less than 50 percent	8	3
More than 50 percent	0	0
Total	276	100

We found it noteworthy that 14 percent of the independent accountants spend at least 15 percent of their audit time evaluating and testing the work of the client company's internal auditors. This implies substantial reliance on internal auditing and should provide a basis of considerable knowledge for their responses to previous questions in this questionnaires.

When asked to compare the internal audit department with other departments in the company, independent accountants are complimentary. They are not as complimentary, however, as were representatives of senior management and members of audit committees. The independent accountants' responses appear in Table 5-29.

Table 5-29
Independent Accountants
Rating of Internal Audit Department Relative to Others in Same Company

Please rate this internal audit department relative to other departments within this company.

	Response Number	Percentage
Very superior	7	3
Superior	109	39
Average	147	53
Disappointing	14	5
Very disappointing	1	0
Total	278	100

A three-way comparison of the ratings from the three groups is interesting. Audit committee members are most complimentary; independent accountants are the least.

Table 5-30
Comparative Ratings of Internal Audit Departments by Representatives of Senior Management, Audit Committees, and Independent Accountants

	Senior Management (%)	Audit Committee (%)	Independent Accountants (%)
Very superior	7	9	3
Superior	48	63	39
Average	43	27	53
Disappointing	2	1	5
Very disappointing	0	0	0
Total	100	100	100

Table 5-31
Independent Accountants
Rating of Internal Audit Departments with Other Internal Audit Departments

	Response No.	%
Very superior	50	18
Superior	116	42
Average	82	30
Disappointing	27	10
Very Disappointing	1	0
Total	276	100

These responses suggest that the internal audit departments covered in this study may be significantly better than the average of audit departments in the United States and Canada. If so, the general need for training programs and other methods of improvement may be greater than one might gather from the foregoing chapters.

Respondents to this questionnaire were also requested to describe the way they work with internal auditors during the performance of the annual independent audit. The same question was directed to directors of internal auditing. Because there are some interesting differences in the responses from the two groups, the data from the directors' responses in included below. Consider that, for the most part, the questionnaire responses are for the same companies.

Table 5-32
Independent Accountants
Work Relationships: Independent Accountants and Internal Auditors

Which of the following statements best describes the way you work with the internal audit department of this company? (Check one.)

	Independent Accountants		Internal Auditors	
	No.	%	No.	%
Members of the internal audit department serve as assistants to the independent auditors by preparing schedules, account analyses, trial balances, etc., in connection with the annual audit.	32	12	38	12

Table 5-32 (continued)

Members of the internal audit department perform audit work in conformity with an audit program provided by the independent auditors.	77	28	48	15
Members of the internal audit department participate with the independent auditors in planning the total audit program which is then divided between the independent and internal audit groups for dependent performance.	90	33	121	37
Members of the internal audit department utilize work done by the independent auditors and extend it where it is not completely appropriate for internal audit purposes.	3	1	11	3
The internal and independent auditors perform their duties independently of one another.	32	12	30	9
Other	37	14	78	24
Total	271	100	326	100

An analysis of the "other" responses finds an encouraging amount of cooperation as well as recognition that the two audit groups have important and different roles to play. These responses reinforce the opinion of both directors and internal audit staff members that internal auditing and independent auditing are substantially different. Some of the responses to this question describe differences in the working relationship. These differences arose only within the last year and are expected to be effetive in the next audit.

The questionnaire to independent accountants, like the ones to audit committee members and representatives of senior management, inquired about reasons why the internal audit department was not as useful as it might be. Table 5-33 presents the results.

Table 5-33
Independent Accountants
Factors Inhibiting Usefulness of Internal Auditing

What factors do you think most inhibit internal auditing from becoming more useful in this company than it now is? (Check as many items as apply.)

	Responses	
	Number	Percentage
Narrow point of view of internal auditors.	32	12
Inadequate appreciation by this company of internal audit capabilities.	93	33
The company's historical experience with internal auditing.	70	25
Limited ability of internal auditors.	45	16
Lack of managerial perspective on the part of internal auditors.	61	22
Lack of adequate supply of qualified internal audit personnel.	81	29
Inadequate incentives for good people to become internal auditors in this company.	69	25
Inadequate programs to keep internal auditors informed of current developments in auditing.	17	6
Other	44	16

Responses in the "other" classification varied greatly. A number pointed to lack of managerial skill within internal auditing. Some noted that, because the internal audit recommendations were frequently negative, management was unenthusiastic about support for that department. Newness of the function and the fact that in many cases the personnel were not yet well trained for any specific activity, including auditing, also received attention. Budget constraints, inability to hold good people in internal auditing, and lack of any attractive career path were frequently mentioned.

Again, it is interesting to compare responses from different groups. Table 5-34 does so.

Table 5-34
Comparative Views
Factors Inhibiting Usefulness of Internal Auditing

	Senior Management (%)	Audit Committee (%)	Independent Accountants (%)
Narrow point of view of internal auditors.	18	9	12
Inadequate appreciation by this company of internal audit capabilities.	41	25	33
The company's historical experience with internal auditing.	27	13	25
Limited ability of internal auditors.	15	7	16
Lack of managerial perspective on the part of internal auditors.	29	17	22
Inadequate supply of qualified internal audit personnel.	23	29	29
Inadequate incentives for good people to become internal auditors in this company.	20	18	25
Inadequate programs to keep internal auditors informed of current developments in auditing.	3	2	6
Other	10	13	16

Respondents' Final Comments

The last question invited additional comments or observations of any kind relevant to the subject of the research. Some very thoughtful comments were received:

> Internal and external auditors have different objectives. Their methods of achieving them are similar; as a result, there is some opportunity for sharing knowledge. However, the extent to which external audit can use the work of internal audit is often less that that understood by audit committees and management. The exception is where the objectives of the two auditors are similar — for example, verification of a division's results or the accuracy of monthly financial reports from branches (e.g., of a bank).
>
> Management has excessively emphasized the director of internal auditing to reduce outside fees. Savings are tangible; however, greater reward may exist in operational areas/special projects.
>
> Many internal audit groups are becoming more concerned about financial reporting merely to reduce external fees. This is a very shortsighted decision since a good operations-oriented group could save many companies more money with

cost-cutting suggestions than is saved on external audit fees. Operations auditing would still highlight weaknesses in financial reporting practices.

Contacts made by internal auditors with financial and operating management at all levels provide unique opportunities for assisting in an organization's communication process. Internal auditors are exposed to both top-down and bottom-up views. They should bring independent, objective, nonpolitical, and nonemotional reasoning and reactions to this process which should help spread top management's views throughout the organization while, at the same time, help ensure a good flow of information upward.

It should never be forgotten that external and internal auditors have two distinct purposes. It would be inappropriate to attempt to move the internal auditor to be more like the external auditor. Rather, he should establish himself as a valued resource to his company, auditing as well as consulting.

The internal audit function is an excellent extension of the internal accounting control of a large organization and provides a safeguard for the assets and liabilities of the enterprise. I have some question as to the advisability of the internal audit function getting more involved in operational/performance and measurements thereof.

There is a substantial difference between those organizations where internal auditing has been an integral part of operations due to cost-benefit considerations and those organizations where internal audit is merely a response to some external force such as the Foreign Corrupt Practices Act. In the former, internal auditing is viewed as a positive influence on profits and achieving corporate goals. In the latter situation, internal auditing is viewed as a cost of compliance.

The company has developed the position of internal auditor as a career choice unlike other firms that use internal auditing as a training ground for financial management. We believe such an approach has not adversely affected the quality or motivation of the internal audit personnel. To the contrary, the staff has the maturity and the experience to be effective; and line management respects their recommendations on financial and operating matters.

Need to differentiate between financial audits and operational audits. Most internal auditors do not change this criteria/definition of what constitutes an error, etc., in completing the very different audits. Objectives need to be better defined. Internal auditors spend too much effort testing compliance with controls. Seldom do they challenge whether existing controls are necessary or redundant.

One of the main reasons for the success of the internal audit function at this company is the high degree of integrity, objectivity, and professionalism of the director of internal auditing. To be effective, the internal audit function must have a highly respected leader. That is the case in this company.

The internal audit function is a necessary evil in this company versus a good career path or stepping stone. Because of this, the department does not attract the best people and is not highly regarded, although this has been recently offset by top management's awareness.

Internal auditing has been upgraded considerably in the past five to ten years to the point where this function is an important management tool. Emphasis has been split appropriately between financial and operational perspectives.

Appendix A

Questionnaire Responses

> Appendix A contains the questionnaires sent to the five participating groups along with the responses to the various questions.

The Institute of Internal Auditors Research Foundation

Research Project on
Developments Influencing Internal Auditing in
U.S. and Canadian Corporations

Questionnaire for
Director of Internal Auditing

This questionnaire is an essential part of a major research project conducted by the Paton Accounting Center at The University of Michigan for the Institute of Internal Auditors. The results, which will be published by the Institute as a monograph, are expected to be directly beneficial in planning future educational and research programs in internal auditing.

All responses will be treated as completely confidential. With this questionnaire, you should receive an addressed, postage-prepaid envelope in which you can mail your completed questionnaire directly to the Paton Accounting Center. No one except members of the research team will ever see your responses. No participating company or person will be mentioned by name or identified in any way. Responses will be reported only in summaries and tabulations.

This questionnaire contains three parts.

    Part I — Personal and departmental information which will provide a basis for demographic analysis

    Part II — Questions directed to your attitude toward internal auditing and the scope and nature of your job

    Part III — Audit activities performed by your staff

Related but similar questionnaires will be completed by your audit staff members, your immediate superior, a representative of your company's audit committee, and a representative of your company's independent audit firm. Please be frank. Opportunity is provided at the end of the questionnaire for you to express yourself freely on any matters not included in specific questions.

If any question is clearly not applicable to your kind of company or your situation, write "N/A" beside the question and continue to the next question.

Your participation in this research is much appreciated.

Part I

1. Present title or rank: _____
2. How long have you held this title or rank?   __1-40__   years.
3. How old are you?   __24-26__   years.
4. How long have you been employed by this company?   __1-46__   years.
5. Please provide the following information about your education.

	Respondents	Acct. 1	Gen. Bus. 2	Engin-eering 3	Computer Science 4	Arts or Science 5	Misc.
High School	330	8	38	1	0	92	191
Institute or college diploma	292	–	–	–	–	–	–
Some university training	29	10	4	2	4	1	8
Bachelor's degree	292	180	53	4	0	26	29
Master's degree or higher	91	31	44	1	0	7	8
Professional Designation:							
C.P.A./C.A. (Canada)	159						
Certified Internal Auditor	78						
Certified Bank Auditor	17						
Certified Management Accountant	3						
Registered Industrial Accountant	2						
Certified General Accountant	3						
Certified Information Systems Auditor	29						
Other (Specify)_____	17						

Major Field of Study (check)

6. Please check the professional organizations to which you belong:

Institute of Internal Auditors	322
American Institute of Certified Public Accoutants	134
The Canadian Institute of Chartered Accountants	16
American Accounting Association	13
Canadian Academic Accounting Association	0
National Association of Accountants	41
The Society of Management Accountants	2
Certified General Accountants Association	3
State C.P.A. Society/Provincial C.A. Institute	102
Bank Administration Institute	60
EDP Auditors Association	49
Other (Specify)_____	64

7. Please provide the following information about your work experience since accepting full time employment.

   a) Work experience with present employer. (*State the number of years worked* at each level for the applicable type of work).

Type of Work	Respondents	Staff	Supervisor	Management
Internal auditing	326	3.0	3.0	4.2
Accounting	47	2.5	2.5	5.4
Finance	18	1.0	1.0	4.0
Production/engineering	5	5.5	2.0	.5
Marketing	4	3.6	—	—
Personnel	0	—	—	—
E.D.P.	8	3.4	4.7	4.4
Other (State) _____	21	2.7	1.7	3.6

   b) Work experience with other employers. (*State the number of years worked* at each level for the applicable type of work).

Type of Work	Respondents	Staff	Supervisor	Management
Internal auditing	128	2.2	1.5	1.8
External auditing	166	3.0	1.6	1.4
Accounting	51	3.7	2.5	2.9
Finance	26	2.3	1.1	3.5
Production/engineering	3	3.2	.5	3.3
Marketing	4	3.0	1.5	2.5
Personnel	1	—	—	2.0
E.D.P.	9	1.8	1.7	1.5
Other (State) _____	31	2.7	1.6	1.5

8. Is your position part of a corporate headquarters staff unit or is it part of an operating unit such as a division, plant, or branch? (Please check one.)

   Corporate headquarters 310
   Operating unit   20

9. To *whom are you responsible* for each of the following purposes? (Check as many items in each column as apply.)

	For Audit Reporting Purposes	For Salary and Promotion Purposes
Audit Committee—Board of Directors	263	22
Chief Executive Officer	141	109
Chief Financial Officer	121	126
Controller	39	36
Treasurer	12	12
Administrative Vice President	19	18
Operating Unit Line Management	17	1
Other (Specify) _____	38	51

10. What is the organizational level of the Director of Internal Auditing in relation to that of the:

	Above	Below	Equal to
Chief Financial Officer	11	271	36
Controller	48	116	145
Treasurer	30	139	116

11. What is the salary level of the Director of Internal Auditing in relation to that of the:

	Above	Below	Equal to
Chief Financial Officer	1	306	6
Controller	28	214	65
Treasurer	22	206	52

12. Are all employees performing auditing functions within your company called internal auditors?

Yes	No
265	60

13. All employees performing auditing functions in your company may be centrally located in a corporate staff unit or some may be part of operating units such as divisions, plants, or branches. State the percentage in each of these locations.

	Percentage
Corporate headquarters	83 %
Operating units	17
Total	100%

14. If some employees performing auditing functions are part of operating units, to whom are they responsible for each of the following purposes? (Check as many items in each column as necessary.)

	For Assignment of Duties	For Audit Reporting Purposes	For Salary and Promotion Purposes
Corporate Director of Internal Audit	55	74	49
Other executive at Corporate Headquarters	4	5	7
Corporate Audit Committee	2	7	0
Operating Unit Management	67	61	68

15. What percentage of the personnel newly assigned to internal audit are generally hired directly from outside the company and what percentage are transferred from other departments within your company?

Percentage	
72%	New hiring
28%	Transfers from other departments
100%	

16. Does your company move either all or certain classes of employees through the internal audit department as part of their career development?

Yes	No
78	241

17. Do you, as Director of Internal Auditing, have the right to refuse to accept transfers to your department if you feel they do not meet your requirements?

    Yes   No
    319   2

18. In comparison with hirings in other areas of your company, recent new company hirings for the internal audit department, in your view, have been: (Please check one)

    75 Substantially above average potential
    184 Above average potential
    50 Average potential
    0   Below average potential
    1   Substantially below average potential

19. In comparison with personnel in other areas of your company, recent transfers into your internal audit department from other departments of your company, in your view, have been: (Please check one)

    38 Substantially above average potential
    137 Above average potential
    46 Average potential
    7   Below average potential
    1   Substantially below average potential

20. Please provide the following information about the size of your internal audit department and your company:

	1974 fiscal year	1977 fiscal year	1978 fiscal year	1981 fiscal year	Current fiscal year (1982)	Best Estimate Available for 1983 fiscal year	Best Estimate Available for 1984 fiscal year
Number of internal audit positions	13.3	15.5	16.4	18.6	18.9	19.5	20.3
Number of internal audit positions unfilled	.5	.6	.7	.9	.8	.4	.4
Number of specialists on internal audit staff	.8	1.4	1.9	2.7	3.0	3.2	3.5
Number of internal audit management personnel	1.8	2.5	2.8	3.4	3.6	3.6	3.7
Departmental audit time spent away from home office (in days)	393	520	570	788	790	790	790
Internal audit travel expenses	30	47	60	125	145	146	152
Internal audit salaries and wages	244	344	405	601	668	732	805
External audit fee for the year (audit services only)	290	383	439	527	552	581	621
Total number of company employees	19.9	20.4	21.4	21.7	21.2	21.4	21.9
Company gross revenues (as per Income Statement)	.85	1.12	1.27	1.93	2.02	2.23	2.48
Company total assets	1.31	1.67	1.93	2.73	2.89	3.16	3.45

21. Do you plan to remain in internal auditing throughout your career?

	Yes	No
	121	200

If *No:*

a) How long do you expect to stay in the internal audit department?

Less than 1 year	1-3 years	4-6 years	More than 6 years
7	108	63	18

b) What type of work do you expect to transfer to if you leave the internal audit department?

Type of Work	Please check one
Accounting	37
Finance	57
Production/engineering	0
Marketing	0
Personnel	0
Operating management	60
Electronic data processing management	4
Other (State) _____	41

22. Please check the level of influence that each of the following has on the content and scope of your company's annual internal audit program using the scale provided:

	Very Substantial Influence	Substantial Influence	Significant Influence	Some Influence	No Influence
Director of Internal Audit	271	46	5	4	0
Controller	9	27	52	143	76
Chief Financial Officer	29	48	69	133	32
Corporate Audit Committee	37	55	72	123	19
Chief Executive Officer	38	49	67	130	36
External C.P.A./C.A.	15	35	95	156	18
Operating Management	3	19	65	168	61
Other (State) _____	10	9	9	11	5

23. What is the average length of time between regularly scheduled audits of your company's departments, divisions, branches, etc. (Please check one)

Less than 1 year	1 year	1½ years	2 years	2½ years	3 years
30	87	58	63	25	44

3½ years	4 years	4½ years	5 years	More than 5 years
1	7	0	4	2

24. In what year was your company's audit committee established? _____

25. If your audit committee was established within the past ten years, please check the statement below which best describes your understanding of the reason for its establishment.
    - 13 We added such a committee in direct response to a specific recommendation from the SEC.
    - 22 We added such a committee because of the requirements of the New York Stock Exchange.
    - 17 We added such a committee because of the FCPA of 1977.
    - 132 We added such a committee as a natural development of our sub-committee structure for our Board of Directors.
    - 50 Other (Please explain)_____

26. Please indicate the number of company directors in each of the following membership categories for the years indicated for your company's Board of Directors and Audit Committee.

		1974	1978	1982
A.	Board of Directors			
	1. Inside members (current management or officers)	3.75	3.46	3.20
	2. External members having no affiliation with the company other than directorship responsibility	8.80	8.90	9.20
	3. External members having some affiliation with the company (company counsel, former management, officers of affiliated companies or major suppliers, etc.)	1.77	1.70	1.88
	4. Other (Please explain) _____	.30	.46	.48
	Total Board of Directors Membership	14.62	14.52	14.76
B.	Audit Committee	1974	1978	1982
	1. Inside members (current management or officers)	.25	.30	.25
	2. External members having no affiliation with the company other than directorship responsibility	3.50	3.50	3.68
	3. External members having some affiliation with the company (company counsel, former management, officers of affiliated companies or major suppliers, etc.)	.35	.40	.40
	4. Ex officio members (Please explain)_____	.10	.10	.10
	5. Other (Please explain) _____	.10	.10	.15
	Total Audit Committee Membership	4.30	4.40	4.58

27. Please provide the following information regarding the relationship between the Director of Internal Audit and the Audit Committee:

    a) Which of the following statements best describes your reporting relationship with the Audit Committee: (Check one)
    - 59 All audit reports go to the Audit Committee.
    - 151 Report summaries are furnished to the Audit Committee on a regular basis.
    - 33 Oral reports only are made to the Audit Committee on a regular basis.
    - 47 Report summaries and/or oral reports are made to the Audit Committee on an irregular basis.
    - 5 No reports are made to the Audit Committee.

    b) How often does the Director of Internal Audit report in person to the Audit Committee? _____ times per year.

    c) Does the Director of Internal Audit regularly meet with the Audit Committee without any other members of management present?

Yes	No
168	145

Internal Auditing: Directions and Opportunities 159

d) Does the Director of Internal Audit ever receive *direct* requests from the Audit Committee for special assignment work to be done for the Audit Committee?

	Yes	No
	144	169

If *Yes*:

1) How many times in the past year did your department undertake such special assignments? _____ times.

2) Do you as Director of Internal Audit feel obligated to report such requests to other members of management if they have not already been informed?

	Yes	No
	87	70

e) Does the Audit Committee ask the Director of Internal Audit for his opinion about the work of the independent C.P.A/C.A.?

	Yes	No
	187	117

f) Does the Director of Internal Audit have the right to take specific matters directly to the Audit Committee on a confidential basis?

	Yes	No
	283	24

If *Yes*:

a) Have you ever done so: Yes 62   No 220

b) Which of the following matters *would* you take directly to the Audit Committee?

	Would take directly to audit committee	Would not take directly to audit committee
1) Significant misuse of corporate assets by a corporate officer.	208	67
2) Noncompliance with capital budgeting requirements by the vice president of manufacturing.	13	239
3) A shortage in the cash receipts from a substantial branch office which the controller acknowledges but contends is not of sufficient importance to bring to the attention of the Audit Committee.	111	159
4) Information that leads you to believe that the chief financial officer is pressuring the controller to make some accounting changes in order to increase current earnings.	156	115
5) Failure by your superior to fund three new internal audit positions which you as director of internal audit feel are essential.	134	141
6) Reduction by your superior of funds available for internal audit training.	72	203

28. In your opinion, how actively is the Audit Committee interested in the internal control concerns of your company? (Check one)

    109 Very actively
    132 Actively
    48 Neither actively nor passively
    11 Passively
    8 Very passively

29. In your opinion, how actively does senior management in your company support the internal audit function? (Please check one)

    138 Very actively
    136 Actively
     40 Neither actively nor passively
     13 Passively
      2 Very passively

30. Which of the following statements best describes your internal audit department's work relationship with your company's independent auditors? (Please check one)

    38 Members of the internal audit department serve as assistants to the independent auditors, preparing schedules, account analyses, trial balances, etc., in connection with the annual audit.

    48 Members of the internal audit department perform audit work in conformity with an audit program provided by the independent auditors.

   121 Members of the internal audit department participate with the independent auditors in planning the total audit program which is then divided between the independent and internal audit groups for independent performance.

    11 Members of the internal audit department utilize work done by the independent auditors and extend it where it is not completely appropriate for internal audit purposes.

    30 The internal and independent auditors perform their duties independently of one another.

    78 Other (Please describe.) _____

31. Which of the following statements best describes the attention given to recommendations made by the internal audit department in your company? (Check one)

    17 Recommendations by the internal audit department are a matter of record but there is no internal audit follow-up on their implementation until the following audit.

   196 Recommendations made by the internal audit department must be answered in writing within a stated time period.

    72 Recommendations made by the internal audit department are maintained in an "open file" until settled by implementation or mutual agreement.

    12 Recommendations by the internal audit department must be complied with unless factually in error.

    25 Other (Please describe.) _____

32. Using the scale provided, please indicate the extent to which the work of the internal audit department is relied upon in evaluating the work of each of the following:

	Very Little or no Reliance	Little Reliance	Some Reliance	Substantial Reliance	Very Substantial Reliance
Accounting and/or financial personnel	12	26	101	132	53
Operating personnel	16	28	163	93	24
Middle management	23	46	150	85	20
Senior management	78	72	101	56	17

Part II

A. The questions in this section generate information about your company, your internal auditing job, and your work related attitudes and preferences. *Your responses will be most helpful if you base them on your experiences as an employee in the company, and, where applicable, on your personal attitudes and preferences towards your work and your career.* All the questions are typical statements about companies, internal auditing, and work related attitudes and preferences. Please indicate your level of agreement with each statement by using the following scale, which will appear to the right of each statement.

Strongly Agree	Agree	Slightly Agree	Neither Agree Nor Disagree	Slightly Disagree	Disagree	Strongly Disagree
StA	A	SA	N	SD	D	StD

	StA	A	SA	N	SD	D	StD
1. You are encouraged to use your initiative in developing the annual audit program.	263	56	4	1	2	2	1
2. Those discretionary decisions permitted you are clearly specified.	37	84	46	38	13	75	35
3. Most internal audit decisions are made by a small number of people in the internal audit department.	120	135	32	13	11	13	6
4. You would not leave your company if a job were offered you with no significant change in compensation by a company you considered to be better managed.	80	99	25	36	18	48	22
5. Your work in the internal audit department calls for frequent exercise of discretionary judgment.	180	135	8	4	0	1	1
6. There are very few people in your department with whom you can discuss professional auditing interests.	25	24	16	22	13	127	100
7. Salary levels are a general indication of one's contribution to the company.	27	118	53	43	30	41	17
8. In your company, getting the work done depends on informal relationships and cooperation.	56	137	68	24	15	26	2
9. You would leave your company if a job at a lower salary were offered you by a company you considered to be better managed.	6	7	7	36	26	110	137
10. More varied assignments are an indication of approval by one's superiors.	26	141	63	70	10	17	2
11. When you find inefficient activities in your work, you feel a responsibility to get them corrected.	156	162	10	0	0	2	0
12. Tasks which require significant ability are more likely to be assigned to those who have displayed significant expertise.	89	197	30	7	2	3	2
13. Barring unforeseen developments, you have every intention of pursuing your career with this company.	126	143	20	17	6	14	4
14. In your company, people communicate only along the channels indicated in the organization chart.	7	14	24	27	40	148	70
15. You get most of your professional auditing stimulation from your department associates.	9	48	48	56	51	95	19

		StA	A	SA	N	SD	D	StD
16.	Barring unforeseen developments, you have no plans to leave your company.	128	134	17	22	9	16	4
17.	To meet your commitment as a professional internal auditor, you should:							
	a) Meet the standards of the Institute of Internal Auditors.	143	163	17	7	0	0	0
	b) Perform assigned tasks with the highest professional competence.	232	96	2	0	0	0	0
	c) Sacrifice personal time to keep abreast of current developments.	67	142	85	17	9	7	2
	d) Rely on your professional judgment as to adequacy of audit procedures needed in specific cases.	90	183	29	9	12	7	0
	e) Avoid relationships with company personnel that might appear to influence your independence.	68	104	57	48	24	22	6
	f) Be an active member of the Institute of Internal Auditors.	62	132	65	44	9	15	3
	g) Participate in formal continuing education.	143	144	35	7	0	1	0
	h) Pass the Certified Internal Audit examination (or its equivalent).	63	82	62	78	9	22	13
	i) Pass the CPA/CA examination (or its equivalent).	48	65	55	90	19	33	15
	j) Accept company policy as your professional priority.	20	66	76	62	49	50	4
	k) Avoid conflicts with company personnel that threaten your promotability.	9	18	25	50	46	133	48
	l) Understate actual hours worked rather than exceed time budgets.	1	0	3	8	6	135	176
	m) Satisfy budgeted time contraints on assignments regardless of their adequacy for the assignment at hand.	3	4	5	10	15	133	158
18.	You would accept demotion rather than leave your present employer.	1	6	11	36	18	120	137
19.	It is not important to you that your company have a reputation as an efficient and well-managed organization.	14	11	4	5	15	137	144
20.	People who aggressively seek promotion are often rewarded beyond their contribution.	7	51	73	75	41	67	16
21.	As long as you perform your internal audit duties adequately, you have no further responsibility to assure the efficient operation of your company.	10	16	4	5	31	142	122
22.	You request or volunteer for demanding committee or special service assignments.	18	127	75	72	15	20	1
23.	You are expected to follow a detailed audit manual for all assignments.	3	25	44	35	45	114	63
24.	Your company offers incentives to its employees in order to attain its objectives.	20	107	68	34	22	56	21

		StA	A	SA	N	SD	D	StD
25.	Your company rewards employees for following directions without question.	3	12	27	60	53	139	3
26.	As an employee, your primary loyalty belongs to your employer.	28	123	72	33	25	35	1
27.	Managers of audited departments tolerate the internal audit function as a necessary business practice.	9	100	95	29	43	51	2
28.	Your company makes decisions using committees of those managers who are responsible for implementing the decisions.	7	105	81	43	36	46	1
29.	When changes are made, your company involves all those who are most likely to be affected in the planning and implementation of the changes.	11	92	96	22	55	44	8
30.	Those who think of new and better ways of doing a task are more likely to be promoted.	12	126	113	46	18	10	3
31.	In your company the expert in a given situation makes the decision even if it means bypassing the formal line of authority.	1	19	52	63	74	105	13
32.	You are impatient when your increased abilities are not recognized by advancement.	20	103	104	46	26	28	1
33.	Your discretionary judgments are reviewed by superiors.	8	94	101	38	37	48	3
34.	You would leave your company if a job at a higher salary were offered you by a company you considered to be better managed.	67	85	61	59	19	33	4
35.	You prefer a position for which there are detailed written procedures describing the responsibilities of the job.	15	47	70	55	40	70	32
36.	You get most of your professional auditing stimulation from people that you meet at professional meetings.	10	46	85	68	55	57	8
37.	Titles are unimportant to you as long as you feel you are making a contribution to your company.	21	73	82	25	69	52	7
38.	You would leave internal auditing if a better job were offered you in another department of your company.	40	133	61	33	8	40	13
39.	Your company's communication channels are highly structured.	5	34	60	44	80	83	22
40.	Your company uses solutions proposed by outside experts in dealing with problems.	5	61	103	56	43	43	16
41.	You are generally uncertain about all the specific job aspects on which your performance will be evaluated.	10	45	75	23	44	108	23
42.	Managers of audited departments in your company tend to look upon the internal audit function as a source of constructive assistance.	5	127	139	22	29	6	1
43.	Members of the internal audit department with little audit experience are not permitted to make judgment decisions.	11	71	53	23	86	75	5

	StA	A	SA	N	SD	D	StD
44. If you discovered practices which discredit corporate officers, you could report them to the proper authorities without fear of jeopardizing your position.	97	146	38	15	16	11	6
45. You get most of your professional auditing stimulation from professional journals.	3	27	107	77	56	50	10
46. Managers of audited departments in your company tend to look upon the internal audit function largely as a policing activity.	10	32	102	28	65	87	6
47. Your company institutes changes without explaining or justifying them to the affected employees.	7	27	71	32	73	102	17
48. If your superior requested you to perform an audit in a manner you felt not to be in accordance with appropriate internal audit standards, you would refuse to comply with his request.	41	113	66	45	38	20	4
49. You get most of your professional auditing stimulation from company continuing education seminars.	4	25	63	50	47	101	36
50. You consider your time in internal auditing as a training period for other positions in your company.	18	62	62	36	24	97	29
51. Your company uses a participative approach to decision-making (specific courses of action are selected only after full discussion leading to a consensus.)	4	80	93	34	49	55	15
52. You understand completely the specific duties for which you will be held responsible.	62	148	59	5	37	15	1
53. There are times when executive expectations with regard to your position appear to conflict.	19	74	87	46	33	60	11
54. In the performance of your internal auditing duties, you seek to find areas or activities where your company's profitability could be improved.	109	162	45	7	3	4	0

For the next question please use the following response scale:

Very Satisfied	Satisfied	Slightly Satisfied	Neither Satisfied Nor Dissatisfied	Slightly Dissatisfied	Dissatisfied	Very Dissatisfied
VS	S	SS	N	SD	D	VD

55. In your present job, how satisfied are you with the opportunities available to:

	VS	S	SS	N	SD	D	VD
1. Make full use of your knowledge and skills.	120	137	40	5	12	13	2
2. Learn new knowledge and skills.	97	138	47	14	25	6	2
3. Earn a satisfactory salary.	68	167	51	9	23	9	2
4. Advance within the company.	45	116	59	30	37	22	9
5. Improve your technical competence.	58	157	68	21	14	8	1
6. Associate with personnel senior to your position.	128	137	38	11	8	4	1
7. Build your professional reputation.	103	156	41	16	7	5	1
8. Work on difficult and challenging problems.	103	155	43	7	13	6	2
9. Make constructive suggestions.	104	177	35	3	6	2	2
10. Be in the company of people you like.	72	177	50	24	5	1	1
11. Enjoy your work.	111	157	42	6	6	7	2
12. Influence company policy.	80	157	67	4	12	6	3

B. Check one response for each question.

56. Do you find your work to be routine or is it a real challenge to your ability or ingenuity? Your work is
    - 54 Almost always a challenge to your ability or ingenuity
    - 149 Usually challenging
    - 109 About half routine and half challenging
    - 14 Usually routine
    - 3 Almost always routine

57. When you don't like restrictions placed on the scope of the internal audit program, how often do you express your opinion to your superior?
    - 3 Never
    - 22 Occasionally
    - 6 Approximately half of the time
    - 69 Most of the time
    - 74 All of the time
    - 148 Never encounter such situations

58. In your job, how often do unanticipated audit problems come up which require your personal attention?
    - 7 On every assignment
    - 60 On most assignments
    - 88 On about half of the assignments
    - 172 On only a few assignments
    - 1 Never encounter such situations

59. Standard audit programs are used:
    - 36 On all assignments
    - 150 On most assignments
    - 55 On about half of the assignments
    - 66 On only a few assignments
    - 21 On no assignments

60. When unanticipated audit problems come up, how seriously do they challenge your expertise?
    - 0 You never solve such problems, but refer them to your superior to decide what to do
    - 31 Almost always a challenge to your expertise
    - 146 Usually a challenge
    - 107 About half challenging and half not challenging
    - 39 Usually not challenging
    - 6 Almost always not challenging

61. In order to do your job right, you may have to: disagree with fellow employees, allocate minimum time over competing needs, resolve difficult accounting or auditing issues, evaluate the importance of errors and irregularities.

    How often do you encounter such situations?
    - 29 Once or more for every assignment
    - 83 Once or more for most assignments
    - 105 Once or more for about half of the assignments
    - 111 Once or more for few assignments
    - 1 Never encounter such situations

62. How tight are time commitments for the responsibilities of your position? Time commitments usually allow:
    - 4 Much more than enough time to fulfill your responsibilities
    - 114 Ample time
    - 75 Just the right amount of time
    - 111 Not quite enough time
    - 25 Much too little time to fulfill your responsibilities

63. If you suggest to the managers of audited departments better ways of doing some job, how often do they go along with your suggestions? They go along with your suggestions:
    - 3 Up to 10 percent of the time
    - 16 About 25 percent of the time
    - 80 About 50 percent of the time
    - 205 About 75 percent of the time
    - 13 100 percent of the time
    - 8 No means to convey this information
    - 2 You never make such suggestions

64. In connection with your job, how much chance do you get to learn new things about your company?
    - 0 Very little or no chance
    - 0 Little chance
    - 26 Some chance
    - 138 A good chance
    - 165 An excellent chance

65. How much will your internal audit experience contribute to your ability to succeed in almost any department of your company?
    - 0 Very little or no contribution
    - 5 Little contribution
    - 32 Some contribution
    - 160 A good contribution
    - 132 An excellent contribution

66. In social conversation, you usually refer to yourself as: (Check one.)
    - 20 An accountant
    - 95 An auditor
    - 0 A public auditor
    - 97 An internal auditor
    - 0 An EDP auditor
    - 0 A systems analyst
    - 40 A manager
    - 5 A businessman
    - 22 An executive
    - 2 A consultant
    - 46 Other (State) _____

67. Most people find some portions or features of their work more appealing than others. Using the list of job features provided below:

   a) Rank order the three features of your work that you find most appealing (use "1" as most appealing).

   b) Rank order the three features of your work that you find least appealing (use "1" as least appealing).

Job Features	Most Appealing			Least Appealing		
	1	2	3	1	2	3
Travel	2	7	25	96	27	45
Intellectual challenge of work	89	64	41	9	6	7
Variety of assignments	74	82	46	2	9	4
Status and prestige of position	26	27	33	20	33	19
Contribution to success of company	74	73	49	3	13	9
Compensation	10	16	39	17	34	36
Authority accompanying auditor's position	13	18	18	21	28	26
Association with other internal auditors	1	2	10	15	23	25
Relationship with independent accountants	0	4	6	30	48	35
General work atmosphere	17	10	24	24	31	31
Others (Describe)_____						

68. If you were to look for another job, you would look for a position in:

   (Please rank order the three most preferred jobs using "1" as most preferred)

	1	2	3
Internal auditing	111	38	41
External auditing	2	14	20
Accounting	8	38	44
General management	80	71	59
Financial management	92	81	40
Operations	12	35	45
Marketing	0	6	6
Personnel	0	4	10
E.D.P.	5	9	18
Others (state) _____	12	5	16

Part III

The questions in this part generate information about your company's internal audit activities from a number of alternative perspectives and elicit your response to specific recent and prospective developments affecting internal auditing. This part is divided into A, B and C sections.

A. The internal audit function, broadly defined, may be characterized as consisting of a wide range of activities. Not all internal audit departments will perform all of the activities listed below. Please indicate the extent to which your internal audit department performs each of the following activities by using the following scale:

Never Performed NP	Rarely Performed RP	Occasionally Performed OP	Normally Performed but Occasionally Omitted NP-OO	Normally Performed and Rarely Omitted NP-RO	Always Performed AP

	NP	RP	OP	NP-OO	NP-RO	AP
1. Review the extent to which *external* financial statements comply with generally accepted accounting principles.	118	82	62	13	25	27
2. Review the extent to which *internal* financial statements comply with company accounting policies.	27	34	78	59	66	66
3. Consult with divisional and/or unit personnel on accounting matters.	5	21	105	66	90	41
4. Review compliance with established control procedures.	0	2	4	20	89	215
5. Review and comment on the adequacy of internal control procedures.	0	1	1	8	78	241
6. Make (as opposed to review) bank reconciliations.	216	57	28	6	7	15
7. Count cash funds.	29	69	93	39	42	58
8. Observe (as opposed to make) physical inventory counts.	45	34	80	44	55	63
9. Recommend improvements in operating controls.	0	1	18	32	116	162
10. Review compliance with company system for approving vendor invoices.	9	7	51	51	85	125
11. Provide pre-acquisition profit and/or cost reviews of potential acquisitions.	124	75	72	22	15	12
12. Investigate alleged shortages or other irregularities.	2	12	62	36	77	141
13. Audit joint venture or supplier's cost statements.	96	56	65	36	41	19
14. Participate in any of the following phases of management information systems development:						
System specification	47	50	71	63	61	35
Design	57	52	64	61	59	30
Programming	136	64	36	37	23	21
Installation	103	50	50	54	38	25
Post-installation testing	24	26	82	61	74	60

	NP	RP	OP	NP-OO	NP-RO	AP
15. Make cost-benefit studies of proposed changes in:						
Operating procedures	75	84	107	30	25	5
Internal control procedures	49	61	94	40	59	23
16. Audit expense reports of:						
Employees	22	29	74	47	70	84
Middle management	20	26	67	50	78	86
Senior management	23	27	60	29	70	119
17. Review usage of company owned aircraft.	143	16	38	13	22	34
18. Investigate regarding conformity with corporate code of conduct for:						
Employees	62	40	59	40	50	71
Middle management	61	30	57	36	60	78
Senior management	65	31	49	36	53	79
19. Review application of product (or service) quality controls.	85	50	81	43	44	17
20. Review analysis of profit or budget variances.	48	39	104	63	49	24
21. Review procedures for developing departmental and/or company budgets.	89	73	95	40	21	8
22. Consult with management about proposed changes in the company's organizational structure.	88	92	85	27	25	10
23. Review the appropriateness of performance evaluation measures for company divisions, departments, branches, etc.	107	80	71	36	27	5
24. Review the conformance of bonus plan administration to company policy.	135	41	52	22	35	24

B. The following questions characterize the internal audit function from a number of alternative perspectives. In responding, please follow the instructions given with each question.

25. Allocate 100 points across the following four activities in such a way as to indicate each activity's proportion of your total current internal audit effort:

__10__ The actual *performance* by internal auditors of internal control procedures such as bank reconciliations, test counts, account analyses, etc.

__41__ The *testing* of the extent to which the work of others *complies* with internal control requirements prescribed by company policy.

__32__ The *evaluation* of the appropriateness of internal control features currently called for by company policy.

__17__ The *initiation* of new or additional internal control features deemed necessary for new or continuing business activities.

__100__ points

26. For the four activities of internal auditing in question 25, please allocate 100 points in such a way as to indicate what you believe *should be* each activity's proportion of your total internal audit effort:

   __8__ Performance

   __41__ Testing compliance

   __34__ Evaluation

   __17__ Initiation

   __100%__ points

27. For the following five activities of internal auditing, please estimate the percentage of total internal audit *time* currently being spent on each activity:

   __20__ Detection of errors and irregularities — this activity is directed at the prevention or timely discovery of errors and irregularities in the processing or recording of transactions.

   __27__ Monitoring management control — management control strives to obtain compliance with the applicable rules and procedures established by company policy.

   __14__ Performance evaluation — this activity assesses the efficiency or effectiveness with which company goals are attained.

   __32__ Monitoring internal accounting control — internal accounting control strives to assure that published financial statements present fairly the financial position and results of operations of the company in accordance with generally accepted accounting practice or other appropriate standards and that assets are appropriately safeguarded.

   __7__ Decision-making review — this activity evaluates the effectiveness of management's operating and financial decisions.

   __100%__

28. For the five activities of internal auditing in question 27, please estimate the percentage of total internal audit time that you believe *will be* spent on each activity five years from now:

   15 Detection of errors and irregularities

   26 Monitoring management control

   19 Performance evaluation

   28 Monitoring internal accounting control

   12 Decision-making review

   __100%__

29. a. Please estimate the percentage of time spent by your internal audit group on audits in the following organizational units.

    22 Corporate headquarters staff units

    36 Plants and departments

    11 Dealers, agencies, and branches

    19 Divisional management units

     4 Outside contractors

     3 Corporate senior management

     5 Other (Specify) _____

  100%

29. b. Please estimate the *percentage of time* spent by your internal audit group in auditing the following activities: (If this question is not applicable to your company, please write "N/A" next to it and continue to the next question.)

     9 Raw material acquisitions

    11 Sales contracts

     3 Labor contracts

     8 Quality controls

    28 Manufacturing operations

     5 Transfers between units of the company

     1 Warranty claims

    35 Other (Describe) _____

  100%

30. Please estimate the percentage of internal audit department time spent on each of the following activities:

    62 Chargeable audit time

     6 Training

     9 Non-controllable time (e.g., vacations, holidays, illness)

     2 Performance evaluations

     6 Planning

     5 Coordination with external auditors and regulators

     2 Interface with audit committee

     2 Recruiting

     5 Internal audit departmental administration

     1 Other (Please describe) _____

  100%

C. The following questions elicit information regarding your company's response to specific recent legislative and business developments and request your opinion with regard to prospective internal audit developments.

31. The following statements describe initiatives companies may have taken in response to the Foreign Corrupt Practices Act (FCPA). Please check *all* the initiatives taken by your company in responding to this Act.

    a) Your company took no specific actions in response to the FCPA. — 49
    b) Your company initiated a formal review of the internal control system. — 180
    c) Your company developed a fully documented internal control file. — 130
    d) Your company initiated new controls or revised existing controls. — 169
    e) Your company took specific actions to create an increased awareness of the importance of internal controls among operating management. — 222
    f) Specific actions were taken to create an increased awareness among internal auditors of the importance of detecting and minimizing fraud possibilities. — 133
    g) Documentation of internal control weaknesses and recommendations for improved controls increased in internal audit reports. — 162
    h) Internal audit emphasis on fraud potential and detection increased. — 89
    i) Internal audit scope expanded to include reviews of more senior management activities. — 88
    j) The audit committee became a more active participant in internal control concerns. — 181
    k) Senior management became a more active participant in internal control concerns. — 192
    l) Revision or initiation of a corporate code of conduct to address issues raised by the FCPA was undertaken. — 138
    m) Annual reports by executives documenting compliance with the corporate code of conduct were initiated. — 98
    n) Internal audit monitoring of management compliance with the corporate code of conduct was initiated or increased. — 118
    o) Revision or initiation of an internal audit charter to address internal control issues raised by the FCPA was undertaken. — 69
    p) The position of Director of Internal Audit was elevated within the company's organizational structure. — 77
    q) A direct reporting relationship between the board of directors and the director of internal audit was instituted. — 52
    r) More frequent or comprehensive audits of foreign operations were initiated. — 30
    s) Specific means were provided for confidential employee reporting of suspected irregularities. — 41
    t) Internal audit resources were increased in response to the FCPA. — 99
    u) Internal audit recommendations gained increased authority. — 126
    v) Others (Describe) _____ — 28

32. Increasing reliance on computers for information processing purposes has created a source of internal control difficulty for many companies' internal audit groups. The statements below characterize several common responses to the internal audit problems associated with assuring internal control over EDP activities. Please consider these statements and *place the number corresponding to the response which best describes your company's current EDP audit strategy in the space provided at the end of the statements.* Please use the "other" option only if none of the statements describes the essence of your company's current response.

Question 32	Question 33	
23	7	1) Your company has taken no special action to assure internal control over EDP systems.
23	9	2) Your company has a group of EDP specialists (not in the internal audit department) which has the responsibility to assure internal control over EDP systems.
114	81	3) Your company has a group of EDP specialists in the internal audit department which works independently to assure internal control over EDP systems.
69	64	4) Your company has a group of EDP specialists which works in teams with non-EDP internal auditors to assure internal control over EDP systems.
15	35	5) Your company has a group of EDP specialists which advises, consults with, and trains internal auditors to assure internal control over EDP systems.
24	105	6) All of your company's internal auditors have sufficient EDP expertise to assure internal control over EDP systems as part of their normal auditing activities.
9	2	7) Your company's internal auditors do not have special EDP expertise, nor do they need it to adequately perform their internal audit duties.
47	15	8) Other (Please explain briefly). _____

Your company's current response to the problems associated with EDP auditing is best described by statement number _____.

33. Many companies have not yet settled on a permanent response to the EDP audit problem. Which of the statements in question 32 would best characterize your view of what EDP auditing will be like in your company in the future? Statement number _____ best describes your company's future response to the problems associated with EDP auditing.

34. Please rate the quality of internal control over EDP systems in your company relative to other activities and functions which are audited by internal auditing.

	Very Superior	Superior	Neither Superior nor Inferior	Inferior	Very Inferior
1. Overall EDP system internal control.	8	73	181	50	8
2. Data base integrity.	4	92	173	37	8
3. File security.	11	113	141	47	9
4. Auditability.	4	92	163	52	11
5. Internal control awareness.	18	106	140	51	5
6. Separation of incompatible duties.	12	106	153	44	6
7. Authorization of system changes.	13	97	136	65	10
8. Report distribution control.	4	79	197	38	3
9. Back-up procedures.	17	124	122	48	9
10. Usefulness of EDP reports.	8	84	200	29	0

35. Please share with us your perspective on any specific difficulties your company experiences in maintaining internal control over EDP systems.
_____
_____
_____

36. Please estimate the percentage of your company's operations in each of the following categories.

Domestic (U.S. & Canada)	92
Nondomestic—Economically developed countries	5
Nondomestic—Economically developing countries	2
Nondomestic—Underdeveloped countries	1
	100%

37. Please estimate the quality of internal control achieved in each of the following categories by checking the appropriate level on the following scale:

Very Poor Quality VPQ	Poor Quality PQ	Neither High nor Poor Quality N	High Quality HQ	Very High Quality VHQ

	VPQ	PQ	N	HQ	VHQ
1. Domestic—U.S. & Canada	1	12	74	195	43
2. Nondomestic—Economically developed countries	2	10	43	55	6
3. Nondomestic—Economically developing countries	4	17	48	11	3
4. Nondomestic—Economically underdeveloped countries	3	13	42	4	2

38. Which of the following statements best describes the manner in which you perform the internal audit function for each of the categories of non-domestic operations of questions 36 and 37? (Please check one statement in each column).

	Nondomestic Economically Developed Countries	Nondomestic Economically Developing Countries	Nondomestic Economically Underdeveloped Countries
The internal audit function is performed entirely by local audit personnel	14	4	2
The internal audit function is performed by local audit personnel with occasional corporate audit on site review	10	6	2
The internal audit function is performed by local audit personnel with regular corporate audit on site review	14	12	5
The internal audit function is performed entirely by corporate audit personnel	69	50	41
Other (Please describe)	7	7	5

For the following questions, you may wish to add additional pages.

39. What changes, if any, do you expect to make in your audit practices for nondomestic operations over the next few years? (Please describe)

40. What, in your opinion, is the most important contribution that your internal audit department has provided for your company over the last few years? (Please describe)

41. What is the most important contribution that you *expect* your internal audit department to provide for your company *over the next few years?* (Please describe)

42. Please describe any significant changes or developments that you believe will occur in your internal audit function *over the next few years.*

43. We are interested in any other comments you may wish to make about internal auditing in general or your present work activities. Please add any additional thoughts you wish to express.

Thank you for your cooperation.

The Institute of Internal Auditors Research Foundation

Research Project on
Developments Influencing Internal Auditing in
U.S. and Canadian Corporations

Questionnaire for
Internal Audit Staff

This questionnaire is an essential part of a major research project conducted by the Paton Accounting Center at The University of Michigan for the Institute of Internal Auditors. The results, which will be published by the Institute as a monograph, are expected to be directly beneficial in planning future educational and research programs in internal auditing.

All responses will be treated as completely confidential. With this questionnaire, you should receive an addressed, postage-prepaid envelope in which you can mail your completed questionnaire directly to the Paton Accounting Center. No one except members of the research team will ever see your responses. No participating company or person will be mentioned by name or identified in any way. Responses will be reported only in summaries and tabulations.

Related but similar questionnaires will be completed by the director of internal auditing, his supervisor, a representative of your company's audit committee, and a representative of your company's independent audit firm. Please be frank. Opportunity is provided at the end of the questionnaire for you to express yourself freely on any matters not included in specific questions.

If any question is clearly not applicable to your kind of company or your situation, write "N/A" beside the question and continue to the next question.

Your participation in this research is greatly appreciated.

Part I

1. Present title or rank: _____
2. How long have you held this title or rank? __1-36__ years.
3. How old are you? __20-66__ years.
4. How long have you been employed by this company? __1-37__ years.
5. Please provide the following information about your education.

	Respondents	Acct.	Gen. Bus.	Engineering	Computer Science	Arts or Science	Misc.
				Major Field of Study (check)			
High School	1,240	24	207	12	1	369	627
Institute or college diploma	1,061	—	—	—	—	—	—
Some university training	100	36	16	3	7	15	23
Bachelor's degree	1,061	630	176	12	10	145	88
Master's degree or higher	225	63	124	1	7	20	10
Professional Designation:							
C.P.A./C.A. (Canada)	301						
Certified Internal Auditor	124						
Certified Bank Auditor	21						
Certified Management Accountant	14						
Registered Industrial Accountant	13						
Certified General Accountant	8						
Certified Information Systems Auditor	81						
Other (Specify) _____	64						

6. Please check the professional organizations to which you belong:

Institute of Internal Auditors	456
American Institute of Certified Public Accountants	195
The Canadian Institute of Chartered Accountants	28
American Accounting Association	9
Canadian Academic Accounting Association	0
National Association of Accountants	79
The Society of Management Accountants	30
Certified General Accountants Association	11
State C.P.A. Society/Provincial C.A. Institute	186
Bank Administration Institute	88
EDP Auditors Association	148
Other (Specify)_____	158

7. Please provide the following information about your work experience since accepting full time employment.

   a) Work experience with present employer. (*State the number of years worked* at each level for the applicable type of work).

Type of Work	Respondents	Staff	Supervisor	Management
			Experience Level	
Internal auditing	1,216	2	1	.6
Accounting	197	2.6	1	.6
Finance	40	2.4	.5	.6
Production/engineering	21	2.2	1.2	.1
Marketing	17	3.3	1.1	—
Personnel	13	1.8	.8	.2
E.D.P.	80	3.0	1.3	.6
Other (State) _____	144	2.9	.9	.4

   b) Work experience with other employers. (*State the number of years worked* at each level for the applicable type of work).

Type of Work	Respondents	Staff	Supervisor	Management
			Experience Level	
Internal auditing	297	2.5	.9	.4
External auditing	322	2.4	.9	.2
Accounting	275	2.0	.7	.6
Finance	65	1.3	.8	.7
Production/engineering	20	2.2	.9	1.1
Marketing	34	1.8	.4	.3
Personnel	16	1.5	.8	.7
E.D.P.	92	3.3	1.1	.8
Other (State) _____	212	2.5	.7	.5

8. If you were transferred to the internal audit department from some other department of your company,

   a) Did you view your transfer to the internal audit department as:

Yes	No	
250	114	A promotion
131	144	A lateral move
128	139	Part of a training program
249	54	Opportunity leading to a management career
6	230	A "dead end"
24	34	Other (describe) _____

   b) Was your transfer to the internal audit department accompanied by:

Yes	No	
295	122	Salary improvement
212	169	An increase in title or rank

9. Is your position part of a corporate headquarters staff unit or is it part of an operating unit such as a division, plant, or branch? (Please check one)

   1,032 Corporate headquarters
   190   Operating unit

   If *Operating unit:*

   To whom are you responsible:

	For Assignment of Duties	For Audit Reporting Purposes	For Salary and Promotion Purposes
Corporate director of internal audit	105	116	117
Other executive at corporate headquarters	5	20	13
Operating unit management	78	72	63

10. Have you seen a formal job description for your position?

    Yes 936   No 301

    If *No:*

    Do you feel that other means have given you a good understanding of the scope of your job?

    Yes 268   No 31

11. To what extent does your understanding of the scope of your job describe your actual activities? (Check one)

    302 Entirely describes your actual activities
    712 Almost entirely describes your actual activites
    190 Describes about half of your actual activities
    23   Describes your actual activities hardly at all
    5   Fails to describe any of your actual activities

12. How often are you requested to perform tasks not included in your understanding of the scope of your job? (Check one)

    12   On every assignment
    58   On most assignments
    110 On about half of the assignments
    733 On only a few assignments
    318 Never requested to perform tasks not included in my understanding of the scope of my job

13. To what extent are you bothered by requests that you perform tasks not included in your understanding of the scope of your job? (Check one)

    3   Makes my job almost intolerable
    30   Bothers me considerably
    131 Bothers me somewhat
    252 Bothers me only a little
    530 Doesn't bother me at all
    267 Never requested to perform tasks not included in my understanding of the scope of my job

14. Do you plan to remain in internal auditing throughout your career?

    Yes 298   No 915

    If *No:*

    a) How long do you expect to stay in the internal audit department?

Less than 1 year	1-3 years	4-6 years	More than 6 years
68	490	282	73

    b) What type of work do you expect to transfer to if you leave the internal audit department?

Type of Work	Please check one
Accounting	266
Finance	246
Production/engineering	9
Marketing	18
Personnel	9
Line management	147
E.D.P.	80
Other (State) _____	140

15. What percentage of your time is spent on each of the following audit activities?

25	Detection of errors and irregularities—this activity is directed to the prevention or timely discovery of errors and irregularities in the processing or recording of transactions.
27	Monitoring management control—management control strives to obtain compliance with the applicable rules and procedures established by company policy.
12	Performance evaluation—this activity assesses the efficiency or effectiveness with which company goals are attained.
27	Monitoring internal accounting control—internal accounting control strives to assure that published financial statements present fairly the financial position and results of operations of the company in accordance with generally accepted accounting practice or other appropriate standards and that assets are appropriately safeguarded.
9	Decision-making review—this activity evaluates the effectiveness of management's operating and financial decisions.
100%	

16. Where in the company do you spend most of your audit time? Place the percentage of time spent next to those company units where you spend your time.

Corporate headquarters staff	33
Plants and departments	42
Dealers, agencies and branches	8
Divisional management	11
Outside contractors	3
Corporate senior management	3
	100%

Internal Auditing: Directions and Opportunities   183

17. Indicate the percentage of your time spent auditing the following types of activites: (If this question is not applicable to your company, please answer with "N/A" next to it and continue to the next question.)

7%	Acquisition of raw materials
5.5	Sales contracts
2.5	Labor contracts
7.0	Quality controls
15.0	Manufacturing operations
14.0	Inventory control
3.0	Transfers between units of the company
1.0	Warranty claims
41.0	Other (Describe) _____
4.0	_____
100%	

18. To what extent do you consider the task of an internal auditor to be different from that of an external auditor?

112	Entirely different
521	Mostly different
434	Half the same and half different
166	Mostly the same
1	Entirely the same

19. Do you consider regular reading of professional and business publications necessary to keep up with current developments in your profession?

    Yes 1,145   No 92

    If *Yes:*

    Indicate the extent to which such reading is done on your own personal time.

101	Entirely on my own time
381	Mostly on my own time
357	Half on my own and half on company time
277	Mostly on company time
31	Entirely on company time

20. Please indicate the frequency with which you read the following journals and magazines:

	Very Infrequently	Infrequently	Neither Frequently Nor Infrequently	Frequently	Very Frequently
Journal of Accountancy	357	241	193	178	69
Fortune	353	279	175	140	63
The Internal Auditor	138	149	191	368	274
Business Week/Forbes	209	225	221	253	137
A state CPA journal	565	104	110	94	34
CA Magazine	689	58	69	31	22
The daily newspaper	25	42	85	256	784
Current popular novels	342	219	197	157	117
Cost and Management	575	142	106	51	12
Wall Street Journal	91	187	221	330	311
The Accounting Review	544	180	128	45	13
Management Accounting	529	175	115	71	26
EDP Auditor	475	159	122	109	110
Other (List) _____	41	6	25	114	196

Instructions for Part II

The questions in this section generate information about your company, your internal auditing job, and your work related attitudes and preferences. *Your responses will be most helpful if you base them on your experiences as an employee in the company, and, where applicable, on your personal attitudes and preferences towards your work and your career.* All the questions are typical statements about companies, internal auditing, and work related attitudes and preferences. Please indicate your level of agreement with each statement by using the following scale, which will appear to the right of each statement.

Strongly Agree	Agree	Slightly Agree	Neither Agree Nor Disagree	Slightly Disagree	Disagree	Strongly Disagree
StA	A	SA	N	SD	D	StD

	StA	A	SA	N	SD	D	StD
1. You are encouraged to use your initiative in developing audit programs.	587	450	98	49	23	21	8
2. Those discretionary decisions permitted you are clearly specified.	70	342	235	231	125	175	50
3. Most internal audit decisions are made by a small number of people in the internal audit department.	247	485	133	123	77	138	31
4. You would not leave your company if a job were offered you with no significant change in compensation by a company you considered to be better managed.	241	321	99	153	116	162	142
5. Your work in the internal audit department calls for frequent exercise of discretionary judgment.	424	578	141	46	19	22	5
6. There are very few people in your department with whom you can discuss professional auditing interests.	48	127	74	103	115	434	333
7. Salary levels are a general indication of one's contribution to the company.	69	251	181	164	166	220	184
8. In your company, getting the work done depends on informal relationships and cooperation.	186	497	276	144	59	59	16
9. You would leave your company if a job at a lower salary were offered you by a company you considered to be better managed.	30	31	50	148	116	410	452
10. More varied assignments are an indication of approval by one's superiors.	147	530	226	220	39	60	13
11. When you find inefficient activities in your work, you feel a responsibility to get them corrected.	469	635	97	26	6	4	1
12. Tasks which require significant ability are more likely to be assigned to those who have displayed significant expertise.	278	640	173	77	26	29	15
13. Barring unforeseen developments, you have every intention of pursuing your career with this company.	314	492	122	147	43	76	44
14. In your company, people communicate only along the channels indicated in the organization chart.	17	108	158	155	209	387	205

		StA	A	SA	N	SD	D	StD
15.	You get most of your professional auditing stimulation from your department associates.	74	362	263	226	121	147	44
16.	Barring unforeseen developments, you have no plans to leave your company.	273	477	98	143	69	113	64
17.	To meet your commitment as a professional internal auditor, you should:							
	a) Meet the standards of the Institute of Internal Auditors.	361	544	147	123	23	24	12
	b) Perform assigned tasks with the highest professional competence.	747	464	21	3	1	0	0
	c) Sacrifice personal time to keep abreast of current developments.	122	400	419	161	71	46	17
	d) Rely on your professional judgment as to adequacy of audit procedures needed in specific cases.	256	665	193	52	49	17	3
	e) Avoid relationships with company personnel that might appear to influence your independence.	209	397	242	153	102	102	30
	f) Be an active member of the Institute of Internal Auditors.	99	209	214	402	77	167	65
	g) Participate in formal continuing education.	397	545	178	73	14	22	7
	h) Pass the Certified Internal Audit examination (or its equivalent).	177	245	198	310	74	147	83
	i) Pass the CPA/CA examination (or its equivalent).	151	210	179	350	82	173	84
	j) Accept company policy as your professional priority.	67	330	333	224	134	116	24
	k) Avoid conflicts with company personnel that threaten your promotability.	50	158	159	221	202	335	110
	l) Understate actual hours worked rather than exceed time budgets.	11	31	43	107	115	490	433
	m) Satisfy budgeted time contraints on assignments regardless of their adequacy for the assignments at hand.	15	27	46	83	115	504	443
18.	You would accept demotion rather than leave your present employer.	9	18	32	125	73	384	595
19.	It is not important to you that your company have a reputation as an efficient and well-managed organization.	25	48	25	48	98	509	484
20.	People who aggressively seek promotion are often rewarded beyond their contribution.	56	151	269	350	185	186	41
21.	As long as you perform your assigned internal audit duties adequately, you have no further responsibility to assure the efficient operation of your company.	8	38	37	65	254	587	249
22.	You request or volunteer for difficult jobs.	144	534	262	249	24	18	2

	StA	A	SA	N	SD	D	StD
23. You are expected to follow a detailed audit manual for all assignments.	24	174	232	127	166	398	118
24. Your company offers incentives to its employees in order to attain its objectives.	39	234	211	183	124	300	145
25. Your company rewards employees for following directions without questions.	8	55	130	314	180	413	137
26. As an employee, your primary loyalty belongs to your employer.	89	436	264	146	134	119	48
27. Managers of audited departments tolerate the internal audit function as a necessary business practice.	64	510	336	96	128	85	19
28. Your company makes decisions using committees of those managers who are responsible for implementing the decisions.	50	457	290	198	84	129	25
29. When changes are made, your company involves all those who are most likely to be affected in the planning and implementation of the changes.	29	255	297	179	215	185	75
30. Those who think of new and better ways of doing a task are more likely to be promoted.	38	356	387	273	92	66	25
31. In your company the expert in a given situation makes the decision even if it means bypassing the formal line of authority.	11	63	169	311	253	367	60
32. You are impatient when your assignments do not recognize your increased abilities.	113	380	386	213	69	70	3
33. Your discretionary judgments are reviewed by superiors.	103	635	323	81	51	38	4
34. You would leave your company if a job at a higher salary were offered you by a company you considered to be better managed.	368	389	219	155	31	51	23
35. You prefer a job for which there are written procedures describing how to do a particular audit task.	52	165	297	264	191	198	70
36. You get most of your professional auditing stimulation from people that you meet at professional meetings.	22	91	196	335	190	313	89
37. Titles are unimportant to you as long as you feel you are making a contribution to your company.	67	277	244	127	275	200	48
38. You would leave internal auditing if a better job were offered you in another department of your company.	265	461	216	143	51	70	30
39. Your company's communication channels are highly structured.	43	239	316	195	212	176	55
40. Your company uses solutions proposed by outside experts in dealing with problems.	32	206	352	306	140	162	37
41. You are generally uncertain about all the specific job aspects on which your performance will be evaluated.	41	118	231	108	167	469	99

	StA	A	SA	N	SD	D	StD
42. Managers of audited departments in your company tend to look upon the internal audit function as a source of constructive assistance.	36	332	458	123	199	75	14
43. Members of the internal audit department with little audit experience are not permitted to make judgment decisions.	31	213	234	150	351	225	26
44. If you discovered practices which discredit corporate officers, you could report them to the proper authorities without fear of jeopardizing your position.	195	527	192	131	86	67	38
45. You get most of your professional auditing stimulation from professional journals.	13	81	251	316	175	304	96
46. Managers of audited departments in your company tend to look upon the internal audit function largely as a policing activity.	33	249	401	155	193	184	21
47. Your company institutes changes without explaining or justifying them to the affected employees.	42	147	328	152	230	294	43
48. If your superior requested you to perform an audit in a manner you felt not to be in accordance with appropriate internal audit standards, you would refuse to comply with his request.	57	284	304	235	200	130	24
49. You get most of your professional auditing stimulation from company continuing education seminars.	27	129	286	264	149	251	121
50. You consider your time in internal auditing as a training period for other positions in your company.	165	312	244	157	99	203	57
51. Your company uses a participative approach to decision-making (specific courses of action are selected only after full discussion leading to a consensus.)	24	219	316	257	175	195	49
52. You understand completely all the aspects of your position for which you will be held responsible.	125	589	285	71	113	40	13
53. There are times when one set of instructions from your superior appears to conflict with another set of instructions.	74	271	345	159	109	241	38
54. In the performance of your internal auditing duties, you seek to find areas or activities where your company's profitability could be improved.	284	618	207	74	26	23	2

For the next question please use the following response scale:

Very Satisfied	Satisfied	Slightly Satisfied	Neither Satisfied Nor Dissatisfied	Slightly Dissatisfied	Dissatisfied	Very Dissatisfied
VS	S	SS	N	SD	D	VD

55. In your present job, how satisfied are you with the opportunities available to:

	VS	S	SS	N	SD	D	VD
1. Make full use of your knowledge and skills.	192	549	279	39	90	60	28
2. Learn new knowledge and skills.	219	499	269	45	113	73	19
3. Earn a satisfactory salary.	151	504	257	79	127	81	38
4. Advance within the company.	94	354	267	154	166	135	64
5. Improve your technical competence.	137	474	314	101	125	67	19
6. Associate with personnel senior to your position.	302	591	173	90	46	20	14
7. Build your professional reputation.	190	586	234	104	73	36	13
8. Work on difficult and challenging problems.	235	550	279	64	72	27	10
9. Make constructive suggestions.	252	632	227	49	50	20	8
10. Be in the company of people you like.	231	600	221	115	40	21	10
11. Enjoy your work.	249	549	257	57	77	38	11
12. Influence company policy.	96	372	302	237	119	69	42

Instructions for Part III

Check one response for each question.

1. Do you find your work to be routine or is it a real challenge to your ability or ingenuity? Your work is
    - 113 Almost always a challenge to your ability or ingenuity
    - 471 Usually challenging
    - 508 About half routine and half challenging
    - 125 Usually routine
    -   19 Almost always routine

2. When you don't like some aspect of the internal audit program, how often do you express your opinion to your superior?
    -   13 Never
    - 278 Occasionally
    - 111 Approximately half of the time
    - 563 Most of the time
    - 263 All of the time

3. In your job, how often do problems come up which were not anticipated in the time budget?
    -   90 On every assignment
    - 397 On most assignments
    - 377 On about half of the assignments
    - 325 On only a few assignments
    -   29 Never encounter such situations

4. Standard audit programs are used:
    - 180 On all assignments
    - 513 On most assignments
    - 176 On about half of the assignments
    - 269 On only a few assignments
    -   95 On no assignments

5. When problems which were not anticipated in the time budget come up, how seriously do they challenge your expertise?
    -   44 You never solve such problems, but refer them to your superior to decide what to do
    - 178 Almost always a challenge to your expertise
    - 496 Usually a challenge
    - 348 About half challenging and half not challenging
    - 129 Usually not challenging
    -   23 Almost always not challenging

6. In order to do your job right, you may have to: disagree with fellow employees, allocate minimum time over competing needs, resolve difficult accounting or auditing issues, evaluate the importance of errors and irregularities.

   How often do you encounter such situations?

151	On every assignment
432	On most assignments
320	On about half of the assignments
312	On only a few assignments
17	Never encounter such situations

7. How tight are time schedules for your audit work? Time schedules are usually set so that there is:

34	Much more than enough time to fulfill your responsibilities
343	Ample time
341	Just the right amount of time
434	Not quite enough time
73	Much too little time to fulfill your responsibilities

8. How often do you suggest to the manager of an audited department a different or better way of doing something on the job?

52	Very infrequently make suggestions for changes
85	Infrequently make suggestions for changes
221	Neither infrequently nor frequently make suggestions for changes
506	Frequently make suggestions for changes
352	Very frequently make suggestions for changes
16	Your superior always makes all suggestions for changes

9. In connection with your job, how much chance do you get to improve your audit expertise?

27	Very little or no chance
91	Little chance
352	Some chance
601	A good chance
166	An excellent chance

10. If you suggest to the managers of audited departments better ways of doing some job, how often do they go along with your suggestions? They go along with your suggestions:

50	Up to 10 percent of the time
120	About 25 percent of the time
324	About 50 percent of the time
589	About 75 percent of the time
40	100 percent of the time
72	No means to convey this information
21	You never make such suggestions

11. In connection with your job, how much chance do you get to learn new things about your company?

6	Very little or no chance
20	Little chance
144	Some chance
618	A good chance
449	An excellent chance

12. How much will your internal audit experience contribute to your ability to succeed in almost any department of your company?

12	Very little or no contribution
29	Little contribution
210	Some contribution
606	A good contribution
376	An excellent contribution

13. In social conversation, you usually refer to yourself as: (Check one)

87	An accountant
436	An auditor
1	A public auditor
434	An internal auditor
123	An EDP auditor
3	A systems analyst
44	A manager
4	A businessman
2	An executive
12	A consultant
75	Other (State)_____

14. Most people find some portions or features of their work more appealing than others. Using the list of job features provided below:

    a) Rank order the three features of your work that you find most appealing (use "1" as most appealing).

    b) Rank order the three features of your work that you find least appealing (use "1" as least appealing).

Job Features	Most Appealing			Least Appealing		
	1	2	3	1	2	3
Travel	45	76	169	250	123	170
Intellectual challenge of work	349	243	132	31	49	42
Variety of assignments	389	323	193	19	18	24
Status and prestige of position	31	73	82	119	159	12
Contribution to success of company	83	124	143	36	66	59
Compensation	76	104	145	139	111	156
Authority accompanying auditor's position	32	60	68	112	140	141
Association with other internal auditors	31	36	61	27	64	44
Relationship with independent accountants	2	9	24	171	159	188
General work atmosphere	98	108	130	89	104	104
Others (Describe)_____	40	13	19	129	49	37

15. If you were to look for another job, you would look for a position in:
    (Please rank order the three most preferred jobs using "1" as most preferred)

	1	2	3
Internal auditing	318	190	143
External auditing	23	37	54
Accounting	111	177	165
General management	174	197	214
Financial management	282	210	160
Operations	69	131	154
Marketing	31	43	56
Personnel	18	31	66
E.D.P.	89	71	73
Others (state) _____	84	36	28

16. We are interested in any other comments you may wish to make about internal auditing in general or your present work activities. Please add any additional thoughts you wish to express.

Thank you for your cooperation.

The Institute of Internal Auditors Research Foundation

Research Project on
Developments Influencing Internal Auditing in
U.S. and Canadian Corporations

Questionnaire for
Representative of Senior Management

This questionnaire is an essential part of a major research project conducted by the Paton Accounting Center at The University of Michigan for the Institute of Internal Auditors. The results, which will be published by the Institute as a monograph, are expected to be directly beneficial in planning future educational and research programs in internal auditing.

All responses will be treated as completely confidential. With this questionnaire, you should receive an addressed, postage-prepaid envelope in which you can mail your completed questionnaire directly to the Paton Accounting Center. No one except members of the research team will ever see your responses. No participating company or person will be mentioned by name or identified in any way. Responses will be reported only in summaries and tabulations.

Related but similar questionnaires will be completed by the director of internal auditing, internal audit staff members, a representative of your company's audit committee, and a representative of your company's independent audit firm. Please be frank. Opportunity is provided at the end of the questionnaire for you to express yourself freely on any matters not included in specific questions.

If any question is clearly not applicable to your kind of company or your situation, write "N/A" beside the question and continue to the next question.

Your participation in this research is greatly appreciated.

Instructions for Part I

Please provide the following information regarding your internal audit department.

1. Please indicate your present title or rank: _____

2. Has your internal audit department grown in size over the last five years?

                       Yes 217   No 47

   If *yes:*

   Please rank order the three most significant causes of the growth of internal auditing in your company (use "1" as most significant).

1	2	3	
11	37	36	Compliance obligations imposed by the Foreign Corrupt Practices Act and similar requirements. .
131	34	14	Desire by senior management to improve control.
7	33	29	Recommendation of Audit Committee.
3	27	29	Need to reduce errors and irregularities.
10	37	45	Attempt to reduce external audit fees.
35	12	11	Other (State) _____

3. Please indicate the extent to which, in your judgment, senior management *currently* relies on the work of the internal auditing function with regard to each of the following items. Please use the following scale:

No Reliance	Very Low Reliance	Low Reliance	Neither Low nor High Reliance	High Reliance	Very High Reliance	Total Reliance
NR	VLR	LR	N	HR	VHR	TR

	NR	VLR	LR	N	HR	VHR	TR
a) Reliability of company's financial data							
i) reported externally	23	31	34	77	65	30	0
ii) used internally only	14	35	30	67	76	42	0
b) Evaluation of the effectiveness of management's							
i) operating decisions	38	50	42	66	54	14	0
ii) financial decisions	38	43	49	78	44	12	0
c) Integrity of company officers and employees	4	9	15	59	89	81	9
d) Efficiency and effectiveness with which company goals are attained	28	24	54	98	48	14	0
e) Compliance with established rules and procedures	1	1	4	11	86	149	14
f) Adequacy of internal control procedures	0	0	1	6	55	168	36
g) Monitoring the application of internal control procedures	0	0	3	9	56	156	42
h) Detection of errors and irregularities	0	9	12	44	98	89	14
i) Assuring company compliance with all relevant government regulations	7	18	40	60	84	50	7

4. Using the same scale as in question 3, please indicate the extent to which senior management, in your judgment, *would like to* rely on the work of internal auditing with regard to each of the following items (your responses here could be that you would like to place more, less, or the same degree of reliance on the work of internal auditing as indicated in question 3).

	NR	VLR	LR	N	HR	VHR	TR
a) Reliability of company's financial data							
i) reported externally	12	19	25	69	82	51	2
ii) used internally only	8	18	25	57	80	71	2
b) Evaluation of the effectiveness of management's							
i) operating decisions	17	26	40	70	74	31	2
ii) financial decisions	20	23	38	69	78	31	2
c) Integrity of company officers and employees	3	6	8	47	81	100	17
d) Efficiency and effectiveness with which company goals are attained	17	19	31	71	76	46	2
e) Compliance with established rules and procedures	2	1	1	6	61	161	31
f) Adequacy of internal control procedures	1	0	1	3	29	181	48
g) Monitoring the application of internal control procedures	1	0	1	6	33	166	54
h) Detection of errors and irregularities	1	4	11	28	73	115	29
i) Assuring company compliance with all relevant government regulations	5	10	17	50	77	89	14

5. Please describe briefly the major reasons for any differences between the extent of senior management's current reliance on internal audit work and senior management's desired level of reliance.

_____
_____
_____
_____

6. Which of the following statements best describes the attention given to recommendations by the internal audit department in your company? (Check one)

☐ Recommendations by the internal audit department are a matter of record but there need be no internal audit follow-up on their implementation until the following audit.

☐ Recommendations made by the internal audit department must be answered in writing within a stated time period.

☐ Recommendations made by the internal audit department are maintained in an "open file" until settled by implementation or mutual agreement.

☐ Recommendations by the internal audit department must be complied with unless factually in error.

☐ Other (Please explain) _____
_____
_____
_____

7. What, in your opinion, is the most important contribution that your internal audit department has provided for your company over the last few years? (Please describe)

_____
_____
_____
_____
_____

8. What is the most important contribution that you *expect* your internal audit department to provide for your company over the next few years? (Please describe)

_____
_____
_____
_____
_____

9. If there are any particular areas or activities within your company for which you experience unusual difficulty in achieving or maintaining what you consider to be an adequate level of internal control, please describe them briefly.

_____
_____
_____
_____

For the next question, please use the following response scale:

Very Unimportant	Unimportant	Neither Unimportant nor Important	Important	Very Important
VU	U	N	I	VI

10. For each of the following statements indicate senior management's view of the importance of the internal audit function in your company as:

	VU	U	N	I	VI
a) A management training program.	15	40	89	98	23
b) A protection to management.	0	2	19	133	112
c) An essential activity for business success.	3	9	55	139	57
d) A resource to assist audit committee.	2	4	27	103	123
e) A career for loyal but not innovative employees.	155	55	49	3	0
f) A means of reducing external audit fees.	8	25	53	151	28
g) An investigative arm for the company's audit committee.	8	16	75	112	51
h) An investigative arm for senior management.	0	7	36	146	77
i) Consultants to management, at all levels, for improving operating efficiency.	9	30	69	120	37

11. Please rate your internal audit department relative to other departments and activities in your company. (Check one)

    18 Very superior
    127 Superior
    113 Average
    6   Disappointing
        Very disappointing

12. What factors do you think most inhibit internal auditing from becoming more useful in your company than it is now: (Check as many items as apply)

    48 Narrow point of view of internal auditors.
    109 Inadequate appreciation by your company of internal audit capabilities.
    73 The company's historical experience with internal auditing.
    41 Limited ability of internal auditors.
    77 Lack of managerial perspective on the part of internal auditors.
    61 Inadequate supply of qualified internal audit personnel.
    54 Inadequate incentives for good people to become internal auditors in this company.
    9   Inadequate programs to keep internal auditors informed of current developments in auditing.
    26 Other (Please describe). _____

13. In your opinion, how actively does senior management in your company support the internal audit function: (Check one)

    100 Very actively
    121 Actively
    36 Neither actively nor passively
    9   Passively
        Very passively

14. In your opinion, how actively is the Audit Committee interested in the internal control concerns of your company? (Check one)

    129 Very actively
    111 Actively
    15 Neither actively nor passively
    5   Passively
    1   Very passively

Instructions for Part II

The questions in this section generate information about your company—its business environment, production technology, the nature of its products or services, and its management style. Responses to them will enable us to relate internal audit characteristics to specific company characteristics. All the questions listed are typical statements about companies. Please indicate your level of concurrence with each statement by using the scales indicated.

For the following statements please indicate your degree of agreement or disagreement with each statement using this scale:

Strongly Disagree	Disagree	Neither Disagree nor Agree	Agree	Strongly Agree
SD	D	N	A	SA

	SD	D	N	A	SA
1. Your company mainly markets already established products or services.	7	23	17	137	80
2. Responsible management of publicly held companies should avoid high risk activities.	20	94	65	70	11
3. Your company sells a single product line or service.	137	82	7	20	19
4. Your company favors a strategy of cooperative existence with rival firms (within the limits of the anti-trust laws) over a strategy of extreme competition.	49	84	48	70	8
5. Your company holds a dominant position in its primary industry.	27	53	39	88	53
6. Your company sells product lines or services in unrelated market segments.	47	80	26	79	28
7. Your company emphasizes profit measurement as its key success indicator.	4	22	37	143	56
8. Your company makes important decisions without formally quantifying relevent costs and benefits.	72	122	31	36	3
9. Your company uses a participative approach to decision-making (specific courses of action are selected only after full discussion leading to a consensus).	11	34	61	131	27
10. Your company uses solutions proposed by outside experts in resolving problems.	22	78	101	61	1
11. Materials and/or products of your company are readily convertible to personal gain.	60	80	36	56	27
12. Your company's operations and/or sales activities are decentralized.	17	53	29	109	56
13. Major company purchases (source of funds for financial institutions) are made from a small number of suppliers.	58	110	33	51	11
14. In your company a high degree of autonomy is permitted to divisional and other unit management.	10	40	48	116	50
15. Your company places considerable reliance on computer based systems for both operations and business data processing purposes.	0	5	18	159	82
16. In your company, getting the work done depends on informal relationships and cooperation.	4	29	74	138	19

		SD	D	N	A	SA
17.	There is a well understood sequence of steps to follow in performing the principal production or service activities of your company.	1	15	38	174	36
18.	Your company sells in a single market (e.g., retail only, wholesale only, etc.).	59	101	28	55	20
19.	In your company the expert in a given situation makes the decision even if it means bypassing the formal line of authority.	25	125	77	34	1
20.	Your company strives for a constant rate of growth.	5	35	45	146	33
21.	Your company offers incentives to its employees in order to attain its objectives.	14	36	36	139	37
22.	Your company's communication channels are highly structured.	11	94	92	66	1
23.	Your company makes decisions using committees of those managers who are responsible for implementing the decisions.	11	52	61	128	9
24.	Your company emphasizes the use of Operations Research (linear programming, simulation, decision models, etc.) in making decisions.	38	92	71	58	5
25.	Your company institutes changes without explaining or justifying them to the affected employees.	33	164	46	17	3
26.	When changes are made, your company involves all those who are most likely to be affected in the planning and implementation of the changes.	4	27	61	157	14
27.	Operations and/or sales activities of your company are conducted in locations remote from the home office.	12	37	19	125	69
28.	Your company's revenue is produced by a large number of small transactions.	9	51	31	104	68
29.	Your company conducts business in a number of less developed countries.	143	54	10	42	13
30.	Your company is engaged in one or more projects calling for major investments of resources.	12	26	31	135	60
31.	Your company participates in joint ventures with other companies.	39	56	38	99	30

For the following statements, please indicate your perception of each statement's size using this measurement scale:

Very Small VS	Small S	Neither Small nor Large N	Large L	Very Large VL

	VS	S	N	L	VL
32. The amount of thinking time spent dealing with specific problems of your company's production or service activity has been	2	6	43	158	54
33. The number of new problems faced by your company in its production or service activity has been	0	17	65	123	58
34. The amount of customized work demanded of your company by its customers has been	23	78	65	73	58
35. Your company's variance in financial performance from year to year has been	11	52	94	86	19

For the following statements, please indicate your perception of each statement's intensity using this measurement scale:

Very Weak VW	Weak W	Neither Weak nor Intense N	Intense I	Very Intense VI

	VW	W	N	I	VI
36. The competition for technical manpower (managers, engineers, scientists, accountants, computer experts, etc.) experienced by your company is	0	13	104	130	17
37. Price competition in your company's product or service markets is	4	13	37	126	83
38. The competition for basic inputs (raw materials, labor, machinery, sources of funds, etc.) experienced by your company is	9	27	102	95	29
39. The marketing competition (advertising, promotion, distribution, etc.) experienced by your company is	13	16	56	130	48

For the following statements, please indicate your perception of the ease or difficulty of achieving each statement's objective using this measurement scale:

Very Easy	Easy	Neither Easy nor Difficult	Difficult	Very Difficult
VE	E	N	D	VD

	VE	E	N	D	VD
40. Planning day to day work schedules for your company's production or service activity is	2	53	134	64	8
41. The solution of problems in running your company's basic production or service activity is	0	25	114	114	9
42. For your company, compliance with government regulations is	1	23	88	103	48
43. Increasing your company's market share by 10 percent would be	0	2	19	89	151
44. Predicting output on the basis of known inputs of time and material is	8	61	96	73	20

For the following statements, please indicate your preception of each statement's importance using this measurement scale:

Very Unimportant	Unimportant	Neither Unimportant nor Important	Important	Very Important
VU	U	N	I	VI

	VU	U	N	I	VI
45. For your company, a variety of products or services at different quality grades is	34	55	52	90	24
46. For your company's success the development of new products or services is	5	13	28	109	107

For the following statements, please indicate your perception of the extent of control which your company can exercise over each factor of production (service) and distribution, using this measurement scale:

No Control	Some Control	Considerable Control	Extensive Control	Total Control
NC	SC	CC	EC	TC

	NC	SC	CC	EC	TC
47. The sources of major raw materials used in operating plants (major sources of funds for financial institutions).	18	100	88	42	4
48. The supply of parts and components required in operating plants (for financial institutions, the degree to which various customer services are supplied internally).	14	58	115	56	6
49. The wholesale distribution system for your products/services.	13	66	76	62	20
50. The retail distribution system for your products/services.	27	66	71	54	20

For the following statement, please indicate your perception of the rate of change using this measurement scale:

Very Slow	Slow	Neither Slow nor Rapid	Rapid	Very Rapid
VS	S	N	R	VR

	VS	S	N	R	VR
51. The rate of innovation in your company's production or service technologies is	7	47	91	77	42

For the following statements, please indicate your perception of the extent to which the chief executive of your company has delegated authority to others to make each of the following types of decisions. Please rate the actual rather than the formal delegation of authority, using the following scale:

Very Little or no Delegation	Little Delegation	Neither Little nor Extensive Delegation	Extensive Delegation	Very Extensive Delegation
VLD	LD	N	ED	VED

	VLD	LD	N	ED	VED
52. The raising of long term capital.	34	44	65	86	26
53. Development of new products/services.	5	13	47	159	39
54. Marketing strategy for a new product/service and changes in the marketing strategy for existing products/services.	5	16	59	151	31
55. Pricing of products/services transferred between company units.	6	12	50	125	48
56. Selection of large new investments.	36	92	74	52	8
57. Pricing of new products/services and significant price changes in existing products/services.	5	23	59	129	38
58. The magnitude and direction of research into new products/services.	12	30	81	121	19
59. Selection of sources for production/services inputs (sources of funds for financial institutions).	8	14	74	130	30

60. Please add any comments or observations that you may wish to make about the internal audit function in your company, or any other concerns you consider relevant to this study.

_____
_____
_____
_____
_____
_____

Thank you for your cooperation.

The Institute of Internal Auditors Research Foundation

Research Project on
Developments Influencing Internal Auditing in
U.S. and Canadian Corporations

Questionnaire for
Independent Certified Public Accountant/Chartered Accountant

This questionnaire is an essential part of a major research project conducted by the Paton Accounting Center at The University of Michigan for the Institute of Internal Auditors. The results, which will be published by the Institute as a monograph, are expected to be directly beneficial in planning future educational and research programs in internal auditing.

All responses will be treated as completely confidential. With this questionnaire, you should receive an addressed, postage-prepaid envelope in which you can mail your completed questionnaire directly to the Paton Accounting Center. No one except members of the research team will ever see your responses. No participating company or person will be mentioned by name or identified in any way. Responses will be reported only in summaries and tabulations.

Related but similar questionnaires will be completed by the director of internal auditing, his superior, internal audit staff members, and a representative of this company's audit committee.

Please answer all questions in terms of your experience with this specific company. Your participation in this research is greatly appreciated.

Please use the following response scale for questions 1 and 2.

Very Unimportant	Unimportant	Neither Unimportant nor Important	Important	Very Important
VU	U	N	I	VI

1. Internal audit departments perform a variety of assignments that can be summarized under the purposes listed below. Using the response scale provided, please rate the degree of importance of each of the following internal audit purposes to this company.

	VU	U	N	I	VI
a. Detection and correction of unintentional errors.	6	28	66	145	33
b. Prevention or reduction of improprieties and irregularities.	1	4	25	148	99
c. Improvement of internal control.	1	3	14	94	166
d. Assistance to independent CPA in performance of the annual audit.	6	12	48	149	63
e. An investigative arm for the company's audit committee.	7	23	101	107	36
f. An investigative arm for senior management.	4	18	53	150	53
g. Monitoring the performance of internal control procedures.	1	3	15	98	16
h. Other (please describe). _____	0	0	1	14	17

2. For each of the following statements indicate your view of the importance of the internal audit function in this company as:

	VU	U	N	I	VI
a) A management training program.	27	64	108	69	9
b) A protection to management.	2	14	51	172	39
c) An essential activity for business success.	19	38	107	93	21
d) A resource to assist the audit committee.	8	16	62	136	52
e) A career for loyal but not innovative employees.	124	76	63	11	2
f) A means of reducing external audit fees.	10	29	63	144	32
g) A means for ensuring compliance with government regulations.	19	40	92	112	15
h) An aid for evaluating the efficiency and effectiveness of management performance.	14	38	87	118	20
i) Other (Please explain) _____	0	0	1	1	10

3. The primary responsibility of the director of internal auditing in this company is to: (Check one)
    - 89 The company's audit committee
    - 43 The company's chief executive officer
    - 64 The audit committee and chief executive officer equally
    - 81 Some other (Please explain) _____

4. The company's audit committee meets with the director of internal auditing with no other members of management present: (Check one)
    - 52 Annually
    - 47 Semi-annually
    - 63 Quarterly
    - 8 Monthly
    - 47 Never
    - 45 Other (Please explain) _____

5. Please indicate the extent to which you agree or disagree with each of the items below as applied to this company, using the following scale:

Strongly Agree SA	Agree A	Neither Agree nor Disagree N	Disagree D	Strongly Disagree SD

	SA	A	N	D	SD
a) Internal audit possesses sufficient independence to fulfill its function.	108	137	17	15	0
b) Internal audit receives adequate support from management.	78	153	23	19	4
c) The audit committee has access to the director of internal auditing for special assignments:					
With management's consent	64	107	45	19	8
Without management's consent	49	92	69	31	9
d) The director of internal auditing has authority to bring matters directly to the audit committee without notification to management when he deems this is necessary.	85	109	35	23	12

6. Which of the following statements best describes the attention given to recommendations by the internal audit department in this company? (Check one)

    23 Recommendations by the internal audit department are a matter of record but there need be no internal audit follow-up on their implementation until the following audit.

  168 Recommendations made by the internal audit department must be answered in writing within a stated time period.

    56 Recommendations made by the internal audit department are maintained in an "open file" until settled by implementation or mutual agreement.

    11 Recommendations by the internal audit department must be complied with unless factually in error.

    16 Other (Please explain) _____

7. What, in your opinion, is the most important contribution this internal audit department has provided for this company over the last few years? (Please describe)

8. What is the most important contribution that this company should expect from its internal audit department over the next few years? (Please describe)

9. Please rate the degree to which you rely on the work of this company's internal audit function in audit matters related to forming your audit opinion.

    46 Very high reliance
  133 High reliance
    56 Neither high nor low reliance
    23 Low reliance
     8 Very low reliance
     8 No reliance

10. Please indicate the manner and extent to which each of the following items has influenced your judgment regarding the degree of reliance to be placed on this company's internal audit work, using the scale below:

Very Positive Influence VPI	Positive Influence PI	Neither Positive nor Negative Influence N	Negative Influence NI	Very Negative Influence VNI

	VPI	PI	N	NI	VNI
a. The position of the person or group to whom the director of internal auditing reports.	63	134	62	17	1
b. The responsibilities assigned by written policy to internal audit.	25	108	134	7	2
c. The professional competence of internal audit staff members.	91	132	32	19	3
d. The extent of control and supervision of work within the internal audit department.	65	142	47	22	1
e. The degree to which internal audit has access to company records, documentation, and personnel.	108	128	39	1	1
f. The quality of internal audit programs.	52	139	66	16	3
g. The quality of internal audit working papers.	41	139	71	25	1
h. The extent of internal audit coverage.	64	140	53	18	2
i. The nature, frequency, and response to reports issued by internal audit.	47	139	72	16	3
j. Knowledge of company operations, processes, and procedures exhibited by internal audit personnel.	75	151	43	8	0
k. Knowledge of new trends and techniques in auditing exhibited by internal audit personnel.	19	96	125	35	2
l. The existence of a continuing education program for internal audit personnel.	27	105	117	24	4

11. What percentage of your audit time budget is spent evaluating and testing the work of this company's internal audit function?
    - 121 Less than 5 percent
    - 117 More than 5 percent but less than 15 percent
    - 30 More than 15 percent but less than 25 percent
    - 8 More than 25 percent but less than 50 percent
    - 0 More than 50 percent

12. Please rate this internal audit department relative to other departments and activities within the company. (Check one)
    - 7 Very superior
    - 109 Superior
    - 147 Average
    - 14 Disappointing
    - 1 Very disappointing

13. Please rate this company's internal audit department relative to other internal audit departments with which you are familiar.

    - 50 Very superior
    - 116 Superior
    - 82 Average
    - 27 Disappointing
    - 1 Very disappointing

14. Which of the following statements best describes the way you work with the internal audit department of this company? (Check one)

    - 32 Members of this internal audit department serve as assistants to the independent auditors preparing schedules, account analyses, trial balances, etc., in connection with the annual audit.
    - 77 Members of the internal audit department perform audit work in conformity with an audit program provided by the independent auditors.
    - 90 Members of the internal audit department participate with the independent auditors in planning the total audit program which is then divided between the independent and internal audit groups for independent performance.
    - 3 Members of the internal audit department utilize work done by the independent auditors and extend it where it is not completely appropriate for internal audit purposes.
    - 32 The internal and independent auditors perform their duties independently of one another.
    - 37 Other (Please describe) _____

15. What factors do you think most inhibit internal auditing from becoming more useful in this company than it now is: (Check as many items as apply)

    - 32 Narrow point of view of internal auditors.
    - 93 Inadequate appreciation by this company of internal audit capabilities.
    - 70 The company's historical experience with internal auditing.
    - 45 Limited ability of internal auditors.
    - 61 Lack of managerial perspective on the part of internal auditors.
    - 81 Lack of adequate supply of qualified internal audit personnel.
    - 69 Inadequate incentives for good people to become internal auditors in this company.
    - 17 Inadequate programs to keep internal auditors informed of current developments in auditing.
    - 44 Other (Please describe) _____

16. Please add any comments or observations you think might be appropriate in explaining your views about internal auditing or which might be relevant to our research in ways not specifically addressed in the questionnaire.

Thank you for your cooperation.

The Institute of Internal Auditors Research Foundation

Research Project on
Developments Influencing Internal Auditing in
U.S. and Canadian Corporations

Questionnaire for
Chairman or Member of Audit Committee

This questionnaire is an essential part of a major research project conducted by the Paton Accounting Center at The University of Michigan for the Institute of Internal Auditors. The results, which will be published by the Institute as a monograph, are expected to be directly beneficial in planning future educational and research programs in internal auditing.

All responses will be treated as completely confidential. With this questionnaire, you should receive an addressed, postage-prepaid envelope in which you can mail your completed questionnaire directly to the Paton Accounting Center. No one except members of the research team will ever see your responses. No participating company or person will be mentioned by name or identified in any way. Responses will be reported only in summaries and tabulations.

Related but similar questionnaires will be completed by the director of internal auditing, his superior, internal audit staff members, and a representative of your company's independent audit firm. Please be frank. Opportunity is provided at the end of the questionnaire for you to express yourself freely on any matters not included in specific questions.

Your participation in this research is greatly appreciated.

Internal Auditing: Directions and Opportunities

1. Internal audit departments perform a variety of assignments that can be summarized under the purposes listed below. Using the response scale provided, please rate the degree of importance of each of the following internal audit purposes to your company.

	Very Unimportant VU	Unimportant U	Neither Unimportant nor Important N	Important I	Very Important VI

	VU	U	N	I	VI
a. Detection and correction of unintentional errors.	11	21	47	126	26
b. Prevention or reduction of improprieties and irregularities.	9	0	5	69	147
c. Improvement of internal control.	5	1	1	56	167
d. Assistance to independent CPA in performance of the annual audit.	8	2	32	143	45
e. An investigative arm for the company's audit committee.	11	14	42	100	62
f. An investigative arm for senior management.	8	13	39	102	66
g. Monitoring the performance of internal control procedures.	5	1	3	86	32
h. Other (please describe). _____	0	0	2	14	8

2. Please indicate the number of times per year that each of the following groups meets:

	Times Per Year
Full Board of Directors	9
Audit Committee	4
Audit Committee with External CPA/CA	3
Audit Committee with Internal Auditor	4
Audit Committee with corporate management	4

3. Does the director of internal auditing have an explicit invitation to bring any concerns he may have directly to the audit committee without prior notification of company management?

                 Yes 206   No 24

If yes, how recently has this occurred?
- 57 Within the past year.
- 32 Within the past five years but not the past year.
- 101 Never to your knowledge.
- 15 Other (Please explain.) _____

4. Please indicate how strongly the audit committee has become involved in active consideration of the following business concerns using the scale below:

Very Strongly Involved VSI	Strongly Involved SI	Neither Strongly nor Weakly Involved N	Weakly Involved WI	Very Weakly Involved VWI

	VSI	SI	N	WI	VWI
a. The reliability of externally reported financial data.	66	81	52	18	8
b. The reliability of financial data used only internally.	15	66	88	35	20
c. The evaluation of the effectiveness of management's operating decisions.	8	38	93	48	37
d. The evaluation of the effectiveness of management's financial decisions.	15	57	84	36	29
e. Monitoring the integrity of officers and employees.	40	97	59	16	14
f. The efficiency and effectiveness with which company goals are attained.	13	53	89	38	29
g. The adequacy of internal control.	127	79	13	5	2
h. Assuring compliance with established company rules and procedures.	61	111	37	12	5
i. Monitoring the application of internal control procedures.	70	104	34	14	3
j. Detection of errors and irregularities.	32	99	65	15	14
k. Assuring company compliance with all relevant government regulations.	40	78	62	30	16
l. Resource allocation to internal auditing.	34	105	55	18	12
m. Detection of fraud.	58	93	49	13	12

5. Please indicate the extent to which the audit committee relies on internal auditing to assure the adequacy of company control over each of the following items, using the scale below:

No Reliance NR	Very Low Reliance VLR	Low Reliance LR	Neither High nor Low Reliance N	High Reliance HR	Very High Reliance VHR	Total Reliance TR

		NR	VLR	LR	N	HR	VHR	TR
a.	The reliability of externally reported financial data.	11	13	18	49	81	44	8
b.	The reliability of financial data used only internally.	8	20	26	54	61	45	12
c.	The evaluation of the effectiveness of management's operating decisions.	29	30	29	80	37	14	5
d.	The evaluation of the effectiveness of management's financial decisions.	25	21	27	90	36	18	7
e.	Monitoring the integrity of officers and employees.	2	14	13	36	66	77	18
f.	The efficiency and effectiveness with which company goals are attained.	27	23	28	84	35	20	6
g.	The adequacy of internal control.	2	3	0	6	50	118	47
h.	Assuring compliance with established company rules and procedures.	2	6	4	16	64	109	25
i.	Monitoring the application of internal control procedures.	3	2	1	6	53	115	47
j.	Detection of errors and irregularities.	1	5	4	18	80	90	28
k.	Assuring company compliance with all relevant government regulations.	8	10	16	49	68	58	17
l.	Detection of fraud.	2	4	4	23	65	85	42

6. If you would like to be able to place greater reliance on your company's internal audit function for any of the items in Question 5, or any other activities, please describe them below:

_____
_____
_____
_____
_____
_____
_____

7. The primary responsibility of the director of internal auditing in this company is to: (Check one)
    - 60 The company's audit committee
    - 32 The company's chief executive officer
    - 87 The audit committee and chief executive officer equally
    - 47 Some other (Please explain) _____

_____
_____

8. The audit committee should meet with the director of internal auditing with no other members of management present: (Check one)

    65 Annually
    71 Semi-annually
    49 Quarterly
    5 Monthly
    6 Never
    33 Other (Please explain) _____

9. Please indicate the extent to which you agree or disagree with each of the items below using the following scale:

Strongly Agree SA	Agree A	Neither Agree nor Disagree N	Disagree D	Strongly Disagree SD

	SA	A	N	D	SD
a. The audit committee has had a direct impact on the amount of resources allocated to the internal audit function.	66	107	39	11	7
b. Internal audit possesses sufficient independence to fulfill its function.	99	116	11	4	0
c. Internal audit receives adequate support from management.	101	117	8	4	0
d. A periodic oral report from the director of internal auditing is all that the audit committee needs from him unless unusual occurrences take place.	14	60	15	88	53
e. The audit committee should have access to the director of internal auditing for special assignments:					
With management's consent	42	69	17	23	18
Without management's consent	72	66	14	29	12
f. The director of internal auditing should have authority to bring matters directly to the audit committee without notification to management when he deems this is necessary.	156	67	3	3	2

10. Which of the following statements best describes the attention given to recommendations by the internal audit department? (Check one)

    1 Recommendations by the internal audit department are a matter of record but there need be no internal audit follow-up on their implementation until the following audit.

    117 Recommendations made by the internal audit department must be answered in writing within a stated time period.

    73 Recommendations made by the internal audit department are maintained in an "open file" until settled by implementation or mutual agreement.

    21 Recommendations by the internal audit department must be complied with unless factually in error.

    10 Other (Please explain) _____

11. What, in your opinion, is the most important contribution that your internal audit department has provided for your company over the last few years? (Please describe)

12. What is the most important contribution that you expect your internal audit department to provide for your company over the next few years? (Please describe)

13. Please rate your internal audit department relative to other departments and activities in your company. (Check one)
    - 21 Very superior
    - 142 Superior
    - 62 Average
    - 1 Disappointing
    - 0 Very disappointing

14. What factors do you think most inhibit internal auditing from becoming more useful in your company than it is now: (Check as many items as apply)
    - 20 Narrow point of view of internal auditors.
    - 59 Inadequate appreciation by your company of internal audit capabilities.
    - 30 The company's historical experience with internal auditing.
    - 17 Limited ability of internal auditors.
    - 40 Lack of managerial perspective on the part of internal auditors.
    - 67 Inadequate supply of qualified internal audit personnel.
    - 41 Inadequate incentives for good people to become internal auditors in this company.
    - 5 Inadequate programs to keep internal auditors informed of current developments in auditing.
    - 30 Other (Please describe). _____

15. Are there any important areas or activities where internal audit could be more useful to the audit committee? (Please explain)

16. Please add any comments or observations you think might be appropriate in explaining your views about internal auditing or which might be relevant to our research in ways not specifically addressed in the questionnaire.

Thank you for your cooperation.

Appendix B

Discussion Paper for Seminar Participants

To: Participants in IIA's Research Seminars on *The Influence of Current Developments on Internal Auditing*
From: R.K. Mautz and R.H. Colson
Subject: Discussion paper for research seminars

Thank you for accepting an invitation to one of our research seminars. Our purpose in holding them is to expose our preliminary findings and to obtain your views and the views of others on those findings. Attached is a discussion paper that summarizes what we believe to be the major issues emerging from responses to our questionnaires. The paper also includes some of the questionnaire data.

Please read the paper carefully before the meeting date. Make notes of any comments or questions you may have. During the seminar, we will ask you to comment on as many of the specific issues as we can cover. We also hope that you and others present will suggest additional issues, offer your views on our preliminary conclusions, cite experiences or other studies you believe are relevant to our work, and in any other ways you think desirable help us reach valid conclusions.

Our experience with similar seminars in the past has been positive. We expect a free exchange of views and experiences, inlcuding some differences of opinion. Please do not hesitate to speak candidly. We may quote your remarks in our finished report, but there will be no attribution of comments to any identifiable person. If previous seminars offer a precedent, you may count on an interesting and rewarding session.

Only the most relevant questionnaire data are presented in our discussion paper. If you have questions about other portions of the seminar, bring them with you; and we will try to have complete data available so that we can respond to your questions.

Purpose of the Project

Any interested observer of business is aware of a number of recent developments and events that have had an influence on internal auditing. Research is not necessary to tell us anything so obvious, but it can help us understand and anticipate the probable full impact that developments such as the following might have on internal auditing:
- The increased utilization of audit committees.
- The Foreign Corrupt Practices Act of 1977.

- The rapid and continuing application of computers to business needs.
- Continuing diversification of activity within companies.
- Increasing size of companies under a single management.
- Geographic distribution of corporate activities.

Some effects of each of these are readily anticipated. Audit committees will provide additional support for the internal audit function, will call upon it for service from time to time, should bring to the internal audit function increased recognition and opportunity for service, and may claim a degree of loyalty from the internal audit function that conflicts with its loyalty to the chief executive.

The FCPA has also increased the attention given to internal auditing, has increased the support available for that activity, and has opened opportunities for increased internal audit services.

As computers find more uses within business corporations and as technological progress expands the nature and the variety of their usefulness, internal auditors must increase their understanding of them. Computers are influencing the ways in which some business activities are performed as well as the ways in which they are recorded. This may have an influence on the company organization, which, in turn, influences the internal auditor's work.

Diversification within a company, whether resulting from acquisitions or other causes, also complicates internal auditors' duties. Auditors now must frequently be experts in more than one industry. When the need for auditing know-how, computer expertise, and a variety of industry knowledge are all required for competent performance, the educational problems of training internal auditors have increased significantly.

As companies increase in size, many of the segments become so large that a segment's chief executive officer finds need for an internal audit staff of his[1] own. Thus, we find internal auditors working at more than one level within the company: some attached to segment headquarters and some to the company's headquarters.

Geographic distribution of corporate activities increases management's control problems. The farther from headquarters, the more difficult the maintenance of effective control. When the geographic distribution also includes international activities, cultural and language difficulties compound the control problem. From such matters as the necessity for extended periods of travel, communication difficulties, and the necessity to become familiar with income tax and other regulations in a number of countries, internal auditors find the complexity of their tasks increasing.

The combined effect of all these events and developments will vary greatly form one company to another. Any one of them can, in a specific circumstance, have a pronounced effect. All together, they can produce profound problems for internal auditors. Our intention is to identify and discuss as many of these problems as we can.

---

[1]Throughout this paper, use of a masculine pronoun is intended to include both genders.

Research Program

The first step in our research consisted of visits to companies to discuss with selected directors of internal auditing the nature of their duties as they saw them, thereby to obtain a more intimate understanding of how leading members of The Institute saw their responsibilities, organized their departments, and proceeded with their work. At the conclusion of these visits, we proceeded to the second step: the development of questionnaires designed to obtain information relevant to our purpose. We sought to obtain from each company which had volunteered to participate in the research five questionnaires addressed as follows:
1. Director of internal auditing.
2. Representative sample of members of the director's staff.
3. Immediate supervisor of the director of internal auditing.
4. A member of the company's audit committee.
5. The company's external auditor.

Returns of useable questionnaires were:

Directors	330
Staff members	1,240
Senior management	266
Audit committee members	232
Independent CPAs/CAs	277
Companies with 100 percent response:	
All five questionnaires	176
All relevant questionnaires	254

Responses from the questionnaires returned have been tabulated and are in process of analysis which will continue for some time. We have identified a number of issues and possible responses. The purpose of this seminar is to examine these issues and to obtain additional views and experiences. Following the seminars, we will review our conclusions and prepare a final report. The amount and the variety of information obtained are such that only certain portions can be included in this paper.

The Major Issues

Because our emphasis is directed at the future of internal auditing, our attention in this paper will be on four major issues:
1. The role of internal auditing.
2. The appropriate relationships between the internal audit function and other groups and interests within the company.
3. The readiness of internal auditing to expand or change its emphasis.
4. The adequacy of support available to internal auditing.

These four issues are separable, but they are also closely related. Consequently, we find difficulty in addressing them independently of one another. From time to time, we find it necessary to consider the implications that each has for the others, although we will discuss them individually insofar as possible.

The Issue of Role

Does internal auditing have a single role or a multiple role with one dominant activity? Does it consist of an indeterminate number of unrelated services, no one of which is essential? Is there a common thread of interest through all internal audit work? Can such a thread be identified?

Internal auditing now appears to be a collection of different activities utilized to a varying degree. Part III of our director's questionnaire, Questions A to C, lists 33 activities sometimes included within the scope of work performed by an internal audit department. The activities listed range from "make (as opposed to review) bank reconciliations" and "count cash funds" to "consult with management about proposed changes in the company's organizational structure" and "review the appropriateness of performance evaluation measures for company divisions, departments, branches, etc."

Respondents were requested to indicate the extent to which their internal audit departments perform the following activities on a scale that included: never performed, rarely performed, occasionally performed, normally performed but occasionally omitted, normally performed and rarely omitted, and always performed.

Every activity listed was checked "always performed" by some significant number of directors. All but three activities were also checked "never performed" by a significant number of directors. Every activity except these three had multiple responses in every category in the scale. Differences in the responses present some interesting contrasts. For example, the responses to item 7, count cash funds, were:

Response	Percentage
Never Performed	9.0
Rarely Performed	21.0
Occasionally Performed	28.1
Normally Performed but Occasionally Omitted	12.0
Normally Performed and Rarely Omitted	12.7
Always Performed	17.2

A first review of the responses to the question leads one to the conclusion that there is no apparent pattern of activities or responsibilities in the duties assigned to and performed by internal audit departments. Industry differences, the specific needs of companies, and perhaps the absence of a strong and unifying conceptual foundation for internal auditing may each contribute to this impressive diversity.

Cluster analysis. This apparent lack of any overall pattern results partly from the presence in the responses of a number of different patterns of activity. A statistical technique described as "cluster analysis" organizes the respondents into groups of companies with similar patterns of activity. Cluster analysis is a technique for dividing a given population into groups or clusters on the basis of a number of characteristics which individuals in the population might or might not have in common. We took the 24 parts of Question A in Part III of the director's questionnaire and categorized them by nature under the following groups:

	Parts of Question A
Accounting compliance	1, 2

Performing routine accounting control	6, 7
Reviewing compliance with control	4, 8, 10, 24, 19, 20
Performing control procedures	6, 7, 12, 16, 17, 18
Adminstrative assignments	11, 13, 15a, 22, 23
Accounting consultation	3
Controls consultation	5, 9, 14, 15b, 21

The scaling called for in responding to the question was converted to numbers as follows:

NP		Never Performed	1
RP		Rarely Performed	2
OP		Occasionally Performed	3
NP — OO		Normally Performed — Occasionally Omitted	4
NP — RO		Normally Performed — Rarely Omitted	5
AP		Always Performed	6

Note that, even if an activity were never performed, it still received a numerical amount of 1. This should be kept in mind in interpreting the results of the cluster analysis. The maximum variance possible is from 1 to 6 for a range of 5. Note also that the numbers assigned as weights are not intended to suggest the relative quality or desirability of an activity. Rather, it shows the respondent's propensity to perform that activity.

Through application of a computer program for cluster analysis, the 330 director's questionnaire companies were found to fall into eight groups as follows:

		Propensity to Supply						
		Performance of			Review of		Consultation on	
Cluster	Number of Companies in Cluster	Routine Accounting	Control Procedures	Administrative Tasks	Accounting Compliance	Compliance with Control Procedures	Accounting Matters	Control Matters
1	25	4.7400	5.2107	2.8740	4.3400	4.4827	5.0000	4.2956
2	23	4.6087	3.2517	1.7913	2.5217	3.3782	4.2609	3.3816
3	74	2.2635	4.8268	2.6995	2.6148	3.9371	3.2027	3.8004
4	61	2.1475	2.9658	2.0642	2.4098	3.2760	3.2295	3.3916
5	40	1.8125	2.8656	2.2250	3.2375	3.5192	5.3000	3.3430
6	57	2.5789	4.7014	3.1877	3.7895	4.4426	5.1053	4.1579
7	36	2.5694	3.6057	2.7014	5.1944	3.9583	3.8611	3.3729
8	14	2.0357	2.9031	1.3809	1.3214	2.7239	1.6429	2.8026
Total	330							
All companies		2.6166	3.9278	2.5030	3.2060	3.8047	4.0060	3.6504

*Numbers in the rows of the matrix are the means for that cluster of the internal audit activity in the columns.

**1. Never Performed
  2. Rarely performed
  3. Occasionally performed
  4. Normally performed — occasionally omitted
  5. Normally performed — rarely omitted
  6. Always performed

What is one to make of these results? We emphasize that this table is nothing more than one way of describing similarities and dissimilarities in directors' responses. It reveals differences in the activities performed by audit departments and their propensity to perform each identified type of activity.

It is interesting to note that cluster 1 includes 25 companies that have a high propensity to perform almost every activity listed. Their tendency to perform routine accounting and control procedures is matched with strong performance of review and consultation. They are well above the group mean on all accounts.

Cluster 5, consisting of 40 companies, does the least in performance of routine accounting, control procedures, or administrative assignments. One might expect this to be balanced by more attention to review and consultation. This is not so. Companies in that cluster stand out only in their propensity to consult on accounting matters. On every other count, they are close to or below average.

Cluster 8, with only 14 companies, appears to be the least aggressive of any group in attempting to take on duties; yet its emphasis is on control procedures rather than on performance, seemingly the least demanding activity.

Interesting as the cluster analysis is, it does not point to any one activity of internal audit departments that stands out as a center of interest. The impression of a variety of services which may be utilized in differing combinations remains.

Other Indications of Diversity. Two other questions in Part III of the director's questionnaire also contribute to the conclusion that present practice in internal audit departments is an unspecified kind of activity. Question 25 asked respondents to allocate 100 points across the following four activities in such a way as to indicate each activity's proportion of the respondents' total audit effort. The results were:

Activity	Percentage
Performance of internal control procedures	10
Testing the work of others for compliance with company's internal control requirements	41
Evaluation of the appropriateness of present internal controls	32
Initiation of new or additional internal controls	17
Total	100

Question 27 listed five activities and requested respondents to estimate the percentage of total audit time currently spent on each activity. The results follow:

Activity	Percentage
Detection of errors and irregularities	20
Monitoring controls established by management to obtain compliance with company policy	27
Evaluation of the efficiency or the effectiveness with which company goals are obtained	14
Monitoring controls intended to assure that published financial statements are in accordance with standards and that assets are safeguarded	32
Evaluation of the effectiveness of management's operating and financial decisions	7
Total	100

Implications of Reported Diversity. The extent of diversity indicated in the responses to our questionnaire raises some unavoidable questions. For example, what constitutes an internal audit if some auditors never do what other auditors always do? Is there within the total range of services performed some pattern of activities that is generally agreed to constitute an internal audit on which a report may be issued? If so, how can that pattern be identified and established so that those who call for an internal audit or rely on a report based on an internal audit can judge the usefulness of it?

The scope of the work undertaken by internal auditors and the variety in the combinations of these several tasks indicated within the eight clusters encourage inquiry about the common interest of internal auditors. What is it that constitutes their common interest? Which of these activities is essential to internal auditing and which are peripheral or perhaps unrelated? How can one define internal auditing as an activity unless there is a central thread?

The Issue of Relationship

One is always tempted to draw analogies between internal auditing and independent auditing and to use the independent auditor-client relationship as a model by which to judge internal audit independence. We believe a more fruitful approach is to recognize the circumstances and conditions as substantively different. The independent auditor performs in an environment with established professional requirements and legal obligations quite foreign to the internal auditor. On the other hand, the internal auditor faces a range of services and complexities of interrelationships quite unknown to the independent auditor.

Two aspects of the internal auditor's relationships appear crucial. One has to do with the familiar auditor-auditee relationship and the other with the organizational position of the internal auditor. The auditor-auditee relationship requires that the auditor have unhampered access to all information sources relevant to his purpose as an auditor, complete freedom to express his findings, and assurance that the results of his examination will not be ignored. It also requires that the auditor have no conflict of interest that might discourage him from utilizing all sources of information relevant to his purpose, expressing his findings candidly and effectively, and demanding the attention for them that they merit.

Position within the company's organizational structure has much to do with the internal auditor's ability to be effective, but it is not the only factor. The attitudes toward internal auditing expressed by other key people in the company also have an impact. We are concerned as a result of our questionnaire responses with the internal auditor's relationship to:
- The company's audit committee.
- Senior management.
- The company's controller.
- The company's management information systems department.

Relationship with the Company's Audit Committee. For some internal audit departments, an active audit committee is a new and complicating factor in the performance of the internal audit function. For other departments, the relationship is well established. Responses to the audit committee's questionnaire provide us with the following information:

The primary responsibility of the director of internal auditing in this company is to:

	Percentage
The company's audit committee	25.5
The company's chief executive officer	13.8
The audit committee and the chief executive officer equally	41.3
Some other	19.4
Total	100.0

Sixty-nine percent of 199 responses rated "an investigative arm for the company's audit committee" as an "important" or "very important" duty of the internal audit department; 73 percent found "an investigative arm for senior management" equally important.

Senior management is responsible for operations. Audit committees are typically composed of nonofficer directors who are expected to have policy rather than operational responsibilities. Occasionally, although probably rarely, nonofficer directors find themselves critical of management. Can an internal audit department meet a dual responsibility under all circumstances?

To the question "Does the director of internal auditing have an explicit invitation to bring any concerns he may have directly to the audit committee without prior notification of management?" 88 percent of 200 respondents answered affirmatively. Of these, the following experience in bringing such concern to the audit committee was noted:

Within the past year	45 responses
Within the past five years but not the past year	29 responses
Never to your knowledge	87 responses
Other	14 responses

To the question of whether the audit committee should have access to the director of internal auditing for special assignments, 69 percent of 143 audit committee respondents agreed that the audit committee should have access with management's consent, whereas 69.5 percent of 164 audit committee members agreed or strongly agreed that the audit committee should have access to the director of internal auditing without management's consent.

Ninety-six percent of 201 audit committee respondents agreed or strongly agreed that the director of internal auditing should have authority to bring matters directly to the audit committee without notification of management when he deems that is necessary. Audit committee members prefer to meet regularly with the director of internal auditing without any other members of management present with the following frequency:

	Percentage
Annually	29.1
Semiannually	32.2
Quarterly	21.6
Monthly	.5
Never	3.0
Other	13.6
Total	100.0

Responses to the director's questionnaire present a different picture.

- Fifty-three percent of 307 directors "regularly meet with the audit committee without other members of management present."
- Forty-seven percent of 307 directors "never receive direct requests from the audit committee for special assignment work to be done for the audit committee," and 50 percent of those responding in the affirmative have undertaken such work within the past year.
- Fifty-five percent of 155 directors "feel obligated to report requests to other members of management if they have not already been informed."
- Ninety-two percent of 301 directors "have the right to take specific matters to the audit committee on a confidential basis."

Given the close working relationship that a director of internal auditing is likely to have with members of senior management, some difficulty in meeting audit committee expectations under certain conditions is not unlikely.

Responses to the following questions provide some insight into the kinds of matters that directors of internal auditing would take directly to the audit committee.

	Directors of Internal Auditing	
	Would Take (%)	Would Not Take (%)
Significant misuse of corporate assets by a corporate officer	75.6	24.4
Noncompliance with capital-budgeting requirements by the vice president of manufacturing	5.2	94.8
A shortage of the cash receipts from a substantial branch office which the controller acknowledges but contends is not of sufficient importance to bring to the attention of the audit committee	41.4	58.6
Information that leads you to believe that the chief financial officer is pressuring the controller to make some accounting changes in order to increase current earnings	58.1	41.9
Failure by your superior to fund three new internal audit positions which you as director of internal auditing feel are essential	48.3	51.7
Reduction by your superior of funds available for internal audit training	25.8	74.2

We might summarize the relationship between internal audit departments and members of corporate audit committees as still new and developing in many cases. Some audit committee members apparently feel a need for some amount of staff assistance in satisfying themselves that their responsibility for adequate internal control measures has been fulfilled. To obtain such help, they turn to internal auditing. Other audit committee members consider internal auditing to be a part of corporate management's staff and not sufficiently independent to serve the audit committee well. Still others are willing to share the internal audit department with management. No doubt some part of this difference is influenced by the nature of past relationships between the audit committee members and management.

From the internal audit point of view, an unavoidable question is whether it can adequately serve the audit committee and senior management at the same time. Does its loyalty to management necessarily conflict with the needs of the audit committee? Or does access to the board of directors through the audit committee effectively counterbalance its apparent dependence on management for position, promotion, and pay? Responses to Question 9 of Part I of the director's questionnaire may provide a clue

To whom are you responsible for each of the following purposes? (Check as many items in each column as apply.)

	For Audit Reporting Purposes (%)	For Salary and Promotion Purposes (%)
Audit Committee/Board of Directors	78.5	6.4
Chief Executive Officer	41.8	32.4
Chief Financial Officer	36.1	37.6
Controller	11.5	10.6
Treasurer	3.6	3.6
Administrative Vice President	5.8	5.5
Operating Unit-Line Management	4.8	0.3
Other	10.9	15.2

Relationship with Senior Management. The relationship of the internal audit department with senior management raises some additional questions. As implied in the preceding section, internal audit's relationship with the audit committee also affects its relationship with senior management. One possibility is that it will be seen to have a joint responsibility to both the audit committee and senior management which on occasion may provide some interesting decisions for the director of internal auditing.

In addition, responses to the director's questionnaire assert a desire and imply the ability on the part of the internal audit department to undertake both of the following evaluations:

- Performance evaluation — assesses the efficiency or the effectiveness with which company goals are attained.
- Decision-making review — evaluates the effectiveness of management's operating and financial decisions.

Both of these are managerial activities performed at the highest level of management as well as at lower levels. Responses to the director's Question 27 of Part III asserts that significant amounts of internal audit time are now being spent on these activities. Responses to Question 28 indicate the expectation that more will be spent in the future.

	Percentage of Internal Audit Time	
	Now	In Five Years
Detection of errors and irregularities	20	16
Monitoring management control	27	26
Performance evaluation	14	18
Monitoring internal accounting control	32	28
Decision-making review	7	12

In addition, Question 29a in the director's questionnaire shows that 7 percent of internal audit time, when allocated among organizational units, is spent in auditing corporate senior management.

To the extent that internal auditing does review the performance and decisions of senior management, the question of a satisfactory auditor-auditee relationship is crucial. The following questions present information relevant to evaluating that relationship. All are taken from the director's questionnaire, Part I.

10. What is the organizational level of the director of internal auditing in relation to that of:

	Above (%)	Below (%)	Equal to (%)
Chief Financial Officer	3.5	85.3	11.2
Controller	15.7	37.7	46.6
Treasurer	10.7	48.9	40.4

11. What is the salary level of the director of internal auditing in relation to that of:

	Above (%)	Below (%)	Equal to (%)
Chief Financial Officer	0.3	97.7	2.0
Controller	9.2	69.3	21.5
Treasurer	8.0	73.5	18.5

The apparent organizational relationship of internal auditors to members of senior management unavoidably raises questions about the effectiveness with which internal audit personnel can review management decisions and performance.

The following data point up some of the other complexities of internal audit's relationship with management:

14. If some employees performing auditing functions are part of operating units, to whom are they responsible for each of the following purposes? (Check as many items in each column as necessary.)

	For Assignment of Duties (%)	For Audit Reporting Purposes (%)	For Salary and Promotion Purposes (%)
Corporate Director of Internal Audit	42.1	49.7	39.4
Other Executives at Corporate Headquarters	3.2	3.4	4.9
Corporate Audit Committee	1.6	4.8	0.0
Operating Unit Management	53.1	42.1	55.7
	100.0	100.0	100.0

22. Please check the level of influence that each of the following has on the content and scope of your company's annual internal audit program, using the scale provided:

	Influence (Percentage)				
	Very Substantial	Substantial	Significant	Some	None
Director of Internal Audit	82.8	14.3	1.6	1.3	0.0
Controller	2.7	8.9	17.2	46.7	24.5
Chief Financial Officer	9.5	15.1	22.3	43.3	9.8
Corporate Audit Committee	12.3	18.3	24.0	39.0	6.4
Chief Executive Officer	12.1	15.6	21.0	40.1	11.2
External CPA/CA	4.8	10.9	29.7	48.9	5.7
Operating Management	12.9	10.1	16.1	25.8	29.1

The views of senior management on the reliability of internal auditing on some of these same issues were requested in the senior management questionnaire. Responses to the following questions show that some members of senior management place great reliance on internal audit for these services and others do not.

3. Please indicate the extent to which senior management currently relies on the work of the internal audit function with regard to each of the following items:

	\multicolumn{6}{c}{Extent of Reliance (%)}	
	None	Very Low	Low	Neither Low nor High	High	Very High	Total
(b) Evaluation of the effectiveness of management's							
(i) operating decisions	15.0	19.6	16.2	23.3	21.3	4.6	0.0
(ii) financial decisions	15.0	17.1	19.6	27.9	15.8	4.6	0.0
(c) Integrity of company officers and employees	1.7	3.3	5.8	24.0	32.6	29.3	3.3
(d) Efficiency and effectiveness with which company goals are attained	10.7	8.7	20.7	37.2	18.6	4.1	0.0

The following question, also from the senior management questionnaire, changed the query to the extent that senior management would like to rely on internal auditing for the same services.

4. Using the same scale as in Question 3, please indicate the extent to which senior management would like to rely on the work of internal auditing with regard to each of the following items. (Your response here could be that you would like to place more, less, or the same degree of reliance on the work of internal auditing as indicated in Question 3.)

	\multicolumn{6}{c}{Extent of Reliance (%)}	
	None	Very Low	Low	Neither Low nor High	High	Very High	Total
(b) Evaluation of the effectiveness of management's							
(i) operating decisions	6.4	10.6	15.7	25.8	28.8	11.9	0.8
(ii) financial decisions	8.0	9.3	15.2	26.2	28.7	11.8	0.8
(c) integrity of company officers and employees	1.3	2.1	3.0	19.3	30.2	37.4	6.7
(d) Efficiency and effectiveness with which company goals are attained	6.3	7.6	11.4	27.3	29.8	16.8	0.8

Relationship with the Company's Controller's. Internal audit's relationship with the controller's office should, in theory, depend on two factors:
1. The division of responsibility for internal control between the controller and internal audit.
2. Whether the controller is functionally responsible for corporate accounting or stands in a staff position advisory to the CEO.

One possibility is that the controller and his staff accept responsibility for the performance of internal control measures, however broadly internal control is defined, that internal audit serves only in a monitoring role to assure that the measures supposedly in place are being performed effectively, and that they are adequate for the company's needs. Another possibility is that the internal auditor's staff might be expected to participate in the functional performance of internal control measures rather than in their monitoring only.

If the corporate controller is not functionally involved in corporate accounting or in the performance of internal control measures, the internal audit department could fall within the controller's jurisdiction and still be adequately independent of the functions it monitors to have a satisfactory auditor-auditee relationship. On the other hand, if the controller is functionally responsible for these duties, an internal audit department under the controller's supervision would appear to lack audit independence. Because none of our questions bear directly on these points, we seek the experience and advice of seminar participants on this issue.

Relationship with the Company's Management Information Systems Department. In earlier research on internal control, we found two points of view expressed by internal auditors regarding their relationship with management information systems departments. One was that, to maintain appropriate audit independence, they refrained from participating in any way with MIS personnel in the specification, design, development, or testing of EDP. The alternative attitude was that they desired to participate as fully as their resources permitted in those same activities to assure that completed systems incorporated useful and auditable controls.

Questions 32 and 33 of Part III of the director's questionnaire provides the following information which has some implications for the issue of relationship and the importance of specialized training in MIS concepts and procedures for internal audit personnel:

> Question 32. Increasing reliance on computers for information processing purposes has created a source of internal control difficulty for many companies' internal audit groups. The statements below characterize several common responses to the internal audit problems associated with assuring internal control over EDP activities. Please consider these statements and place the number corresponding to the response which best describes your company's current EDP audit strategy in the space provided at the end of the statement. Please use the "other" option only if none of the statements describes the essence of your company's current response.
>
> Question 33. Many companies have not yet settled on a permanent response to the EDP audit problem. Which of the statements in question 32 would best characterize your view of what EDP auditing will be like in your company in the future?

	EDP Audit Strategy	
	Now (%)	In Future (%)
Your company has taken no special action to assure internal control over EDP systems.	7.2	2.2
Your company has a group of EDP specialists (not in the internal audit department) which has the responsibility to assure internal control over EDP systems.	6.9	2.9
Your company has a group of EDP specialists in the internal audit department which works independently to assure internal control over EDP systems.	35.9	25.3
Your company has a group of EDP specialists which works in teams with non-EDP internal auditors to assure internal control over EDP systems	21.1	19.8

Your company has a group of EDP specialists which advises,

consults, and trains internal auditors to assure internal control over EDP systems	4.7	11.2
All your company's internal auditors have sufficient EDP expertise to assure internal control over EDP systems as part of their normal auditing activities.	7.2	33.2
Your company's internal auditors do not have special EDP expertise, nor do they need it to adequately perform their internal audit duties.	2.8	0.6
Other	14.2	4.8
	100.0	100.0

The Issue of Readiness

A profession facing opportunities and even pressures for significant changes in its responsibilities and activities would be wise to give some consideration to the readiness of its members to make substantive changes before charting its course for the future. Readiness, in the sense that it is used here, is a combination of competence or ability and motivation.

We must be careful not to place emphasis on any one question. Nevertheless, questions 25 and 26 of Part III of the director's questionnaire provide cause for concern. The first, as already reported, asks respondents to indicate on a percentage basis how they now spend their audit effort; Question 26 asks how they think that time should be spent. The following summary contrasts the responses to these two questions:

	Audit Effort (Percentage)	
	Now	Should Be
Performing internal control procedures	10	9
Testing the work of others for compliance with company's internal control requirements	41	41
Evaluating the appropriateness of present internal controls	32	33
Initiating new or additional internal controls	17	17
Totals	100	100

In the face of what appear to some observers to be substantive changes affecting internal auditing, directors appear remarkably satisfied that no changes should be made.

Some general information about the educational and experience qualifications of directors and staff members gleaned from a number of questions is found in the following summary.

Extent of education	Directors (%)	Staff (%)
High school	3	4
Institute or college diploma	4	6
Some university training	7	5
Bachelor's degree	59	67
Master's degree or higher	27	18
Totals	100	100
Major field of study for university degrees (bachelor's degree)		
Accounting	69	65
General business	20	18
Engineering	1	1

Computer science	0	1
Arts or science	10	15
Totals	100	100

Some encouraging information is found in the directors' evaluations of the quality of people now coming into internal auditing.

18. In comparison with hirings in other areas of your company, recently new entrants into the internal audit department have been:

	Recently New Hirings (%)	Recent Transfers (%)
Substantially above average potential	23.9	16.5
Above average potential	59.7	59.8
Average potential	16.1	20.5
Below average potential	0.0	2.7
Substantially below average potential	0.3	.5
Totals	100	100

Some of the questions in the staff questionnaire provide a clue as to how entrants to internal auditing view their experience in it and how long other expect to stay in this activity.

8. If your were transferred to the internal audit department from some other department of your company,

(a) Did you view your transfer to the internal audit department as:

	Affirmative (%)
A promotion	31.3
A lateral move	16.9
Part of a training program	16.3
Opportunity leading to a management career	31.7
A "dead end"	0.8
Other	3.0
	100.0

(b) Was your transfer to the internal audit department accompanied by:

	Affirmative (%)
Salary improvement	70.4
An increase in title or rank	55.4

14. Do you plan to remain in internal auditing throughout your career?

	Directors (%)	Staff (%)
Yes	38	24
No	68	76

(a) How long do you expect to stay in the internal audit department?

	Directors (%)	Staff (%)
Less than one year	3.6	7.5
1-3 years	55.2	54.0
4-6 years	32.8	30.6
More than 6 years	8.4	7.9
	100.0	100.0

(b) What type of work do you expect to transfer to if you leave the internal audit department?

	Directors (%)	Staff (%)
Accounting	19.0	28.8
Finance	28.7	27.4
Production-engineering	0.0	0.9
Marketing	0.0	2.0
Personnel	0.0	1.0
Line management	30.3	16.4
EDP	2.0	8.8
Other	20.0	14.7

Perhaps the most encouraging information in these responses is the number of respondents who consider internal auditing to hold promise for a career in management.

The Issue of Support

One of the most interesting results of the questionnaires is the strong support for internal auditing evidenced by the responses of senior managers, audit committee members, and independent CPAs. A very important indication of support is the treatment accorded recommendations of the internal audit department. The following question was included in the three questionnaires:

Which of the following statements best describes the attention given to recommendations by the internal audit department of this company?

	Senior Management (%)	Audit Committee Member (%)	Independent CPA (%)
Recommendations made by the internal audit department are a matter of record, but there need be no internal follow-up on their implementation until the following audit.	3.5	0.5	6.9
Recommendations made by the internal audit department must be answered in writing within a stated time.	56.2	54.8	63.4
Recommendations made by the internal audit department are maintained in an open file until settled by implementation or mutual agreement.	31.0	35.0	20.7
Recommendations by the internal audit department must be complied with unless factually in error.	5.3	8.1	3.3
Other	4.0	1.6	5.7
Total	100.0	100.0	100.0

Another indication of support is found in the ratings given to the internal audit department in comparison with other departments of the company by senior management and members of the audit committee:

Please rate your internal audit department relative to other departments and activities in your company.

	Senior Management (%)	Audit Committee Member (%)
Very superior	7.5	9.2
Superior	46.7	61.9
Average	43.8	28.9
Disappointing	2.0	0.0
Very disappointing	0.0	0.0
Total	100.0	100.0

The following question was directed to senior management with the results noted:

How actively does senior management in your company support the internal audit function?

	Percentage
Very actively	38.4
Actively	45.0
Neither actively nor passively	14.1
Passively	2.5
Very passively	0.0
Total	100.0

Independent CPAs were asked to indicate the degree of reliance they placed on the work of internal auditors in the following question:

Please rate the degree to which you rely on the work of this company's internal audit function in audit matters related to forming your opinion.

	Percentage
Very high reliance	17.1
High reliance	48.4
Neither high nor low reliance	21.5
Low reliance	8.1
Very low reliance	2.0
No reliance	2.9
Total	100.0

The preceding responses evidence a high regard for internal audit quality.

The following question, asked of all three groups outside the internal audit department, seems especially relevant to possible improvement of the internal audit role and performance:

What factors most inhibit internal auditing from becoming more useful in your company than it now is: (Check as many items as apply.)

	Senior Management (%)	Audit Committee Member (%)	Independent CPA (%)
Narrow point of view of internal auditors.	17.7	7.8	10.8
Inadequate appreciation by your company of internal audit capabilities.	36.5	20.3	30.0
The company's historical experience with internal auditing.	23.7	11.6	22.7
Limited ability of internal auditors.	14.7	6.0	15.2
Lack of managerial perspective on the part of internal auditors.	27.4	13.8	19.1
Inadequate supply of qualified internal audit personnel.	21.8	26.7	26.7
Inadequate incentives for good people to become internal auditors in this company.	16.9	16.8	21.7
Inadequate programs to keep internal auditors informed of current developments in auditing.	3.4	2.2	5.8
Other	8.6	12.1	13.4

Issues for Comment and Discussion

We believe that these seminars can advance our research most effectively if participants will be prepared to respond or comment on the following questions closely related to these issues:

I. Can the role of internal auditing be defined with more precision than now found in the *Standards for the Practice of Internal Auditing* ?
   A. Does internal auditing have a single major role?
   B. Does internal auditing have alternate major roles?
   C. Does internal auditing unavoidably have multiple major roles?
      To aid in the discussion of this subject, we suggest the following possibilities: (Participants may wish to suggest others.)
      1. Internal auditing as a protection to senior management and the board.
         a. From the embarrassment and costs of errors and irregularities.
         b. From failure to meet legal requirements (including the FCPA). Responsibility for meeting the FCPA is, for internal accounting control, a relatively narrow term in the minds of many.
      2. Internal auditing as a means of improved management through recognition of management control as a company-wide activity requiring integrated planning, installing, monitoring, and reporting.
      3. Internal auditing as a staff of competent accountants and auditors available to management for the performance of accounting and control tasks, regular and special investigations, and conslutation to staff and operating personnel on:
         a. Financial matters.
         b. Operating and financial matters.
II. What should be the nature of internal audit relationships with the following interests in its work?
   A. The audit committee of the board.
      1. Is internal auditing primarily an investigative arm of the audit committee reporting and responsible to that committee?
      2. Is internal auditing a staff activity responsible to senior management but subject to review by the audit committee?
      3. Is internal auditing a staff activity responsible only to senior management?
   B. Senior management (see "A" above).
      1. How much independence can internal auditing have from senior management?
      2. At what levels can internal auditing review managerial performance and decisions effectively?
   C. The controller.
      1. How are the following responsibilities to be divided between the controller's office and internal auditing?
         a. Performing of transactions and other activities.

- b. Safeguarding assets.
- c. Accounting for transactions, other activities, and assets.
- d. Controlling procedures to provide assurance that transactions are conducted only as authorized, assets are safeguarded, and accounting is reliable.
- e. Monitoring control procedures.
  2. Are there conditions in which internal auditing can properly be included within the controller's responsibilities?
  D. The management information systems function
     1. To what extent should internal audit participate in specifying, designing, developing, and testing new systems?
     2. How is this best accomplished?
        a. Exchange of competent personnel.
        b. Development of experts.
        c. Other.
  E. Operating management.
     1. When operating units become of such size that unit management needs and has internal audit personnel on its staff, what relationship to the director of internal audit should unit internal auditors have?
     2. If internal auditors serve as consultants on accounting and control to unit operating and accounting personnel, does that have any effect on their independence in an audit capacity?
III. Is internal auditing likely to make any substantive changes in its present role in the foreseeable future?
   A. Is their any need? opportunity?
   B. Is internal auditing in a position to make a change?
      1. Recognition of opportunity?
      2. What are resources and constraints?
         a. Quality of personnel; short-term availability.
         b. Training and experience of personnel.
         c. Support of management.
         d. Motivation of personnel.
IV. What can internal auditing do to strengthen its usefulness and opportunities?
   A. Recruiting.
   B. Staff training.
   C. Staff utilization.
      1. Career planning.
   D. Research.
   E. Internal/public relations.

Appendix C

Differences in Audit Expenditures Across Industries
by Charles F. Klemstine

A considerable diversity in the amount of expenditures for internal and external auditing was reported by the respondents to our study. This diversity appears related to the fact that a variety of industries with different control and auditing requirements are represented. This appendix provides an analysis of the financial data presented in Chapter 3 classified by respondents' industries. It also includes some discussion of these differences.

Six broad industry categories are readily identified in the companies responding to our request for information. These are shown in Table C-1 together with their SIC codes and the number and the nationality of the companies. Responses from one or more companies from each of the two-digit SIC groups are included.

Company Expenditures for Audit Purposes

Three types of audit costs are examined in this report: (1) the average number of internal auditors per company, (2) total internal audit salaries, and (3) audit fees paid to independent accountants. Tables C-2 through C-7 show the relevant details within these three classes by industry category. Two tables are shown for each type of audit expenditure. The first presents the average figures for each year for each industry category. The second relates the expenditures to some measure of the size of the companies. Amounts for 1974 and 1977 (before the FCPA), 1978, 1981, and 1982 (after the FCPA), and projections for 1983 and 1984 provided by the respondents are shown for all industries so that trends can be examined.

Table C-1
Average Number of Internal Auditors per Company

Year	Manufacturing	Oil/Mining	Financial	Insurance	Utility	Retail/Service
1974	15.8	12.1	12.9	8.4	9.9	14.4
1977	18.1	13.7	14.6	10.2	11.6	18.4
1978	19.8	13.9	14.5	11.1	12.8	19.9
1981	22.7	18.0	16.3	12.3	14.9	21.2
1982	22.7	19.0	16.7	12.8	16.4	21.0
1983	23.3	19.1	17.4	13.2	17.0	21.5
1984	24.5	19.4	18.2	13.6	17.7	22.1

Table C-2
Distribution of Respondents by Industry

Category	Industries Represented by One or More Respondents	SIC Code	U.S.	Canada	Total	%
Manufacturing	Food	20	96	7	103	31
	Textile	22				
	Lumber/Wood	24				
	Furniture	25				
	Paper	26				
	Printing	27				
	Chemicals/Drugs	28				
	Rubber	30				
	Glass	32				
	Steel	33				
	Machinery	35				
	Electrical	36				
	Autos/Trucks/Aircraft	37				
Oil and Mining	Metal Mining	10	15	7	22	7
	Petroleum/Gas	13				
	Nonmetal Minerals	14				
	Petroleum Refining	29				
Financial	Banks	60	94	3	97	29
	Credit Institutions	61				
Insurance	Life/Property/Health	63	29	4	33	10
Utilities	Electric/Gas/Water	49	21	3	24	7
Retail/Service	Construction	15,16,17	45	6	51	16
	Air/Rail/Truck Freight	40,42,47				
	Wholesale Products	51				
	Retail Stores	52,53,54,58,59				
	Hotels/Motels	70				
	Advertising/Consulting	73				
	Motion Pictures	78				
			300	30	330	100

Just over 30 percent of the companies are in manufacturing. Slightly under 30 percent are financial institutions, mostly small banks. The remaining 40 percent are distributed among the other industries. Ten percent were Canadian companies. Because the small number of Canadian firms in each industry group may be unrepresentative, no breakdown between these groups is included in this appendix.

Table C-3
Average Number of Internal Auditors per 1,000 Employees

Year	Manufacturing	Oil/Mining	Financial	Insurance	Utility	Retail/Service
1974	.57	1.02	12.31	5.23	2.90	1.08
1977	.79	1.38	13.54	6.62	3.31	1.06
1978	.88	1.30	13.39	6.73	3.69	1.05
1981	1.27	1.72	13.75	7.56	4.33	1.22
1982	1.31	1.83	13.97	7.65	4.40	1.28
1983	1.33	1.80	14.21	8.13	4.55	1.41
1984	1.37	1.95	15.09	8.73	4.72	1.51

Table C-2 shows that the average number of auditors differs across industries, although perhaps not as much as one might expect. Manufacturing and the retail/service industries employ more auditors, whereas the insurance industry employs the fewest internal auditors per company. As a percentage of the workforce, however, internal auditors in the insurance companies outnumber those in all other industry groups except the financial industry (see Table C-3). Table C-2 also shows that the number of internal auditors in all industries has increased from 1974 through 1982. The average size of the internal audit department in the manufacturing and retail/service categories grew more than 40 percent during this time period. It grew more than 50 percent in the oil/mining and insurance industry companies and more than 60 percent in utility companies. The actual and projected growth rates across all the categories from 1974 to 1984 averaged 5 percent per year. Only the oil/mining firms appear to have had more growth in the three-year period following passage of the FCPA (1978-81) than in the prior three-year period (1974-77).

This growth in internal audit positions comes at a time when total firm employment is not growing or is slightly declining in some industries. This can be seen in Table C-3, where the average number of auditors per 1,000 employees is shown. Except for a few minor decreases, there is a steady increase in the number of internal auditors per 1,000 employees. This increase is expected to continue in all industries for the next several years.

Another interesting observation from Table C-3 is the number of internal auditors employed in financial institutions, even though the participating organizations are primarily small banks. In terms of auditors employed, the average financial organization appears similar to many of the other industries in Table C-2. Only the insurance industry appears to employ fewer auditors than banks over the years reported. As a percentage of the firm's workforce, however, internal auditors constitute a substantial portion, thereby reflecting the generally greater need for and emphasis on control and auditing in that industry.

Expenditures on internal audit salaries are shown in tables C-4 and C-5.

Table C-4
Average Expenditures on Internal Audit Salaries (in thousands)

Year	Manufacturing	Oil/Mining	Financial	Insurance	Utility	Retail/Service
1974	$385.6	$235.8	$166.8	$108.1	$147.7	$272.8
1977	501.8	347.4	255.4	151.2	217.2	426.8
1978	590.1	400.3	299.7	168.3	292.5	496.0
1981	875.5	646.4	451.7	248.9	495.2	667.5
1982	961.4	829.5	487.3	274.2	570.9	745.9
1983	1,046.7	909.4	522.8	308.8	641.4	831.7
1984	1,151.4	976.5	577.2	338.7	700.5	923.8

Table C-5
Average Expenditures on Internal Audit Salaries per $1,000,000 of Revenue

Year	Manufacturing	Oil/Mining	Financial	Insurance	Utility	Retail/Service
1974	$246.4	$104.2	$2,783.8	$666.5	$411.9	$231.3
1977	254.8	249.8	2,868.8	672.2	337.7	252.8
1978	288.7	266.3	2,651.7	616.0	405.9	257.0
1981	334.5	277.4	6,167.7	635.5	651.6	237.9
1982	372.8	291.4	7,041.9	684.8	641.0	246.0
1983	363.8	276.0	5,243.6	633.2	657.4	257.0
1984	366.3	264.3	4,758.7	641.8	655.2	261.8

All industry groups show substantial increases from 1974 to 1982 and projected increases for 1983 and 1984. The oil/mining and utility firms have more than tripled their expenditures over this eight-year period. All other groups have more than doubled theirs.

In terms of dollars spent, the manufacturing group projects average expenditures of more than $1,000,000 per company on internal audit salaries by 1984. The oil/mining and retail service groups will average almost as much. Although the insurance industry projects less dollar growth, the average company in that industry expects to spend over $300,000 per year on internal audit salaries by 1984. The financial group is also on the lower end, expecting expenditures for audit salaries of just under $600,000 on the average. Some of these disparities, no doubt, result from differences in the sizes of the companies in one industry as compared with the others.

As evident in Table C-5, there are substantial differences across the industry categories in internal audit salaries as a percentage of company revenues. The manufacturing, oil/mining, and retail/service industries are larger in terms of revenues per company than are the companies in the other industries. They also show the highest totals for internal audit salaries but are the lowest in terms of salary expenditures per million dollars of revenue. Financial institutions are on the low end of the spectrum in salary dollars spent, but they spend a relatively high percentage of their revenues on internal audit salaries. In all years, as a percentage of revenues, financial institutions spent considerably more than any other industry group. In 1982, financial companies averaged .7 of one percent of their gross revenues on internal audit salaries.

Once again, some of this difference results from disparities among industries in the average revenues of the member companies. In 1982, the manufacturing firms had average revenues of $2.7 billion per company, while the financial institutions had average revenues per company of less than $600 million.

Expenditures on auditing performed by independent accountants are reported in tables C-6 and C-7.

Table C-6
Average Expenditures on External Audit Fees (in thousands)

Year	Manufacturing	Oil/Mining	Financial	Insurance	Utility	Retail/Service
1974	$ 519.9	$434.4	$112.4	$ 93.6	$115.1	$238.9
1977	653.1	536.3	179.3	139.4	144.7	366.8
1978	751.5	655.6	206.7	161.6	149.3	394.4
1981	885.0	737.1	271.4	194.4	206.2	483.3
1982	922.8	870.5	276.2	203.4	197.5	496.2
1983	976.1	918.8	277.2	220.3	211.4	536.2
1984	1,048.8	995.6	285.9	239.6	223.9	562.5

Table C-7
Average Expenditures on External Audit Fees per $1,000,000 of Revenue

Year	Manufacturing	Oil/Mining	Financial	Insurance	Utility	Retail/Service
1974	$630.0	$641.6	$1,481.5	$287.2	$325.7	$428.8
1977	566.7	584.7	1,335.4	290.2	291.2	372.5
1978	585.6	712.4	1,263.4	299.0	284.6	360.9
1981	496.5	487.2	1,549.3	291.0	285.6	311.3
1982	516.7	476.6	1,467.3	334.0	232.7	301.0
1983	498.8	416.2	1,160.0	294.8	204.5	280.2
1984	480.1	407.5	1,006.8	292.6	193.8	267.8

Considerable differences exist across industries in the amounts spent on external audit fees. The manufacturing and oil/mining industry groups spend by far the largest amounts, while insurance companies and utilities spend the least. Variance in the sizes of the companies within these industries affects these amounts. Table C-7 presents the amount of external audit fees per $1,000,000 of company revenue. The industry with the most striking results is the financial group. In Table C-6, financial institutions, insurance companies, and utilities are the lowest as far as expenditures for audit fees are concerned. As a percentage of revenues, however, these amounts take on greater importance. As a percentage of revenues, expenditures on external audit fees by the financial industry are several times greater than those of the other industry groups.

Table C-6 shows that expenditures on external audit fees grew from 1974 to 1982. All industry groups except manufacturing and utilities experienced more than 100 percent growth in their average external audit expenditures over these eight years. This growth was particularly explosive in the 1974-1977 period for the financial, insurance, and retail/service groups, which averaged more than 50 percent growth over those three years. In the later years, growth in all industries slowed somewhat. Growth over 1983 and 1984 was projected at less than 6 percent per year over all industries. This is different from the pattern (Table C-4) of expenditures for internal audit salaries which shows all industry groups experiencing growth of 150 percent or more from 1974 to 1982 and average-projected growth across groups of 10 percent per year for 1983 and 1984.

Despite this growth, most industries have experienced a general downward trend in external auditing fees as a percentage of revenue since 1978 except for financial companies which did not peak until 1981 (see Table C-7). Projections suggest that this trend is expected to continue.

One final measure to be presented is the average internal audit salary in each industry.

Table C-8
Average Internal Audit Salaries

Year	Manufacturing	Oil/Mining	Financial	Insurance	Utility	Retail/Service
1974	$20,924	$18,503	$13,653	$15,244	$13,696	$19,377
1977	22,788	25,857	16,244	16,958	16,741	22,708
1978	24,282	29,752	18,098	17,272	18,929	24,216
1981	30,648	35,759	20,594	23,096	27,546	27,283
1982	34,600	39,485	22,442	24,435	28,178	29,265
1983	37,624	43,985	23,500	26,652	31,246	31,524
1984	39,968	46,646	24,242	28,198	33,534	33,580

Of all groups presented, financial institutions spend the largest percentage of revenues on internal audit salaries and also pay the lowest average internal audit salary. This is true for all the years reported, and the distinction is expected to continue. Companies in the oil and mining category pay the highest average salaries, possibly because their internal auditors need technical, engineering, and auditing expertise. Manufacturing companies are not far behind in paying high average salaries to internal auditors. The growth rate of average internal audit salary over the years 1974-1982, across all groups, averaged more than 9 percent per year, while projections indicated a slight drop in 1983 and 1984.

Industry Expenditures Profiles

Based on the preceding data, the following profiles emerge:

Manufacturing. The companies in this category report high expenditures on internal and external auditing and spent more on external auditing than they did on internal auditing through 1981. Since then, expenditures on internal auditing have exceeded those for external auditing. This industry group pays a very high average salary. The number of auditors employed is the highest of all industries (along with the retail/service group), but the number of auditors per 1,000 employees is the lowest.

Oil/Mining. This industry group also reports high internal and external costs and is the only one in which expenditures on external auditing on average exceed those for internal auditing. The difference is narrowing, however; and the emphasis in the future appears oriented toward internal auditing. This industry pays the highest average salary of all industries, and projections indicate that it will continue to do so — even though the average salary will level off.

Financial. This group is characterized by extremely high expenditures as a percentage of revenue for internal and external auditing. Dollar expenditures for external auditing are low; those on internal auditing are moderate. Expenditures on internal auditing are approximately twice as high as those on external auditing and are projected to remain that way. On an average, more than one percent of the workforce in these firms is directly employed in internal auditing. The lowest average salaries for internal auditors paid by any industry are paid by this group.

Insurance. Firms in the insurance industry are the only ones characterized by low expenditures on both external auditing and internal auditing, although they do spend more on internal auditing. This difference is expected to widen, while expenditures on external auditing are projected to remain fairly constant and internal audit expenditures are expected to increase. These firms report the fewest number of auditors but rank second in the percentage of auditors in the workforce. This industry group pays the second lowest internal audit salaries.

Utilities. Utilities have the smallest external audit fees of all industry groups and spend considerably more on internal auditing than on external audit fees. They appear similar to financial institutions in terms of dollars spent. Utilities rank near the middle of all industries for number of audit positions and internal audit salaries.

Retail/Service. The companies in this category have high expenditures for internal auditing but spend only a moderate amount on external audit fees. They pay a moderately high average salary.

Appendix D

Differences in the Responses of Career and Noncareer Internal Auditors

The research team was concerned that the descriptive statistics based on the overall sample of internal audit directors and internal audit staff members might mask some significant differences between the attitudes of those who consider themselves "career" internal auditors and those who consider their internal auditing assignment to be only temporary. The section of our questionnaire that would be most sensitive to those potential attitudinal differences is Part II of both the staff's questionnaire and the director's questionnaire.

We stratified our sample of directors and of staff members into two groups each. One group consisted of career internal auditors and the other included those who regarded themselves as temporarily involved in internal auditing. We then recalculated the descriptive statistics for the questions in Part II of each questionnaire for both "career" and "temporary" internal auditors. Responses to the questions in Part II indicated the respondents' extent of agreement or satisfaction with a series of positive statements. Respondents were offered seven choices. They could check any of the following options:

Score
Strongly agree	1
Agree	2
Slightly agree	3
Neither agree nor disagree	4
Slightly disagree	5
Disagree	6
Strongly disagree	7

To provide a basis for comparing the two sets of responses, each was scored as shown. Averages were computed for responses from career internal auditors and from noncareer internal auditors and appear in the following tables:

Table D-1
Differences in the Attitudes of Career and Temporary Directors of Internal Auditing.

Table D-2
Differences in Job Satisfaction: Career and Temporary Directors of Internal Auditing.

Table D-3
Differences in the Attitudes of Career and Temporary Internal Audit Staff Members.

Table D-4
Differences in Job Satisfaction: Career and Temporary Internal Audit Staff Members.

Differences in Directors' Responses

Three hundred and twenty-one directors of internal auditing responded to our questionnaire. Of these, 121 (38 percent) stated they plan to remain in internal auditing throughout their careers, while 200 (62 percent) plan to move into management. Analysis of the questions in Part II of the director's questionnaire revealed slight differences between the attitudes of directors of internal auditing who consider themselves to be career internal auditors and those who plan to remain in their present positions only temporarily. These differences relate principally to a respondent's commitment to the company of current employment, the importance of professional certification, and job satisfaction.

Career internal audit directors are slightly more committed to pursuing careers within their present company than are temporary internal audit directors. In each of the questions related to leaving their positions (4, 9, 13, 18, and 34), career directors indicated greater willingness to remain with their current employer. Temporary directors showed more interest in changing employers if there was an opportunity to increase compensation or to work for a better managed company.

As might be expected, there also are some differences between the two classes of directors with respect to meeting their commitments as professional internal auditors (Question 17). Career directors agree that they "should be an active member of The Institute of Internal Auditors" with an average score of 2.24. Temporary directors scored 3.33. These are not very important differences. It is actually remarkable, we believe, that two groups with such different career interests agree so often. With respect to the importance of relying on personal professional judgment, the temporary directors agree more strongly than do the career directors (1.97 versus 2.23).

Not surprisingly, the 121 career directors indicated slightly greater job satisfaction than did the 200 directors who do not intend to stay in their present positions. Career directors were more satisfied on every one of the 12 aspects of job satisfaction with an average of 1.93 versus 2.37 for the temporary directors.

Differences in Staff Members' Responses

Internal audit staff members responding to their questionnaire numbered 1,212. Of these, 914 (75 percent) indicated that they did not plan to remain in internal auditing throughout their careers; and 298 (25 percent) responded that they plan a career as an internal auditor. Responses to the attitudinal questions in Part II are classified according to "career" and "temporary" internal audit staff members. The differences which emerge are described in the following paragraphs. Please note that they are all minor. Overall, the attitudinal profile of the career internal auditor is remarkably similar to that of the temporary internal auditor.

There is some indication that career internal audit staff members place a greater emphasis on aspects of professional commitment than do temporary internal auditors. For example, career staff members agree more strongly than noncareer members that they should "meet the standards of The Institute of Internal Auditors" (2.01 versus 2.28); that they should "sacrifice personal time to keep abreast of current developments" (2.72 versus 2.96); that they should "be an active member of The Institute of Internal Auditors" (3.23 versus 3.92); and that they should "pass the Certified Internal Audit examination" (3.01 versus 3.70).

On the other hand, temporary internal audit staff members agree more strongly than do their career counterparts with "passing the CPA/CA examination" (3.64 versus 3.92) and with "avoiding conflicts with company personnel that threaten your promotability" (4.39 versus 4.70). In each case, however, the difference between the two average scores is so slight that it could be argued that they are indistinguishable for all practical purposes.

Like the directors of internal auditing, career staff members appear to be marginally more committed to their current company than are the temporary internal auditors. Responses to questions 4, 9, 13, 18, 26, 34, and 38 spow them more committed than noncareer auditors. Note, however, that their average scores do not differ as much as a full point — the difference between any two adjacent responses.

Responses to other questions indicate that career staff members perceive their working conditions differently than do temporary staff members. For example, Question 1 responses show that career staff members believe more strongly that they are encouraged to use their initiative than do temporary staff (1.64 versus 1.91). Likewise, questions 2 and 53 show that they perceive their decision-making authority to be more clearly spelled out than do the temporary members (3.32 versus 3.69 and 4.07 versus 3.53).

Question 55 (Table D-4) is concerned with 12 aspects of job satisfaction. Career staff members are consistently more satisfied than temporary staff members on all 12 dimensions. Even so, the total difference does not seem very significant. The average satisfaction level for all aspects of satisfaction is 2.4 for career staff versus 2.8 for temporary staff.

Conclusion

Classification of responses to attitudinal and job satisfaction questions between internal auditor respondents who are committed to a career in internal auditing and those who are not so committed uncovers remarkably few significant differences.

Table D-1
Differences in the Attitudes of Career and Temporary Directors of Internal Auditing

		Average Scores	
		Career Internal Auditors	Temporary Internal Auditors
1.	You are encouraged to use your initiative in developing audit programs.	1.9	1.3
2.	Discretionary decisions permitted you are clearly specified.	3.85	3.85
3.	Most internal audit decisions are made by a few people in the internal audit department.	2.03	2.24
4.	You would not leave your company if a job were offered you with no significant change in compensation by a company you considered better managed.	2.26	3.62
5.	Your work in the internal audit department calls for frequent exercise of discretionary judgment.	1.46	1.58
6.	There are few people in your department with whom you can discuss professional auditing interests.	5.32	5.32
7	Salary levels are a general indication of one's contribution to the company.	3.17	3.44
8.	In your company, getting the work done depends on informal relationships and cooperation.	2.88	2.55
9.	You would leave your company if a job at a lower salary were offered you by a company you considered to be better managed.	6.11	5.77
10.	More varied assignments are an indication of approval by one's superiors.	2.90	2.85
11.	When you find inefficient activities in your work, you feel a responsibility to get them corrected.	1.50	1.63
12.	Tasks which require significant ability are more likely to be assigned to those who have displayed significant expertise.	1.81	2.02
13.	Barring unforeseen developments, you have every intention of pursuing your career with this company.	1.57	2.37
14.	In your company, people communicate only along the channels indicated in the organization chart.	5.39	5.49
15.	You get most of your professional auditing stimulation from your department associates.	4.5	4.52
16.	Barring unforeseen developments, you have no plans to leave your company.	1.55	2.49
17.	To meet your commitment as a professional internal auditor, you should:		
	a. Meet the standards of The Institute of Internal Auditors.	1.61	1.70
	b. Perform assigned tasks with the highest professional competence.	1.31	1.30
	c. Sacrifice personal time to keep abreast of current developments.	2.27	2.42

Table D-1 (continued)

	d. Rely on your professional judgment as to adequacy of audit procedures needed in specific cases.	2.23	1.97
	e. Avoid relationships with company personnel that might appear to influence your independence.	2.94	2.80
	f. Be an active member of The Institute of Internal Auditors.	2.24	2.80
	g. Participate in formal continuing education.	1.77	1.72
	h. Pass the Certified Internal Audit examination (or its equivalent).	2.54	3.33
	i. Pass the CPA/CA examination (or its equivalent).	3.53	3.28
	j. Accept company policy as your professional priority.	3.52	3.75
	k. Avoid conflicts with company personnel that threaten your promotability.	5.29	5.03
	l. Understate actual hours worked rather than exceed time budgets.	6.40	6.44
	m. Satisfy budgeted time constraints on assignments regardless of their adequacy for the assignments at hand.	6.20	6.25
18.	You would accept demotion rather than leave your present employer.	5.32	6.33
19.	It is not important to you that your company have a reputation as an efficient and well-managed organization.	6.07	5.95
20.	People who aggressively seek promotion are often rewarded beyond their contribution.	3.99	4.13
21.	As long as you perform your internal audit duties adequately, you have no further responsibility to assure the efficient operation of your company.	5.84	5.85
22.	You request or volunteer for demanding committee or special service assignments.	3.02	2.45
23.	You are expected to follow a detailed audit manual for all assignments.	5.03	5.13
24.	Your company offers incentives to its employees in order to attain its objectives.	3.21	3.76
25.	Your company rewards employees for following directions without questions.	5.26	5.05
26.	As an employee, your primary loyalty belongs to your employer.	2.97	3.27
27.	Managers of audited departments tolerate the internal audit function as a necessary business practice.	3.75	3.35
28.	Your company makes decisions by using committees of those managers who are responsible for implementing the decisions.	3.44	3.60
29.	When changes are made, your company involves all those who are most likely to be affected in the planning and implementation of the changes.	3.16	3.76
30.	Those who think of new and better ways of doing a task are more likely to be promoted.	2..72	3.03
31.	In your company, the expert in a given situation makes the decision even if it means bypassing the formal line of authority.	4.75	4.68

Table D-1 (continued)

32.	You are impatient when your assignments do not recognize your increased abilities.	3.31	3.03
33.	Your discretionary judgments are reviewed by superiors.	3.56	3.47
34.	You would leave your company if a job at a higher salary were offered you by a company you considered to be better managed.	3.65	2.57
35.	You prefer a position for which there are detailed, written procedures describing the responsibilities of the job.	4.09	4.28
36.	You get most of your professional auditing stimulation from people that you meet at professional meetings.	3.72	4.11
37.	Titles are unimportant to you as long as you feel you are making a contribution to your company.	3.79	3.63
38	You would leave internal auditing if a better job were offered you in another department of your company.	3.97	2.44
39.	Your company's communication channels are highly structured.	4.37	4.57
40.	Your company uses solutions proposed by outside experts in dealing with problems.	4.00	3.69
41.	You are generally uncertain about all the specific job aspects on which your performance will be evaluated.	4.59	4.30
42.	Managers of audited departments in your company look upon the internal audit function as a source of constructive assistance.	2.64	3.05
43.	Members of the internal audit department with little audit experience are not permitted to make judgment decisions.	3.96	4.14
44.	If you discovered practices which discredit corporate officers, you could report them to the proper authorities without fear of jeopardizing your position.	2.24	2.34
45.	You get most of your professional auditing stimulation from professional journals.	4.17	4.00
46.	Managers of audited departments in your company look upon the internal audit function largely as a policing activity	4.53	4.01
47.	Your company institutes changes without explaining or justifying them to the affected employees.	4.98	4.30
48.	If your superior requested you to perform an audit in a manner you felt not to be in accordance with appropriate internal audit standards, you would refuse to comply with his request.	3.02	3.01
49.	You get most of your professional auditing stimulation from the company's continuing educaiton seminars.	4.84	4.62
50.	You consider your time in internal auditing as a training period for other positions in your company.	5.46	3.43
51.	Your company uses a participative approach to decision making (courses of action are selected only after full discussion leading to a consensus.)	3.67	3.87

Table D-1 (continued)

52.	You understand completely all the aspects of your position for which you will be held responsible.	2.19	2.79
53.	There are times when instructions from your superior appear to conflict with other instructions.	3.96	3.55
54.	In the performance of your internal auditing duties, you seek to find areas or activities where your company's profitability could be improved.	1.97	1.90

	Score
Strongly agree	1
Agree	2
Slightly agree	3
Neither agree nor disagree	4
Slightly disagree	5
Disagree	6
Strongly disagree	7

Table D-2
Differences in Job Satisfaction: Career and Temporary Directors of Internal Auditing

		Average Scores	
		Career Internal Auditors	Temporary Internal Auditors
55.	In your job, how satisfied are you with the opportunities available to:		
	a. Make full use of your knowledge and skills.	1.62	2.36
	b. Learn new knowledge and skills.	1.84	2.54
	c. Earn a satisfactory salary.	2.15	2.47
	d. Advance within the company.	2.73	3.19
	e. Improve your technical competence.	2.03	2.63
	f. Associate with personnel senior to your position.	1.92	1.91
	g. Build your professional reputation.	1.80	2.19
	h. Work on difficult and challenging problems.	1.78	2.27
	i. Make constructive suggestions.	1.73	202
	j. Be in the company of people you like.	1.98	2.24
	k. Enjoy your work.	1.63	2.24
	l. Influence company policy.	1.98	2.35

	Score
Very satisfied	1
Satisfied	2
Slightly satisfied	3
Neither satisfied nor dissatisfied	4
Slightly dissatisfied	5
Dissatisfied	6
Very dissatisfied	7

Table D-3
Differences in the Attitudes of Career and Temporary Internal Audit Staff Members

		Average Scores	
		Career Internal Auditors	Temporary Internal Auditors
1.	You are encouraged to use your initiative in developing audit programs.	1.64	1.91
2.	Discretionary decisions permitted you are clearly specified.	3.32	3.69
3.	Most internal audit decisions are made by a few people in the internal audit department.	2.75	2.91
4.	You would not leave your company if a job were offered you with no significant change in compensation by a company you considered better managed.	2.97	3.71
5.	Your work in the internal audit department calls for frequent exercise of discretionary judgment.	1.90	2.02
6.	There are few people in your department with whom you can discuss professional auditing interests.	5.28	5.21
7.	Salary levels are a general indication of one's contribution to the company.	3.92	4.32
8.	In your company, getting the work done depends on informal relationships and cooperation.	2.76	2.68
9.	You would leave your company if a job at a lower salary were offered you by a company you considered to be better managed.	5.86	5.63
10.	More varied assignments are an indication of approval by one's superiors.	2.67	2.80
11.	When you find inefficient activities in your work, you feel a responsibility to get them corrected.	1.64	1.82
12.	Tasks which require significant ability are more likely to be assigned to those who have displayed significant expertise.	2.26	2.26
13.	Barring unforeseen developments, you have every intention of pursuing your career with this company.	1.87	2.86
14.	In your company, people communicate only along the channels indicated in the organization chart.	4.96	4.94
15.	You get most of your professional auditing stimulation from your department associates.	3.42	3.49
16.	Barring unforeseen developments, you have no plans to leave your company.	2.02	3.18
17.	To meet your commitment as a professional internal auditor, you should:		
	a. Meet the standards of The Institute of Internal Auditors.	2.01	2.28
	b. Perform assigned tasks with the highest professional competence.	1.36	1.45
	c. Sacrifice personal time to keep abreast of current developments.	2.27	2.96

Table D-3 (continued)

	d. Rely on your professional judgment as to adequacy of audit procedures needed in specific cases.	2.20	2.23
	e. Avoid relationships with company personnel that might appear to influence your independence.	2.91	3.00
	f. Be an active member of The Institute of Internal Auditors.	3.23	3.92
	g. Participate in formal continuing education.	1.99	2.11
	h. Pass the Certified Internal Audit examination (or its equivalent).	3.01	3.70
	i. Pass the CPA/CA examination (or its equivalent).	3.92	3.64
	j. Accept company policy as your professional priority.	3.26	3.43
	k. Avoid conflicts with company personnel that threaten your promotability.	4.70	4.39
	l. Understate actual hours worked rather than exceed time budgets.	5.97	5.79
	m. Satisfy budgeted time constraints on assignments regardless of their adequacy for the assignments at hand.	6.04	5.81
18.	You would accept demotion rather than leave your present employer.	5.55	6.21
19.	It is not important to you that your company have a reputation as an efficient and well-managed organization.	5.95	5.90
20.	People who aggressively seek promotion are often rewarded beyond their contribution.	3.81	4.01
21.	As long as you perform your internal audit duties adequately, you have no further resonsibility to assure the efficient operation of your company.	5.67	5.63
22.	You request or volunteer for difficult jobs.	2.62	2.63
23.	You are expected to follow a detailed audit manual for all assignments.	4.46	4.56
24.	Your company offers incentives to its employees in order to attain its objectives.	4.15	4.33
25.	Your company rewards employees for following directions without questions.	5.11	4.87
26.	As an employee, your primary loyalty belongs to your employer.	2.89	3.42
27.	Managers of audited departments tolerate the internal audit function as a necessary business practice.	3.00	3.04
28.	Your company makes decisions by using committees of those managers who are responsible for implementing the decisions.	3.22	3.26
29.	When changes are made, your company involves all those who are most likely to be affected in the planning and implementation of the changes.	3.86	3.97
30.	Those who think of new and better ways of doing a task are more likely to be promoted.	3.25	3.27
31.	In your company, the expert in a given situation makes the decision even if it means bypassing the formal line of authority.	4.76	4.64

Table D-3 (continued)

32.	You are impatient when your assignments do not recognize your increased abilities.	3.27	2.87
33.	Your discretionary judgments are reviewed by superiors.	2.57	2.58
34.	You would leave your company if a job at a higher salary were offered you by a company you considered to be better managed.	3.07	2.25
35.	You prefer a job for which there are written procedures describing how to do a particular audit task.	3.90	4.03
36.	You get most of your professional auditing stimulation from people that you meet at professional meetings.	4.42	4.56
37.	Titles are unimportant to you as long as you feel you are making a contribution to your company.	3.64	3.92
38.	You would leave internal auditing if a better job were offered you in another department of your company.	3.73	2.31
39.	Your company's communication channels are highly structured.	4.05	3.78
40.	Your company uses solutions proposed by outside experts in dealing with problems.	3.80	3.77
41.	You are generally uncertain about all the specific job aspects on which your performance will be evaluated.	4.89	4.60
42.	Managers of audited departments in your company look upon the internal audit function as a source of constructive assistance.	3.25	3.34
43.	Members of the internal audit department with little audit experience are not permitted to make judgment decisions.	3.78	4.22
44.	If you discovered practices which discredit corporate officers, you could report them to the proper authorities without fear of jeopardizing your position.	2.65	2.82
45.	You get most of your professional auditing stimulation from professional journals.	4.47	4.53
46.	Managers of audited departments in your company look upon the internal audit function largely as a policing activity.	3.87	3.64
47.	Your company institutes changes without explaining or justifying them to the affected employees.	4.29	4.11
48.	If your superior requested you to perform an audit in a manner you felt not to be in accordance with appropriate internal audit standards, you would refuse to comply with his request.	3.55	3.58
49.	You get most of your professional auditing stimulation from the company's continuing education seminars.	4.39	4.30
50.	You consider your time in internal auditing as a training period for other positions in your company.	5.04	2.90

Table D-3 (continued)

51.	Your company uses a participative approach to decision making (courses of action are selected only after full discussion leading to a consensus.)	3.95	3.90
52.	You understand completely all the aspects of your position for which you will be held responsible.	2.59	2.73
53.	There are times when instructions from your superior appear to conflict with other instructions.	4.07	3.53
54.	In the performance of your internal auditing duties, you seek to find areas or activities where your company's profitability could be improved.	2.21	2.21

	Score
Strongly agree	1
Agree	2
Slightly agree	3
Neither agree nor disagree	4
Slightly disagree	5
Disagree	6
Strongly disagree	7

Table D-4
Differences in Job Satisfaction: Career and Temporary Internal Audit Staff Members

		Average Scores	
		Career Internal Auditors	Temporary Internal Auditors
55.	In your job, how satisfied are you with the opportunities available to:		
	a. Make full use of your knowledge and skills.	2.20	2.81
	b. Learn new knowledge and skills.	2.52	2.76
	c. Earn a satisfactory salary.	2.72	3.01
	d. Advance within the company.	3.16	3.61
	e. Improve your technical competence.	2.68	2.98
	f. Associate with personnel senior to your position	2.17	2.32
	g. Build your professional reputation.	2.36	2.62
	h. Work on difficult and challenging problems.	2.11	2.56
	i. Make constructive suggestions.	2.05	2.35
	j. Be in the company of people you like.	2.01	2.51
	k. Enjoy your work.	1.83	2.67
	l. Influence company policy.	3.01	3.30

	Score
Very satisfied	1
Satisfied	2
Slightly satisfied	3
Neither satisfied nor dissatisfied	4
Slightly dissatisfied	5
Dissatisfied	6
Very dissatisfied	7

Appendix E

Influence of Nondomestic Activities on Internal Auditing

Some members of the advisory committee expressed concern with our conclusions regarding the responses to questions 36, 37, and 38 in Part III of the director's questionnaire. These questions are concerned with performance of the internal audit function in companies engaged in nondomestic operations. To discover whether we had missed any significant differences, we undertook additional analysis of the responses to those questions. That analysis is reported in this appendix.

Of the 330 companies represented in our data, 204 have no operations in foreign countries; 126 do. We divided the companies into four groups as follows:

Group	Percentage of Activity in Nondomestic Countries	Number of Companies	Percentage of Companies
1	0	204	62
2	1 to 9	40	12
3	10 to 29	49	15
4	30 and more	37	11
		330	100

On the supposition that participation in internal auditing in nondomestic countries might influence responses to other questions, we analyzed the responses to questions 25, 26, 27, 28, 31, 34, 37, and 38 in terms of the four groups above.

Except for Question 31, which sought information on the initiatives undertaken by companies following passage of the FCPA, the additional analysis was not very enlightening. The evidence is clear that companies engaged in operations in nondomestic countries were more responsive to the passage of that Act. Responses indicate that increased attention was given to internal control and to involving senior management and the audit committee in internal control considerations. Outside of "internal audit monitoring of management's compliance with the corporate code of conduct was initiated or increased" and "internal audit resources were increased in response to the FCPA," there is little significant difference between Group 1 and the other three groups. Thus, we conclude that internal auditing was not affected as directly or as much as were other aspects of the responding companies' activities.

There are some interesting differences in the responses among the three groups, but it is not easy to fit them into a meaningful pattern. In most cases, Group 3 (the 10-to-29-percent-nondomestic-activity category) shows the greatest response throughout the questions.

This leads to an "evolutionary theory" something like this: When a company first moves into nondomestic operations, the problems of dealing with language, currency, customs, practices, restrictions, and requirements demand primary attention. Internal auditing, therefore, gets relatively little. By the time the nondomestic activities have increased to more than 10 percent of the company's operations, their importance is evident; and the internal audit department is called on to play a larger role. Finally, by the time nondomestic activities exceed 30 percent of the company's operations, its foreign relationships have matured, its internal audit department is experienced, and special attention to internal auditing of foreign activities is no longer needed. We emphasize that this is no more than speculation. Additional research on internal audit of foreign activities might provide far better explanations.

Table E
Director's Questionnaire
Responses to Selected Questions Classified by Percentage of Nondomestic Operations

	Percentage of Operations in Nondomestic Countries			
	Group 1 0	Group 2 1-9	Group 3 10-29	Group 4 30 & More
25. Allocate 100 points across the following four activities in such a way as to indicate each activity's proportion of your total internal audit effort:				
The performance by internal auditors of internal control procedures such as bank reconciliations, test counts, account analyses, etc.	11.9	8.0	6.4	9.2
The testing of the extent to which the work of others complies with internal control requirements prescribed by company policy.	40.1	47.9	39.3	41.4
The evaluation of the appropriateness of internal control features currently called for by company policy.	30.6	30.6	36.3	33.2
The initiation of new or additional internal control features deemed necessary for new or continuing business activities.	17.4	13.5	18.0	16.2
26. For the four activities of internal auditing in question 25, please allocate 100 points in such a way as to indicate what should be each activity's proportion of your total internal audit effort:				
a. Performance.	9.4	6.1	6.4	9.9
b. Testing compliance.	39.9	45.3	39.1	38.9
c. Evaluation.	33.2	31.6	35.5	34.3
d. Initiation.	17.5	17.0	19.0	16.9
27. For the following five activities of internal auditing, please estimate the percentage of total internal audit time being spent on each activity:				

Detection of errors and irregularities — this activity is directed at the prevention or timely

	discovery of errors and irregularities in processing or recording transactions.	22.2	20.5	14.6	14.8
	Monitoring management control — management control strives to obtain compliance with the applicable rules and procedures established by company policy.	26.2	27.3	27.4	30.4
	Performance evaluation — this activity assesses the efficiency or the effectiveness with which company goals are attained.	13.3	11.1	16.9	14.2
	Monitoring internal accounting control — internal accounting control strives to assure that published financial statements present farily the financial position and results of operations of the company in accordance with generally accepted accounting practice or other appropriate standards and that assets are appropriately safeguarded.	30.0	35.2	34.5	35.3
	Decision-making review — this activity evaluates the effectiveness of management's operating and financial decisions.	8.3	5.9	6.6	5.3
28.	For the five activities of internal auditing in question 27, please estimate the percentage of total internal audit time that will be spent on each activity five years from now:				
	a. Detection of errors and irregularities.	16.0	17.1	12.5	12.0
	b. Monitoring management control.	25.6	26.9	25.9	28.1
	c. Performance evaluation.	18.4	15.6	20.8	18.0
	d. Monitoring internal accounting control.	25.9	30.0	29.4	30.8
31.	The following statements describe initiatives companies may have taken in response to the FCPA. Please check all the initiatives taken by your company in responding to this Act.				
	a. Your company took no specific action in response to the FCPA.	20	10	4	5
	b. Your company initiated a formal review of the internal control system.	47	65	73	62
	c. Your company developed a fully documented internal control file.	30	48	57	59
	d. Your company initiated new controls or revised existing controls.	47	53	61	59
	e. Your company took specific actions to create an increased awareness of the importance of internal controls among operating management.	58	75	82	89
	f. Specific actions were taken to create an increased awareness among internal auditors of the importance of detecting and minimizing fraud possibilities.	38	35	49	46
	g. Documentation of internal control weaknesses and recommendations for improved controls increased in internal audit reports.	47	40	57	59
	h. Internal audit emphasis on fraud potential and detection increased.	26	25	31	27
	i. Internal audit scope expanded to include reviews of more senior management activities.	23	20	37	43
	j. The audit committee became a more active participant in internal control concerns.	49	58	73	62
	k. Senior management became a more active				

		participant in internal control concerns.	50	58	80	73
	l.	Revision or initiation of a corporate code of conduct to address issues raised by the FCPA was undertaken.	34	43	59	62
	m.	Annual reports by executives documenting compliance with the corporate code of conduct were initiated.	23	30	49	43
	n.	Internal audit monitoring of management's compliance with the corporate code of conduct was initiated or increased.	26	43	55	57
	o.	Revision or initiation of an internal audit charter to address internal control issues raised by the FCPA was undertaken.	18	20	24	32
	p.	The position of director of internal audit was elevated within the company's organizational structure.	20	25	31	32
	q.	A direct-reporting relationship between the board of directors and the director of internal auditing was instituted.	16	10	20	14
	r.	More frequent or comprehensive audits of foreign operations were initiated.	0	15	14	38
	s.	Specific means were provided for confidential employee reporting of suspected irregularities.	9	10	24	19
	t.	Internal audit resources were increased in response to the FCPA.	26	33	37	41
	u.	Internal audit recommendations gained increased authority.	34	33	47	57
34.		Please rate the quality of internal control over EDP systems in your company relative to other activities and functions which are audited by internal auditing. (Rating on a basis of 5 points with 1 as "very superior.")				
	a.	Overall EDP system internal control.	2.9	2.9	2.9	3.1
	b.	Data-base integrity.	2.8	2.8	2.9	3.0
	c.	File security.	2.8	2.8	2.7	2.9
	d.	Auditability.	2.9	3.2	2.8	2.9
	e.	Internal control awareness.	2.7	3.1	2.7	2.9
	f.	Separation of incompatible duties.	2.8	2.9	2.7	2.8
	g.	Authorization of system changes.	2.8	3.1	2.8	3.1
	h.	Report-distribution control.	2.8	3.1	2.8	2.9
	i.	Backup procedures.	2.6	2.8	2.9	2.7
	j.	Usefulness of EDP reports.	2.7	2.8	3.0	2.7
37.		Please estimate the quality of internal control achieved in each of the following categories by checking the appropriate level on the following scale: (Rating on a basis of 5 points with 5 as "very high quality.")				
	a.	Domestic — United States and Canada	3.7	4.0	3.9	4.2
	b.	Nondomestic — Economically developed countries.	—	3.3	3.5	3.7
	c.	Nondomestic — Economically developing countries.	—	2.6	2.9	3.0
	d.	Nondomestic — Economically underveloped countries	—	2.7	2.9	2.7

	A Groups			B Groups			C Groups		
	2 1-9%	3 10-29%	4 30% & More	2 1-9%	3 10-29%	4 30% & More	2 1-9%	3 10-29%	4 30 & More

38. Which of the following statements best describes the manner in which you perform the internal audit function for each of the categories of nondomestic operations of questions 27 and 36? (Please check one statement in each column.)

		A2	A3	A4	B2	B3	B4	C2	C3	C4
a.	The internal audit function is performed entirely by local audit personnel.	3	4	4	3	0	1	2	0	0
b.	The Internal audit function is performed by local audit personnel with occasional corporate audit on-site review.	3	3	3	1	1	2	1	0	1
c.	The internal audit function is performed by local audit personnel with regular corporate audit on-site review.	1	5	8	4	3	5	0	2	3
d.	The internal audit function is performed entirely by corporate audit personnel.	19	30	20	8	21	21	6	16	17

A Group — Nondomestic Economically Developed Countries.
B Group — Nondomestic Economically Developing Countries.
C Group — Nondommestic Economically Underdeveloped Countries.

Appendix F

Package Mailed to Directors of Internal Auditing

To Directors of Internal Auditing
Participating in The Institute of Internal Auditors' Research on "Developments Influencing Internal Auditing in U.S. and Canadian Corporations."

    We greatly appreciate your offer to participate in The Institute's research project on "Developments Influencing Internal Auditing in U.S. and Canadian Corporations." Directors of internal auditing constitute the key element in our efforts to obtain necessary data; without your cooperation, we would have little possibility of success. Hence, we have tried to hold to a minimum our requests for information from your files.

    Please write your Standard Industrial Classification number or major SIC number at the top of your questionnaire.

    Enclosed you will find a number of questionnaires, each with an addressed, postage-paid, return envelope. In order to avoid any question of violation of confidentiality, each completed questionaire should be mailed to me by the person asked to complete it. Please give each person who receives a questionnaire a return envelope with the questionnaire.

    In addition to the director's questionnaire, which we hope you will complete and return, you will find a short questionnaire for each of the following:

- The chairman or member of the audit committee.
- The senior executive to whom you report.
- The independent accountant in charge of your annual audit.

    You will also find a number of questionnaires for members of your staff. Using the best information available to us, we have sent you enough questionnaires to comply with our distribution rule which runs as follows: ten percent of your total audit staff with a maximum of 15 questionnaires and a minimum of four. If your audit staff is less than four, please ask each member to respond. No person should complete more than one questionnaire. If the number of staff questionnaires is inadequate to meet our distribution rule, please call me for more copies.

    The staff questionnaires should be distributed across your staff in such a manner as to provide us with a representative sample, taking into account years of experience, rank within the staff, and any other factors you consider important to obtaining a representative distribution.

    Please encourage all those receiving questionnaires to complete and return them by July 31. If you have any difficulty in applying these guidelines, please call me at (313) 763-1292. Thank you very much.

If you can arrange to send us a copy of your latest annual report and any board of directors' resolution or an official charter that states or describes the mission of the internal audit function in your company, we will find such items very helpful in our research.

Very truly yours,

R.K. Mautz
Director

July 12, 1982

The Institute of Internal Auditors Research Foundation: 1984-1985

Board of Trustees

Charles W. Gissel, CIA, CPA, Foundation President — Morton Thiokol Corporation
William C. Anderson, CIA, CBA — Continental Illinois Bank & Trust Co.
Jean A. Bernard — Bell Canada
Donald F. Clark, CIA — Copley Newspapers
William B. Costill, CIA — The Harris Corporation
Roy C. Culbertson, CIA — Pacific Gas & Electric Company
Emmet E. De Lay — General Electric Company
F. Thomas Fanning, CIA — Getty Oil Corporation
Robert N. Feltes — ITT Corporation
Paul E. Heeschen, CIA — Lockheed Corporation
James A. Hooper, CIA — Southern California Edison
James R. Kelly, CIA, CPA — Investors Diversified Services
O. Jack McGill — Gulf Oil Corporation
Frederick L. Neumann, Ph.D., CPA — University of Illinois at Urbana-Champaign
Malcom J. Parker, CIA — Omega Associates
Walter D. Pugh, CDP, CISA, CPA — Price Waterhouse
Lewis J. Qualkenbush, CIA — Marathon Oil Company
Jerry D. Singleton, CIA — South Central Bell Telephone

The Institute of Internal Auditors International Research Committee: 1984-85

O. Jack McGill, Committee Chairman — Gulf Oil Corporation
Kathryn L. Auten — California First Bank
Etienne Barbier — L' Oreal
Michael J. Barrett, DBA, CIA — University of Illinois at Chicago
Kenneth D. Carner, CIA — Security Pacific Corp.
John H. Cary, CPA — Price Waterhouse
Jennifer M. Fox, CIA — Southern Company Services
Arthur R. Gates, CIA, CPA — Norton Company
Joseph P. Greene — The Gillette Company
Michele Guenard, CPA — Peugeot Citroen
Keith R. Howe, DBA, CIA — Brigham Young University
James G. Johnston, CPA
Danny R. Kelly, CPA — Koch Industries, Inc.
Jean-Pierre Larrivee, CA — Metro-Richelieu, Inc.
Richard N. Lemieux, CPA — Ernst & Whinney
C. Richard MacWilliams, CISA — Union Mutual Life Insurance Company
Robert T. Mitchell — McIlwraith-Davey Industries, Ltd.
Lindsey S.W. Montgomery
Wayne G. Moore, CIA — Conoco, Inc.
Paul E. Nelson, CIA — 3M Company
Claire B. Nilsen, Wilmington Savings Fund Society
Frederick L. Page — Silver State Mining
James W. Pattillo, CMA, CPA — Indiana University
Walter D. Pugh, CDP, CISA, CPA — Price Waterhouse
Donald E. Ricketts, DBA — University of Cincinnati
David H. Rosenstein, CISA — Deloitte Haskins & Sells
Hanan Rubin, CIA — Metropolitan Life Insurance Company
Rudolph H. Schellenberger — Penn Central Corporation
Melvin F. Skindzier, CIA — JCPenney Co., Inc.
Oscar Suarez, CIA, CMA — Great West Life Assurance Company
Mark P. Thornton — Barnett Bank of Central Florida
William W. Warrick, III, CPA — Coopers & Lybrand
Timothy M. Wise — Veterans Administration
John P. Dattola — Staff Liaison of The Institute of Internal Auditors, Inc.